BALI

Also in the Series

BALI

A Cultural History

ARTHUR COTTERELL

Interlink Books

An imprint of Interlink Publishing Group, Inc.
Northampton, Massachusetts

First published in 2016 by
INTERLINK BOOKS
An imprint of Interlink Publishing Group, Inc.
46 Crosby Street, Northampton, Massachusetts 01060
www.interlinkbooks.com

Library of Congress Cataloging-in-Publication Data
Cotterell, Arthur, author.
Bali, a cultural history / Arthur Cotterell.
    pages cm
Includes bibliographical references and index.
ISBN 978-1-56656-081-8
1. Bali Island (Indonesia)--Civilization. 2. Bali Island (Indonesia)--History. I. Title.
DS647.B2C68 2015
959.8'62--dc23
                        2015025233

Front cover photo: Nataliya Hora/Shutterstock
Photographs: Yong Yap Cotterell
Maps and Illustrations: Ray Dunning

Printed and bound in the United States of America

To request our complete 48-page full-color catalog, please call us toll free at
1-800-238-LINK, visit our website at www.interlinkbooks.com, or write to
Interlink Publishing 46 Crosby Street, Northampton, MA 01060
e-mail: info@interlinkbooks.com

Contents

Preface and Acknowledgements

My own relationship with maritime Southeast Asia stretches back almost half a century, yet my amazement at its culture still grows year by year. While I have lived in Borneo, traveled to other islands, and written about the region's history, nothing prepared me for what can only be described as the culture shock of a visit to Bali. This beautiful island is literally steeped in traditional beliefs. International tourism has begun to have an effect but the friendliness of the Balinese people ensures that there is always something new to discover.

Bali never really attracted writers of note, its allure being most influential with artists and dancers, who have responded intensely to the island's rich heritage. Even a cursory glance at the Neka Museum of Art at Ubud, an important town in central Bali, reveals how intertwined dance-drama and painting have been in Balinese culture. Besides works showing the splendid dances performed at temple ceremonies, this museum's collection includes paintings by Arie Smit, a Dutchman who in 1950 became an Indonesian citizen. His paintings seem to capture quintessential Bali—its shores, hills, mountains, forests, fields, villages, and temples. During the 1960s Smit also encouraged young Balinese artists to develop their own talents. It proved to be one aspect of an artistic renaissance centered upon Ubud.

I must express my special thanks to my wife Yong Yap, who tolerates an absorbing interest in things Southeast Asian. That she hails from Sarawak, and my initial journey east was the result of our engagement as students in England, perhaps explains her understanding attitude toward my research. Residence in Borneo had a profound effect on me, but hardly compares with the impact of coming face to face with Bali. Now both of us have become enthusiastic visitors to a truly remarkable island, which I hope this book goes some way to elucidate.

For assistance with drawings and maps I am grateful once again to Ray Dunning, with whom I have collaborated over many years. All the photographs were, however, taken by my wife.

Introduction

Because all the beliefs of maritime Southeast Asia find their focus on Bali, the island is an ultimate landscape of the imagination. Not only have the Balinese embraced Hinduism, but even more they piously respect their own ancestors and carefully placate the indigenous spirits dwelling in the island.

Offerings placed outside doorways are intended to satisfy the demonic spirits while those on special shrines in gardens seek the goodwill of ancestors. From Gunung Agung, Bali's highest volcano, the gods are said to descend periodically to temples left open to the sky in order to assist their arrival. That there is no strict taboo about eating beef, except for priests and worshippers actually attending temples, indicates just how far the Balinese have transformed the imported Hindu faith. Even though a caste system does exist, its social distinctions are not rigidly applied and there are no untouchables, long the bane of Indian society. In contrast to the leaden atmosphere of the subcontinent, Jawaharlal Nehru on a visit in 1950 described Bali as "the morning of the world."

What makes Bali so unique is an untroubled acceptance of reincarnation alongside ancestor worship and the spirit world. The Balinese never adopted the entire Hindu pantheon with the result that there are gods and goddesses who are not Indian at all, such as the rice goddess Dewi Sri. Another element of Balinese religion is trance, a means of communication with spirits that is common throughout Southeast Asia. Professional mediums communicate with the unseen powers through trance, although this exulted state is often reached during a performance of dance-drama, a prominent feature of Balinese culture.

Underlying the importance placed upon communication with the spirit world is a conviction that nothing in fact is inanimate. Everything possesses a spirit: animals, rocks, and trees are the most obvious examples. Yet during the Hindu festival of the New Year, the same reverence is also extended to machines, when the hoods of buses, trucks, and cars are adorned with the sacred cloth usually wrapped around the trunks of trees and prominent rocks.

RITUAL AND RULERS

So crucial has irrigation been for growing rice that the holiness of water is taken for granted. Fast-running streams always delight visitors to Bali, even though they may be quite unaware of the complex arrangements by which this life-giving resource is distributed from springs arising near the island's three great mountain lakes. Priests stationed at water temples are as much hydraulic engineers as experts in religious ritual. Renowned for his water-control schemes was a Balinese prince by the name of Erlanga, who became king of eastern Java. Having reunited this part of Java after almost thirty years of unrest in 1037, Erlanga restored its prosperity through the placement of dams along rivers so as to prevent flooding and provide a regular supply of water for irrigation.

For this water miracle Erlanga is still remembered with gratitude by the Javanese to this day. He did not succeed, however, in transplanting Bali's belief in the sanctity of water to Java, despite his personal association with the savior god Vishnu. When he died in 1044, the ashes of Erlanga were enclosed in a stone casket and buried beneath a mountain spring, a clear reference to the end of the Indian epic the *Ramayana*, when Rama disappears in a river. Water is the favorite element of Vishnu, whose avatar Rama was.

At this period Bali was not yet Hindu. Erlanga had been introduced to this religion through marriage to a Javanese princess and residence in his father-in-law's court. Unlike Erlanga, the early Balinese rulers made no claim to divinity. King Udayana, Erlanga's own father, had also married a Javanese princess shortly after 989, and so Hinduism was beginning to penetrate Balinese high society, but not for another three centuries would the Indian faith make serious inroads. The catalyst was the Javanese conquest of 1284 which, though short-lived, allowed Hindu ideas to travel eastwards. But the decisive factor in the conversion of Bali was undoubtedly the rise of Majapahit, a powerful kingdom in eastern Java which within fifty years came to dominate much of the Indonesian archipelago. Situated on Majapahit's doorstep, Bali had no chance of remaining independent. A Javanese monk-chronicler by the name of Prananca records how in 1343 the "vile, long-haired princes of Bali" were wiped out and "all the customs changed to those of Java."

At first, Bali was treated as no more than a colony until Balinese resentment at its blatant exploitation obliged Majapahit to install a vassal king. He was Ketut Kresna Kapakisan, a Javanese priest who changed his status to that of a warrior so that he could rule. With the support of a group of prominent Balinese nobles, he established a dynasty that would last until the twentieth century. King Kapakisan is credited with the construction of temples at Besakih on the southern slope of Gunung Agung, where according to legend the first Hindu rituals were performed in Bali, apparently by a priest who arrived from Java in the eighth century. Today the Pura Besakih complex, spread over one-and-a-half square miles, is still the premier religious site with its administration overseen by descendants of the Klungkung royal house.

In 1710, the royal court had moved to Klungkung in eastern Bali. Although the king became known as Dewa Agung, or "supreme one," the island had become a patchwork of squabbling kingdoms. Nominal as each Dewa Agung's political influence progressively became, the Klungkung monarch remained for the Balinese people a supreme being, the inheritor of an entitlement to rule which was put into dramatic form during impressive festivals. So splendid and frequent were these events, in Klungkung and other royal courts, that pre-colonial Bali has been called with some justification a theater state.

A Balinese ruler was always portrayed as more than the apex of a hierarchical society: through his close relationship with the supernatural powers, he guaranteed the kingdom's prosperity. Whether in demon exorcisms conducted on the seashore, or celebrations at his own palace, the king was always the great rajah whose ceremonial umbrella was large enough to ensure the island's safety. Obsessed though historical Bali may seem to have been by elaborate ceremony and startling display, its approach was no different from other Indian-influenced Southeast Asian countries. Perhaps the real distinction was the sheer exuberance which informed these hallowed rituals, a legacy still evident in contemporary Balinese art, music, and dance-drama.

Although the Balinese recognize the decisiveness of Majapahit's involvement with their island, and indeed the nobility trace with pride family trees going back to the reign of Kapakisan, they are intrigued by earlier times, the era of the old Balinese kings who lived during the first millennium. The earliest known ruler is Kesari Warmadewa, three of whose inscriptions have survived at his capital of Pejeng in central Bali. Yet these are comparatively late and date only from the tenth century. More is known about Udayana and his energetic son Erlanga. Udayana sought alliances with Javanese kings, married one of their daughters, and even issued his edicts in the Javanese language. He seems to have commissioned the famous Goa Gajah, or "Elephant Cave," not far from Ubud. Carved out of solid rock, this priestly hermitage reflects an ancient veneration for stone which survives today in the megalithic thatched roofs rising high above Balinese temples.

Not the first inhabitants of Bali, but the ancestors of the present-day Balinese were the Austronesian peoples of southern China and especially the Yangtze delta. When they began to migrate by sea, not later than 3000 BC, this area was not, of course, Chinese. The cradle of China's civilization was located much farther north on the flood plain of the Yellow River. Inveterate mariners, the Austronesians settled in Taiwan, the Philippines, central Vietnam, southern Thailand, the Malayan peninsula, and the Indonesian archipelago. They even populated islands as far west as Madagascar and as far east as Hawaii. But the vast majority of the Austronesians occupied the Indonesian archipelago where today 300 distinct peoples live and speak 250 separate languages.

That was the reason why Sukarno, the Republic of Indonesia's first president, insisted that teachers in primary schools should use Bahasa Indonesia, the national language. Based on the Malay spoken in central Sumatra, it contains additional elements from other Indonesian tongues, above all Javanese. From his earliest years, Sukarno had been aware of language differences because his Javanese father was a teacher in the employ of the Dutch, who married a local girl when he was working in Bali. Despite his hatred of tourism, Sukarno's spirit is believed by the Balinese to inhabit a palatial government guest house next to the Pura Tirta Empul, a popular spring temple and source of holy water in central Bali.

The spirit-haunted Austronesians were deeply influenced by the environment in which they settled. Open though Southeast Asia has always been to the outside world, located as it is at the junction of several ocean routes, the region's unusual character essentially stems from an adaptation to landscape, water, and climate. Active volcanoes and high mountains, great rivers and turbulent seas, dense jungle and teeming wildlife, monsoon rain and seasonal drought—these are the factors that have shaped one of the most fascinating parts of the globe. And Bali itself comprises this dramatic background in miniature. The island is not quite the continuous slope as some visitors would suggest, but its hills and valleys are notable features in a landscape over which loom the peaks of volcanoes.

FOREIGN INFLUENCES

Outside influences have been important for Balinese culture. Yet as no full-scale Indian migration or conquest ever occurred in the Indonesian archipelago, the adoption of Indian ideas must have met local needs. The contrast between attitudes towards India and China could not be starker: India provided spiritual guidance, China offered political stability. Tributary relations with the Chinese empire were a regular part of maritime Southeast Asian diplomacy, since they gave access to the largest market for trade goods in the world. By simply acknowledging the Chinese emperor as the Son of Heaven, seaborne commerce was permitted to flourish without hindrance.

All this changed with the arrival of the European powers. Had China not chosen to run down its navy after 1433, the Portuguese, the Dutch, the French, and the English sailing eastwards in search of spices would not have gained the false impression that they were the earliest navigators of Asian waters. On rounding the Cape of Good Hope seventy years before his first voyage to India in 1498, Vasco da Gama could well have found his few vessels of 300 tons sailing alongside a Chinese armada containing ships of over 1,500 tons. No vessel in the Royal Navy could match such a tonnage until the eighteenth century.

By the Portuguese capture of Malacca in 1511, China had ceased to bother with the sea altogether, possibly for the reason that the removal of its capital northward to Beijing had focused attention on the Great Wall as the empire's critical line of defense. As a result, local states in maritime Southeast Asia were left to resist European colonialism on their own. A Javanese king twice invested Batavia, the headquarters of the Dutch East India Company on the site of modern Jakarta, but without a navy he could not stop the city's resupply by sea. After the failure of a second siege in 1629, the Javanese realized that the Dutch were there to stay.

Dutch encroachment in Bali only began at the start of the early nineteenth century and did not stop until 1908. Then at Klungkung, the last supreme Balinese king Ida I Dewa Agung Jambe, along with his wives, his children, and his courtiers marched straight into Dutch machine-gun fire. Having purified themselves for death, dressed in white, and armed with no more than spears and swords, the Klungkung aristocracy strode calmly into battle. Pausing only to dispatch the wounded, the last independent Balinese ruler led his family and followers until virtually everyone had perished. The island's freedom was over in a fashion that horrified the Western world.

In spite of present-day Japanese tourists showing sympathy at Klungkung for this parallel of the glorious self-destruction expected of soldiers in the Imperial Japanese Army during the Second World War, they are incorrect in supposing that any military impulse lay behind *puputan*, or "until the last." Mass suicide is in fact a consequence of reincarnation, an Indian concept the Balinese fully absorbed following the Majapahit conquest. That there was a long-standing belief in multiple reincarnation meant that *puputan* was far from the end for the Klungkung victims, one of whom was even said to have been reincarnated in a number of different persons.

During the thirty-four years of Dutch colonial rule in Bali royal authority barely existed. The Balinese kingdoms were not formally abolished until 1950, one year after Indonesia secured its independence from Holland, but the old ways were gone forever. Even worse, between 1942 and 1945 Japanese officials exercised almost unlimited control over daily affairs. They even recruited Balinese to work on coastal defenses, simple fortifications of tree trunks, rocks, and earth. The Imperial Japanese Army was not overly pleased about the project, because it was unsure whether an invasion could be repulsed, but with the growing weakness of Japan in the face of the Allied counterattack, there needed to be some enlistment of local support. In comparison with Java, where local recruits were put through a guerrilla warfare program, young Balinese men hardly received any military training at all. Yet Tokyo's promise of independence in 1944 was sufficient to encourage opposition to any return to Dutch colonial rule.

A consequence of this promise was that in Bali the Dutch faced both armed and passive resistance after the surrender of Japan. An attempt to relax colonial control by means of a confederation of self-governing Indonesian states under the Dutch crown failed to head off nationalist demands for outright independence, and in 1949 Bali found itself a province within the Republic of Indonesia. The political traumas of this new country did not spare Bali, which suffered greatly during the military coup that overthrew President Sukarno. An estimated 80,000 Balinese people were killed in 1965–66, around five percent of the population. The conflict in the island reflected those of the nation at large, with communists espousing the cause of the peasantry and landlords refusing to accept land reform. Yet the Communist Party of Indonesia aggravated an already tense situation at Klungkung by an attempted desecration of an important Hindu funeral. Both troops from Java and local people took a terrible revenge, dumping in the sea or mass graves thousands of communists, executed either with guns or knives.

Since this bloodbath, an event the Balinese are even now most reluctant to discuss, there has been peace and progress. The enforced retirement in 1998 of General Suharto, Sukarno's successor as president, largely passed the island by. Even the financial crisis at the time, during which the value of Indonesia's currency plunged by eighty percent, had only a temporary impact because a tourist boom was already underway. Renowned though Bali had always been as an exotic destination for globe-trotters, the growth of tourist numbers since then was exponential. Rising from 1.4 million visitors in 2000 to over 4 million now, the island's popularity was not even affected by Islamic terrorism. The 2002 and 2005 bomb blasts at the seaside resort of Kuta, in southern Bali, killed over 200 people and shocked the Balinese, who could not understand why Javanese terrorists should target their island. Anger only subsided after priests performed a cleansing ritual on Kuta beach, which was intended to release the spirits of the dead and purify the town.

Cultural tourism—the notion that exposing visitors to Bali's rich heritage in a controlled manner can be beneficial for all concerned—was the basis of government-sponsored advertising from the 1970s onwards. And it has to be said that this approach has stimulated the visual arts, in particular painting and sculpture. The sheer number of tourists, however, poses a threat to Balinese culture over the longer term. At the moment the island is able to accommodate beach lovers as well as culture vultures; providing both groups of visitors recognize local sensibilities, such an arrangement is likely to last without undue stress. So far the Balinese themselves have managed to keep a sensible balance between family ritual and public ceremony, and they have also resisted the temptation to turn out too many cheap souvenirs. That is why their beautiful island remains unique, a landscape of the imagination in an increasingly commercialized world.

Part One

LANDSCAPES

Gunung Kawi paddies

Chapter One

THE PHYSICAL LANDSCAPE

"Where volcanoes rise up and rivers run down their sides, where sun
and moon shine, divine blessings are bestowed upon people."

Balinese saying

Possibly the most complicated geological part of the planet, the Indonesian
archipelago comprises an immense chain of islands stretching from the
Asian continent to New Guinea, the world's second largest island lying to
the north of Australia. If compared with a map of Europe, the archipelago
would begin in the Irish Sea and end in the Caspian Sea, so far does it
extend from west to east. At the last count, fewer than a quarter of its
13,677 islands were inhabited. The reason for an uncertainty over the total
is that some are no more than coral reefs, while in the 1970s Singapore was
accused of purloining tiny islands to increase its own physical size.

That the dimensions of the islands vary so much explains the cultural
diversity of the present-day Republic of Indonesia. Sumatra alone is twice
the size of the United Kingdom, while even modest Bali is some twenty
times bigger than the Isle of Wight. The name of the archipelago only
dates from 1850, when a British scholar resident in Singapore cast about
for a suitable designation. James Logan coined Indonesia by combining the
Greek words *indos*, "Indian," and *nesoi*, "islands," and thereby launched the
name on its triumphant career. Taken up with such enthusiasm by the
nationalists, the notion of Indonesia encompassing the whole archipelago
in a single, independent country had by 1928 become an article of faith.
That year an Indonesian journalist wrote a tune entitled "Great Indonesia,"
the state's future national anthem.

As a consequence, the Dutch colonial authorities announced that the
word "Indonesia" could no longer be used. Relations between the Dutch
and the Indonesians then hit rock bottom as police surveillance was
stepped up: even the popular village sport of pigeon racing was outlawed
to prevent the spread of bad news. The fall of the Netherlands to Germany
in 1940 could not be kept a secret forever, but the feebleness of Dutch

resistance to the Japanese two years later still astonished the local population.

During the last great ice age, which lasted from about 100,000 to 9,500 years ago, so much water was locked up in ice and glaciers that the sea level in Southeast Asia was nearly 394 meters lower than today. Vast expanses of the relatively shallow seabed around the Indonesian archipelago were then dry land. The islands of Sumatra, Java, Borneo, and Bali actually lie on a once-exposed continental shelf known as Sundaland, while to the east, Australia, New Guinea, and the island of Tasmania formed a single land mass called Sahul. The islands between them, such as Sulawesi, the Moluccas, Amboina, Banda, Lombok, Timor, and the Lesser Sundas, always seem to have been surrounded by water, however.

This circumstance must account for marked differences in flora and fauna between Bali and Lombok, which was noticed by the British naturalist and colleague of Charles Darwin, Sir Alfred Wallace. The large mammals of Bali and Java, such as elephants, tigers, and rhinoceros, give way in Lombok to marsupials and birds common to Australia. Therefore Wallace concluded that the Lombok Strait, which is much deeper than the channel separating Bali from Java, defined an ecological divide between the Asian and Australian continents. Although the so-called Wallace Line has been modified by subsequent research, so that Bali and Lombok are now viewed as a transitional zone rather than a definite break, Wallace's observation was fundamentally correct.

Archaeological finds show that people had crossed from Sundaland to Sahul about 50,000 years ago. Since the oldest stone tools of the sort necessary to make dugout canoes are only 20,000 years old, these intrepid voyagers would have constructed rafts of lashed logs. Taking advantage of a now invisible chain of small islands, these earliest long-distance mariners had largely migrated eastward before a new group of mariners began to arrive from southern China some 5,000 years ago. The ancestors of the present-day inhabitants of the Indonesian archipelago, these Austronesian-speakers came in ocean-going craft equipped with sails.

That the first people who had lived in Sundaland, before moving on to Suhal, were exchanging one kind of environment for another was dramatically demonstrated in the 1930s, when the last Balinese tiger fell victim to a Dutch big-game hunter. But the monkeys that Wallace realized had trekked across Asia during the ice age are still living in Bali. According to the Balinese, the monkeys now occupying their forested hills are the remnants of the monkey god Hanuman's victorious army. In the *Ramayana*, the epic Indian account of Rama's defeat of the demon Ravana, Hanuman rendered invaluable service. The chief demon, and Rama's bitter enemy, Ravana had increased his own strength by his devotion to the creator god Brahma, from whose feet demons are supposed to have sprung.

When Hanuman leapt across the sea to Ravana's stronghold in the island of Sri Lanka, a female demon named Surasa tried to swallow him bodily. To avoid this interception Hanuman distended his body, forcing Surasa to elongate her mouth, then he shrank to the size of a thumb, shot through her head and emerged from her ear. Landed safely in Sri Lanka, he dealt the forces of Ravana mighty blows and burned down the demon's citadel. In gratitude for this daring assault, Rama granted Hanuman the gift of perpetual life and youth. Yet the Balinese do not worship Hanuman as a monkey god: rather he is an ambiguous figure, an immortal straddling both the animal and demonic worlds.

A mask of Hanuman, the monkey king

POWER OF NATURE

Volcanoes form a notable feature of the Indonesian archipelago. Through a major fault in the bed of the Indian Ocean to its south, an amazing alignment of active volcanoes runs through Sumatra, Java and Bali. The most famous is Krakatoa, situated between Java, and Sumatra. For several months in 1883 a series of explosions shook the region: the biggest one was heard in Australia over 1,864 miles away, and ranks with the loudest noise ever recorded on Earth. Wind-blown ash fell at an even greater distance, and waves rose on shores as remote as South Africa, Cape Horn, and India. The sky was black with smoke for two and a half days; hot ash and pumice rained down on crops and livestock; and sea floods killed nearly 37,000 people. Fortunately for Indonesia, tropical rainfall limited permanent damage to agriculture by quickly washing away the layer of dust.

More recently the Indian Ocean has dramatically reminded us of its latent power. In 2004 a giant tsunami, a Japanese word meaning "harbor wave," was triggered by a massive earthquake off the western coast of Sumatra. The quake at the interface between the India and Burma tectonic plates lifted up the sea floor several meters, causing a tremendous displacement of water which struck Sumatra within half an hour, causing 98,000 deaths on this island alone. Such sudden violence in the past doubtless gave rise to the idea of a malignant sea goddess, whom the Javanese call Ratu Lara Kidal. Her body comprises the hair and bones of her drowned victims.

Although volcanoes can be as dangerous as the sea, their peaks have always been regarded as the home of the gods. Sumatran and Javanese kings styled themselves "lords of the mountain," each occupant of a throne claiming a special authority granted by the deities and the ancestral spirits who dwelt on the upper slopes of volcanoes. For the Balinese a similar belief predates the conquest of their island by the Javanese state of Majapahit in 1343. The subsequent installation of a vassal king led to the adoption of Hinduism, although not its entire pantheon. Many Hindu gods were, however, added to the ancestral inhabitants of Gunung Agung, or "the great mountain," Bali's highest volcano.

So deeply rooted is belief in the holiness of Gunung Agung that, when in 1963 the volcano erupted unexpectedly, many people refused to leave

Gunung Agung, Bali's highest volcano

their endangered homes, preferring to die together on the spot. They saw the eruption as a supernatural event, which priests confirmed to have been the case. Important rituals scheduled to take place a few years later at the Pura Besakih temple complex, on the southern slope of the volcano, had been brought forward to 1963 at the insistence of Bali's governor, Bagus Suteja. In spite of warnings from concerned religious leaders, the governor insisted on having his own way because he thought this would convince the Balinese people of his personal adherence to the island's traditional values. There had been persistent rumors about his sympathetic attitude to the Communist Party of Indonesia. In the event, the great ceremony at Pura Besakih was not enough to save Bagus Suteja, and he died in the bloody anticommunist purge of 1965–66.

Even though the destruction around Gunung Agung in 1963 proved to be less severe than was originally feared, the volcano's height was actually reduced to 9,186 feet from 10,308 feet before the eruption. But Balinese caution over the two great volcanoes of Gunung Agung and Gunung Batur is understandable, because the latter is still visibly active. And as it is surrounded by a spectacular caldera, Gunung Batur must have been once much bigger than at present, having blown away its top during a particularly violent eruption.

Given the dominance of Gunung Agung and Gunung Batur, Balinese respect for stone is not unexpected. An echo of this pre-Majapahit attitude is apparent in the unique construction of temples in Bali. Towering thatched pagodas resembling stacked megaliths are a reminder of the intrinsic value accorded to rocks and mountains, while in their openness to the sky, temple sites preserve the ritual descent of the gods and the ancestral spirits.

The whole of the Indonesian archipelago falls within the tropics and high temperatures are normal. As the equator itself passes through Sumatra, Borneo, and Sulawesi, Bali is situated barely 560 miles to its south. Climate has always been a critical factor in human settlement close to the equator, not least because soils tend to be infertile clays, with the exception of areas where volcanic activity has laid down tracts of land more suited to cultivation. As in Sumatra and Java, the fertile soil of Bali is a gift from its volcanoes, but there are climatic differences in the island that impact agriculture. The chain of mountains, which runs from west to east, ending with Gunung Agung, is a significant watershed. The steep and dryer northern side of this chain is sparsely populated, since only on the alluvial plain of Singaraja is intensive agriculture possible, and even then dry-land methods of cultivation tend to predominate. Irrigation is restricted elsewhere in the north to the amount of rainwater that can be stored in cisterns during the monsoons. Citrus fruits, vegetables, and coffee are the main crops here rather than rice.

Bali's extensive paddy fields are to be found to the south of the mountain chain in areas such as Tabanan, Badung, Gianyar, Bangli, and Karangasem. Their terraced hillsides, with ingenious irrigation systems employing tunnels as well as channels specially developed to grow wet-rice, have long ensured the prosperity of the Balinese. Here the island's cultural achievements are concentrated, not only at Klungkung but also in other centers of royal patronage. Sacred ceremonies have always involved elaborate dance-drama, these performances attracting vast crowds of worshippers. Even the ill-fated rituals at Pura Besakih in 1963 drew over 100,000 people. That the sounds of gamelan orchestras, the ringing of

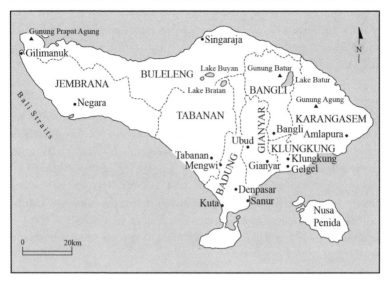

Bali today

bells, the chants of priests, and the singing of hymns were at times completely obliterated by the rumblings of Gunung Agung deterred nobody, since the dances performed to entertain the gods were simply too impressive to be missed. A coating of volcanic ash appeared a very small price for the spectators to pay.

To the south and east of the wet-rice growing area of southern Bali are two unusual features: the island of Nusa Penida and the Bukit Badung peninsula. A narrow land bridge joins the limestone peninsula to the main island, where today are situated the Ngurah Rai airport and Benoa ocean terminal. At the western tip of the Bukit Badung peninsula stands the Pura Luhur Uluwatu, a temple once reserved for the Badung royal family. Its prominent position on a rocky headland, some 328 feet above the sea, was apparently chosen by Danghyang Nirartha, a distinguished Javanese priest who came to Bali in 1537. Immediately pressed into royal service, Danghyang Nirartha is credited with both the reform of Balinese ritual and the island's caste system. Apparently, the offspring of the reformer's five wives were responsible for introducing different levels of seniority within the *ida*, or "brahmin caste." A pagoda at Pura Luhur Uluwatu is dedicated to him.

In western Bali, where the mountains are older than the eastern part of the island, rivers have worn down the landscape more extensively. Trees and bushes extend over hills, providing a convenient refuge for wild pig and game. The Muslim taboo on the consumption of pork was never imported from Java to Bali, where meat is preferred to fish. Hinduism also failed to stop the Balinese from eating beef, since only priests and worshippers attending services at temples are required to abstain. Much of western Bali is now a national park, a circumstance that further reduces the number of inhabitants in an already underpopulated area. It was on the gentle slopes of Gunung Prapat Agung, a low-lying extinct volcano 1320 feet in height, that a Dutchman shot dead Bali's last tiger. The most exotic creature at large in the national park now is the white starling, which has brilliant blue patches around its eyes and black tipped wings. A constant reminder of western Bali's volcanic character, however, are the numerous hot springs.

LAND AND WATER

Bali is subject to monsoon weather. From May until September a monsoon, blowing from Australia towards the equatorial low-pressure zone, brings moderate rainfall. On its short passage across the warm sea, the monsoon can absorb only a small amount of moisture, making this period the island's dry season. In October and November, the trade winds fall away so that rainfall results from thunderstorms arising from convectional air currents. But from late November until March, another monsoon brings high winds, turbulent seas, and heavy downpours. The northern coast of Bali becomes too dangerous for small ships to dock and the ferry service from Java is often inoperable. Called the Javanese monsoon by the Balinese, this powerful weather system provides most of the 80 inches of rain that fall each year in the island.

Bali's mountain chain intercepts rain-laden clouds so that rivers and streams flow down the sides of mountains, cutting deep ravines through the soft volcanic rock. Just a glance at the clouds clustered around the peak of Gunung Batur is enough to remind farmers in southern Bali of the ultimate source of the water arriving in their paddy fields. In the crater of this volcano is a vast freshwater lake, whose custodian is the high priest of Pura Ulun Danu, a temple dedicated to the lake goddess Dewi Danu.

Every year the heads of all the *subaks*, or "irrigation societies," gather at the temple to pay homage to the goddess and agree about the distribution of water to their villages. A network of water temples schedules planting, coordinates irrigation flows, and imposes brief periods of fallow in order to keep pests under control. The water system is quite separate from the provincial government, its operation having always been in the hands of the priesthood.

Legend claims that the lake goddess and the god of Gunung Agung emerged from an erupting volcano and, together with lesser deities, took possession of the land and waters of Bali. The goddess rules the crater lake and Gunung Batur. In precolonial times, the male god was identified with the Hindu god Shiva, who was believed to guarantee kingly authority. Because of this association, the descendants of the royal family of Klungkung remain involved with the running of the Pura Besakih temple complex, situated on the southern slope of Gunung Agung. Should the summit of the volcano be covered by clouds, a Balinese will say that Shiva has gone to sleep.

Not all the streams are so regulated as the water temple system might suggest. Torrential downpours during the Javanese monsoon can totally disrupt drainage, turning paths into torrents, flooding roads, and upsetting arrangements for sewerage. Then the only thing the Balinese can do, other than collect rainwater in buckets for drinking purposes, is to wait for the deluge to stop. On these wet days humidity tops eighty percent, making it feel much hotter than the temperature actually is.

Because Pura Ulan Danu, the temple of the crater lake, is the second most important religious site after Pura Besakih, it comes as no surprise that the goodwill of the lake goddess is considered vital for the successful cultivation of Bali's terraced paddy fields. Yet farmers worship as well the rice goddess Dewi Sri, whose shrines are spread across nearly all the cultivated land. Although an indigenous deity like the lake goddess Dewi Danu, the rice goddess is linked to Shiva in an unusual fashion. Yet she was not identified with Shiva's wife, the Hindu goddess Uma, in spite of Dewi Sri only just avoiding the lustful attentions of Shiva.

As far as we can tell in Bali, human sacrifice was never a part of Dewi Sri's cult. In Cambodia, on the other hand, victims were still being sacrificed to Uma as late as 1877, at the start of the agricultural cycle. The Balinese believe, however, that it was the deliberate slaying of Dewi Sri that inaugurated their island's abundant rice harvests. So attractive was she to Shiva that, in order to prevent her rape, the other gods killed and buried her in the ground. When rice grew from Dewi Sri's corpse, a remorseful Shiva is supposed to have given this new plant to the Balinese as their staple food.

Rice is the world's most valuable crop, feeding at least half its inhabitants. Where rice was first domesticated and grown by farmers is still a matter of dispute, but it looks as if the ancestors of the Balinese people brought rice with them from southern China, after the Austronesian peoples began to disperse around 3000 BC from the Yangtze delta. They appear to have sailed first to Taiwan, then to the Philippines before reaching Bali via Sulawesi. Certainly rice has been grown by the Balinese for several millennia. So famous did their paddy fields become that Chinese visitors named Bali "the rice island."

Equally impressed by Balinese farming methods was Thomas Stanford Raffles, who in 1811 had been appointed as governor general of the Dutch East Indies. When Holland fell under the sway of Napoleon, the Dutch ruler William V fled to England and instructed Dutch colonial officials to hand over their territories to Britain, so that they would not be occupied by the French. In 1815 Raffles visited Bali.

As the English governor general had traveled widely in the Indonesian archipelago, Raffles was in a good position to comment upon what he saw. He noted how

> the inhabitants of Bali, like those of Java, are principally employed in agriculture. The fertility of the island may be inferred from the number of people maintained on a limited spot. Rice is the chief produce of the soil, and of course the chief article of subsistence. From the mountainous nature of the country, advantage cannot be so easily taken of the periodical rains for the purpose of irrigation, but the lands are irrigated by an abundant supply of water from streams and rivers. In some places, as in Karang Asem, two crops of rice are obtained in one year; but over the greatest part of the island only one.

The efficient use of land in Karangasem, a kingdom in eastern Bali, was in fact legendary. Except for Tabanan, visitors always thought its paddy fields were better managed than anywhere else in the island.

The ultimate owners of the land and the water are Bali's gods and goddesses, but they are well served by the diligence of Balinese farmers. Upon their unremitting toil and their mutual support as members of irrigation societies, the survival of Balinese culture has always depended. In the 1970s, on mistaken advice from the Asian Development Bank, the Indonesian government demanded constant cropping. Farmers were forced to abandon traditional ways of growing rice with the result that there was chaos in water scheduling and pests proliferated in paddy fields. A decade passed before the old methods could be fully restored and harvests again reached previous levels. Only then did it become obvious to everyone just how ecologically engineered was Bali's physical landscape.

Working in a paddy field

Chapter Two

THE HUMAN LANDSCAPE

"It neither cracks in the sun nor rots in the rain."

A view of Balinese society

Fossil remains indicate the early presence of humans in the Indonesian archipelago. A number of sites have been excavated in Java, the most recent of which dates from 100,000 years ago. Whether or not Java Man, as these hunter-gatherers are called, merged with later arrivals is uncertain, but there is no doubt about the extinction of Flores Man, whose fossil remains were uncovered in caves on the island of Flores, some 340miles east of Bali. The most remarkable feature of Flores Man was his small size, which led to a comparison with the fictional hobbit. A diminutive stature naturally reignited arguments over human origins: Africa, as Charles Darwin argued, or Asia, according to some modern specialists. That Flores Man existed a mere 12,000 years ago makes his discovery all the more tantalizing, because it means that he had lived there for over half a millennium. A volcanic eruption may well have wiped out the hobbit-like cave dwellers, or possibly newcomers arriving by sea. A vague memory of Flores Man could be contained in a legend about small, flat-headed people who once lived alongside the present-day islanders.

Bali itself bears no trace of early settlement. So far archaeologists have located sites no older than 2,000 years at Gilimanuk, then a tiny island in the channel between Java and Bali, and Sembiran, a mountain village near Tejakula, a town on Bali's northern coast. The finds at Gilimanuk reveal a community of fishermen, hunters, and farmers already in possession of bronze and iron artifacts. Skeletons unearthed near the settlement belong to people of southern Mongoloid descent, Austronesian-speakers like the modern Balinese.

Having acquired the skill to construct ocean-going outriggers, they had sailed from southern China a couple of millennia before Gilimanuk was settled. The invention of the double-outrigger sailing canoe represented a huge advance on the dugout canoe: not only did the two parallel logs, attached to each side of the canoe, prevent it from capsizing in rough seas but also the much improved balance permitted the hoisting of a large sail. The aerodynamically efficient mat-and-batten sail typical of Chinese junks almost certainly derived from the mastery of the winds achieved by the earliest Austronesian mariners. It was the mat-and-batten sail that allowed junks to make headway windward, something the square-sailed vessels of Europe could not do. For this reason Portuguese shipwrights had turned to Arab models when developing long-distance craft. The famous *caravela* (from the Arabic word *karib*) had a wide hull displacing little water, with three masts hoisting triangular sails, hung from long spars. They gave greater scope in maneuvering as well as better use of the wind.

The alignment of burials at Gilimanuk, with the deceased facing north towards Gunung Prapat Agung, points to a continuity of belief with later Balinese respect for volcanoes, since the people living in Gilimanuk must have thought that the summit of this extinct volcano was the home of their deities and ancestral spirits. Inland at Sembiran great care was also taken with the dead, who were placed in two-piece sarcophagi carved from soft volcanic rock. A few of these elaborate coffins have also been excavated at Gilimanuk, where secondary burial sometimes occurred in urns. Examples of turtle-shaped stone sarcophagi are on display today at Museum Purbakala in Pejeng, not far from Ubud. They may date from around 300. Stone coffins were a specialty of prehistoric Bali, the burial practice having started among the mountain dwellers.

A stone sarcophagus dating from the fourth century

Goods from India at Sembiran point to extensive trading activities. Although such finds are not rare in Bali, those discovered at Sembiran strongly suggest that this early settlement participated in an international trading network that exchanged spices for products made in India, and even as far west as the Mediterranean. Yet the most interesting prehistoric find was of local manufacture. It is a stone stamp used to press patterns into wax for bronze casting. The one recovered from Sembiran could well have belonged to the Balinese smiths who were responsible for the famous Moon Drum at Pejeng. Copper, bronze, and iron were imported from the Southeast Asian mainland as finished articles, because the technologies necessary to produce them were slow to transfer to the Indonesian archipelago. During the period Sembiran was involved in international commerce, the so-called Dong Son culture of northern Vietnam was the most advanced in bronze manufacture. Named after the Dong Son excavation site, its defining product were deep-rimmed bronze kettledrums. These richly decorated gong-like instruments were prized by leading families in Sumatra, Java, and Bali, but only the Balinese ever succeeded in their local production.

That is why the Moon Drum or Pejeng Moon, measuring 5 feet in diameter, is considered to be one of the most spectacular specimens of the Southeast Asian Bronze Age. Its sophisticated decoration has fierce human faces between four handles, making it quite clear that no unauthorized person should dare to touch this ritual object during ceremonial events. The largest Dong Son-style bronze drum ever found, the Moon Drum resides now in the Pura Penataran Sasih temple at Pejeng.

Placed on a high ceremonial tower, the Moon Drum is believed to possess tremendous power because it fell from the sky, and was not therefore the handiwork of Balinese craftsmen. Some worshippers at the temple even say that it is an earplug of the moon goddess. Today processions tend to follow bronze drums pushed on small carriages. Behind them walk gamelan orchestras, drummers, and flautists, whose combined noise is supposed to deter any demons attracted to such ceremonial events. When the musicians play loudly, they are trying to drive malignant spirits away.

TRADE AND CONFLICT

Comparatively isolated though Bali was, wedged between eastern Java and Lombok, the island stood close to an important trade route plied by

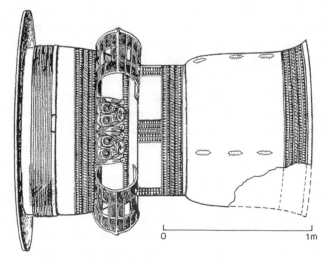

The famous Moon Drum now housed in the Pura Penataran Sasih temple at Pejeng

Indonesian and Indian ships carrying spices and aromatic woods westward. From 1514 onward the Portuguese were to follow the same route to and from Timor because of its abundant sandalwood forests. Here as elsewhere in the Indonesian archipelago, Portuguese merchants would establish themselves temporarily each year and make deals through local chieftains. Something similar must have happened in northern Bali, whenever Indian vessels stopped during their long trading voyages. For the general absence of Indian words in Indonesian languages shows that Indians were uninterested in conquest or migration: their primary objective was the purchase of spices.

Only in Sumatra was there actual conflict between Indian and Indonesian rulers. In 1025 the Tamil king, Rajendra Chola, launched "many ships in the midst of the sea, catching the king of Kedah by surprise, together with the elephants of his glorious army, and then overwhelming the great capital of Srivijaya with its gateway resplendent with great jewels." This inscription at the Tanjavur temple in southern India records the shock of the seaborne assault on peninsular Malaya and Sumatra. For Rajendra Chola's expedition was an unprecedented event in India's history and its otherwise peaceful relations with the maritime states of Southeast Asia, which had already come under Indian cultural influence for almost a millennium. India was, after all, the holy land of Buddhism and Hinduism. The cause of the sudden attack may well have been growing Tamil interest in the China trade, whose passage through the Straits of Malacca was subject to Srivijayan control.

Strategically situated to take full advantage of this India-China trade route, Srivijaya's capital city of Palembang in southern Sumatra was the focus of seaborne commerce passing eastward as well as westward. One of its kings had sent a tributary mission to the Chinese emperor in 695 with the result that Srivijaya was accorded privileged trading relations. But Srivijaya overplayed its hand. In 1017, a Tamil tributary mission returned from China with the news the Chola kingdom was regarded by the Chinese authorities as no more than a dependency of Srivijaya. Nothing could have put out the nose of the Tamil king more than this assertion of his subordinate status. Having just come to the throne, Rajendra Chola was in no mood to tolerate such an insult, and the young king would have enjoyed the support of Tamil traders who were intent on expanding their share of the profitable China trade.

The assault of 1025 does not seem to have weakened Srivijaya's power in the Straits of Malacca, since a second Chola expedition was deemed necessary in the 1070s. But the war did improve the southern Indian kingdom's relationship with the Chinese empire, which allowed Tamil merchants resident in Guangzhou to dedicate a temple there to Shiva, the favorite Chola deity.

The unexpected Chola-Srivijaya conflict was of course the result of China's phenomenal growth as a market for overseas goods. We cannot be certain of the date of Bali's first involvement with the China trade, but Chinese diplomats are known to have visited in the 240s the maritime state of Funan in the Mekong delta. They were amazed at the wealth of this tiny kingdom, in which taxes were paid in gold, silver, pearls, and perfume. At this period, before ships sailed through the Straits of Malacca, cargoes were transported overland across the narrow Isthmus of Kra in southern Thailand, and then onwards by sea to Funan, the final stopping point before the run to China. Whereas the land at Kra was heavily forested and the soils unsuited to intensive cultivation, Funan's alluvial soil could grow rice without irrigation. Regular rice surpluses were thus able to feed large numbers of merchants and seamen while they waited in Funan for a change in the monsoon pattern of winds. Though they might have to stay a couple of months, the wind system provided a swift and reliable means of sailing to China from July each year.

It is not a little ironic that Srivijaya's early supremacy as an Indonesian trading state was undermined not by India but China, once Emperor Gao Zong decided to permit unrestricted commerce in 1145. Because of its advantageous location Palembang did not stop being a major port, but Java soon overtook Sumatra as China's chief trading partner. In the process it nourished the imperial ambitions of Majapahit, a rising power in eastern Java. Already with outposts as far north as the Philippines and as far east as New Guinea, Majapahit constructed the most widespread seaborne empire before to the establishment of the Dutch East Indies. And in 1343 the island of Bali was added to Majapahit's possessions.

Prior to this conquest, Bali was ruled by its own kings. In comparison with the post-Majapahit period, however, little is known about their rule in spite of a number of villages in eastern and northern Bali still holding onto pre-Hindu rituals and social arrangements. At Tenganan, for instance,

A Javanese portrait of King Erlanga as the Hindu god Vishnu

the dead are not cremated in Hindu fashion but they are placed in the village graveyard. Referred to as the Bali Aga, the Tenganans and other like-minded villagers who chose not to accept imported Hinduism cling to ancestor worship and reverence for their own gods in the same manner as the early inhabitants of Gilimanuk and Sembiran. That such communities were termed Bali Aga, or "original Balinese," in edicts issued by pre-Majapahit kings indicates how they have always kept to traditional ways. But they are no different from the rest of the island's population, other than in their personal beliefs.

All that can be concluded is that the Bali Aga became more conspicuous as the old Balinese rulers came under increased Javanese influence. From 989 onward the language of the Balinese court was Javanese: King Udayana had imported a Javanese princess as his queen along with her ideas of how a kingdom should be properly run. Queen Gunapriya Dharmapatni was the great-granddaughter of Sindok, who had consolidated the central Javanese kingdom of Mataram by moving its political center of gravity into the eastern end of the island. In the 930s King Sindok had encouraged the migration of farmers from central Java, where renewed volcanic activity rendered agriculture increasingly precarious. It was during Sindok's reign that the *Ramayana* first appeared in the Javanese language. The translation of Sanskrit texts greatly enhanced the appeal of Hinduism in Java and allowed its spread to Bali, the only Indonesian island faithful to this religion today.

Queen Guapriya Dharmapatni's son Erlanga was to be closely associated with Rama, the divine hero of the *Ramayana*, after he was crowned king of eastern Java. Leaving his brother to rule Bali on his behalf, Erlanga responded to a request to end the turmoil following the collapse of Mataram. A Javanese chronicler tells us that "having placed his feet on the head of his enemies," the new king "ascended the throne of lions, decorated with jewels."

Besides giving birth to this conqueror-king, Udayana's queen is credited with the introduction of sorcery to Bali, but it is far from clear that witchcraft was unknown beforehand. Certainly black magic was widely feared in Java. One of Erlanga's most determined opponents was a woman "endowed with a formidable power, similar to a demon": she devastated much of what had been Mataram with "a tongue like a fiery serpent." Whatever his mother's occult powers, Erlanga overcomes in the myth of

The royal monuments at Gunung Kawi

Colon Arang none other than Rangda, the supreme Balinese witch. Modern Balinese have no doubt about the black magic practiced by women. The main characteristic of these witches is shape changing, the ability to assume a whole range of creatures or objects, such as monkeys, birds, pigs, lights, bicycles, and even motor cars. In spirit-haunted Bali there is plenty of room for spells, so that sudden illness, family disputes, and economic setbacks are often blamed on sorcery. Because of this traditional healers are on occasion consulted instead of scientifically trained specialists. Also invoked against malignant forces is the assistance of ancestral spirits.

Unlike Erlanga who was regarded as an incarnation of the Hindu savior god Vishnu in eastern Java, old Balinese kings never laid any claim to divinity. All this would change with the Majapahit conquest, when a quasi-divine monarch stood at the head of a caste system which divided society into four classes. Yet in preconquest Bali the growth of funeral cults already pointed in this direction. Nowhere is such a development more transparent than the Gunung Kawi monuments near Tampaksiring in central Bali, where a long flight of 276 stone steps descends to a river valley into the sides of which are carved shrines. According to an inscription, the Gunung Kawi, or "mountain of poetry," was completed in 1080 and its stupa-like structures contain the ashes of King Anak Wungsu, Udayana's younger brother, along with those of his wives.

Although this royal funerary cult marked a definite shift towards the reverence shown to god-kings in eastern Java, the continued use of sacred sites devoted to the worship of indigenous Balinese deities meant that imported religious ideas were largely accommodated within the island's Austronesian spiritual heritage. It is indeed the survival of a profound respect for ancestral and local spirits which has shaped Bali's unique culture.

So decisive was the Majapahit takeover of Bali, however, that for most Balinese people it appears to be the origin of almost everything valuable in their lives. The conquest of 1343 was accomplished by Gajah Mada, a renowned minister who guided Majapahit to the peak of its power, following the Mongol intervention of 1292 in eastern Java. The political fallout of the huge seaborne expedition sent by Kublai Khan to punish a recalcitrant ruler by the name of Kertanagara was the establishment of the new state of Majapahit. Satisfactory relations with the Mongol dynasty in China subsequently served Majapahit well because recognition of its commercial connections with the Indian Ocean happened to coincide with an expanding European market eager for spices.

Notwithstanding the last old Balinese king supposedly possessing supernatural powers, the Javanese overran Bali and installed a vassal king named Ketut Kresna Kapakisan. Apparently Bedaulu, the last Balinese ruler of Pejeng, was a semidemonic figure with the head of a wild boar and the body of a man. The magical powers of this king were so impressive that, whenever he concentrated on a particular problem, his head would detach itself from his body and rise into the sky. One day, a courtier became so distressed about this happening that he cut off the head of the nearest animal he could find and placed it on the king's headless torso. When Bedaulu discovered how ugly he now appeared with a boar's head, he forbade his subjects to look upon his face and resided in the seclusion of a tower. But hearing of the boar-headed monarch, Gajah Mada wanted to meet this extraordinary man. With great reluctance, the king of Pejeng finally agreed to share a meal with the Javanese minister but it proved to be his undoing because, overcome by shame at his ugliness, Bedaulu burst into flames.

Despite Bedaulu's sudden disappearance, initial attempts to Javanize the island of Bali made poor progress, especially among the villagers living around Gunung Agung and Gunung Batur, where a Bali Aga outlook was destined to persist right down until today. Under King Kapakisan and his successors, however, not only Bali but also parts of eastern Java as well as the island of Lombok were incorporated into a powerful kingdom. So strong did Bali become during the sixteenth century that it acted as a bulwark against the eastern advance of Islam. As Raffles noted on his 1815 visit, Bali's "iron-bound coast, without good harbors or good anchorages" has "in large measure shut out large vessels," thereby protecting the island from enemy attack. Specifically Raffles was referring to the coral reefs upon which so many ships have foundered.

At this time the *varna*, the Hindu class system, took root. In order of precedence, it divided Balinese society into four classes: they are the *ida* (priestly brahmins), the *satria* (warlike rulers), the *wesia* (nobles), and the *sudra* (the rest of the population). The upper castes are called the *triwangsa*, or "the three peoples": comprising less than ten percent of the Balinese people, the *ida, satria,* and *wesia* alone could claim supravillage authority. In India a distinction had been drawn between farmers and the servant class, the *sudra*, but not in Bali.

The Buddha had opposed the whole caste system. He maintained that a person's social standing should be determined not by birth but worth, by conduct and character, rather than descent. But with the decline in India of the Buddhist faith and the revival of Hinduism during the third century, the lawgiver Manu was able to reassert the role of inherited duties which had to be fulfilled in an endless cycle of death and rebirth. Apart from giving the caste system its classical form, Manu defined Indian kingship when he said that anarchy on Earth obliged

> first-born Brahma to create a king. For this special purpose he mixed together particles of mighty Indra, whose weapon is the irresistible thunderbolt, of the wind god Vayu, the very breath of life, of Yama, the king of the dead, of the sun god Surya, whose ruddy horses pull his chariot across the sky, of Agni, god of fire and sacrifice, and Kubera, god of wealth. Because the king is formed from these great gods, he surpasses all other created beings and, like the sun, he scorches eyes and hearts, so that none may look upon him.

The eventual arrival in Bali of this Indian view of a god-king turned the court into a cosmic focus, the universe in miniature. Balinese temples continued to flourish as cult centers for the worship of local deities, ancestors and sources of fertility, but the pivotal position of the king was manifest in the rise of Shiva worship. Temple priests who survived from pre-Majapahit times were often relegated to commoner status, with newly arrived Shiva specialists from the *ida* caste taking over the most influential places of sacrifice.

But divine rulers conspicuously failed to absorb Balinese villages into a tightly run state. Once there were several kingdoms in existence this proved quite impossible, yet even before political fragmentation set in during the seventeenth century, the autonomy of village communities remained essentially intact. The vital importance of cooperation in wet-rice cultivation, expressed most obviously in the *subaks* or "irrigation societies," drew the villagers together in a tight social organization. That the overall arrangements for irrigation were also handled by a priesthood which managed a network of water temples tended to keep royal power and economic activity well apart. The royal palace might be regarded as the axis of the world by the Balinese, who looked to the ruler for a guarantee of peace and prosperity: yet this expectation did not diminish in any way the importance of religious rituals performed in paddy fields. Nobody could ever afford to neglect the bountiful rice goddess Dewi Sri.

The ruggedness of Bali's physical landscape has always necessitated the digging of tunnels to supply lowland farmers with water from springs that rise close to its mountain lakes. Tunnel building is mentioned in an inscription dated to the ninth century and another refers to an irrigation society 150 years later. We know that old Balinese kings actually offered tax incentives to clear land and construct irrigation systems, but they left their management in the hands of priests and farmers. Just as holy water is always poured over temple offerings, so is it required to purify land before the planting of rice seedlings. As in every aspect of Balinese culture, nothing can hope to succeed without the propitiation of the unseen powers.

Two *nagas* guarding the entrance to one of the pavilions at Museum Bali

Chapter Three
THE SPIRITUAL LANDSCAPE

"Only the gods in the waters can guarantee purification."

Balinese saying

Spirit-haunted as is the whole of Southeast Asia, Bali boasts a unique amalgam of beliefs since the Hindu faith overlays a much older spiritual relationship with the physical world. Already at Gilimanuk, on the extreme western end of the island, its inhabitants had worshipped the deities and spirits who were believed to dwell on the summit of Gunung Prapat Agung, an extinct volcano situated to the north of this prehistoric settlement. Archaeological discoveries at Gilimanuk bear witness to early Balinese reverence for volcanoes which is still evident today. Perhaps such an enduring attitude is to be expected, considering the vital role that volcanoes have always played in Bali's history.

Volcanoes dominate the Balinese consciousness, and the highest one, Gunung Agung, acts as both the focal point of the island and the spiritual source of everything worthwhile. It is not only the abode of the mighty Hindu god Shiva, but also that of the islanders' deified ancestors. That the latter are so closely associated with this powerful Indian deity, who was imported during the Majapahit takeover of Bali, goes to show how deeply embedded Balinese beliefs still are in the chthonic powers, and in particular the honored dead. The special houses, or shrines, erected in gardens testify to a continuing connection between living family members and their deceased forebears. The more esoteric aspects of the Hindu faith, such as asceticism and yoga, never attracted the Balinese, although an acceptance of the divine quality of kingship did transfer from Java to Bali, thanks to the charisma of King Kertanagara. His spiritual elevation of the throne in the eastern Javanese kingdom of Singhasari was inherited by the Majapahit monarchs, who then passed the notion on to Bali.

Significantly, the first Majapahit ruler of Bali, Ketut Kresna Kapakisan, sought to secure his own authority on the island by founding the Pura Besakih temple complex on the southern slope of Gunung

Agung. Today this premier religious site is still managed by this king's descendants. Even though this mother temple of Balinese religion is no longer seen as a guarantor of royal authority, it does remain intimately involved with the preservation of the social order. So much divine goodness is believed to be concentrated in Gunung Agung that even viewing the summit of the volcano from a distance is considered a blessing. When there is any need to placate the hidden powers in a time of illness or death, though, a Balinese person turns away from the mountain and faces the sea. For this reason village cemeteries and cremation sites are always located on downward slopes, facing toward the sea.

Villagers lay out their houses, temples, cemeteries, and cremation grounds in such a way that a satisfactory relationship, or rather a respectful distance, exists between the visible and invisible worlds. The "unseen," or *niskala*, haunts the Balinese and so village worship is as much concerned with placating demons as with pleasing the gods. Members of a village

A grotesque gate guardian

must act as a religious community, keeping up their observances in temples, maintaining their fabric and organizing sacred festivals. Most feared is Kala, a demon given to seeking his prey at crossroads in the middle of the day, or among people outside their houses at night. Elaborately carved figures, akin to the grotesque heads of gargoyles common on medieval Western buildings, are placed near gateways to frighten off such demonic visitors.

The evil nature of Kala, "the lord of darkness," is actually surpassed by Rangda, the chief witch. This vampire-like creature sates herself on the blood of pregnant women and the entrails of unborn children. But in dance-drama, Rangda meets her match in the good lion Barong. At the end of a performance the wicked witch is vanquished and vanishes, even though every Balinese knows that she will be back along with other demons.

An abundance of fresh water has ensured in Bali that this element is viewed as more than a divine blessing: it is a spiritual force in itself. Farming in an extremely hot climate necessitates daily washing of the whole body, not simply to remove particles of dirt but even more the salty sweat that otherwise would clog the pores. Hand in hand with this thorough physical cleansing among the Balinese is a desire for ritual purification. In order to remove any lingering spiritual impurity holy water is liberally employed. It is indeed central to every ceremony, as this sacred substance cleanses, blesses, and purifies. Holy water is poured over offerings, buildings, fields, and people.

For impurity the Sanskrit word *mala* has been borrowed and innumerable versions of this unsatisfactory condition are identified, such as being touched by an unclean person, overflown by a cockerel, or struck by a falling branch. There are even circumstances in which an entire community is defiled by impurity. Sometimes the problem of village impurity can be solved with locally made holy water, although quite often there is a requirement to bring water from an important but distant temple. Village priests as well as temple priests make holy water every day so as to provide an ample supply for ritual ablutions. For domestic purposes, lay people can also make holy water from the family well, but the limits of its effectiveness are the home compound itself. A bowl of water put in an ancestral shrine is believed to produce holy water, provided the correct prayers accompany such a family request.

The most sacred water of all is located in the great crater lake next to Gunung Batur, Bali's second largest and most active volcano. This vast expanse of water belongs the goddess Dewi Danu, whose high priest is called Sanglingan, or "lightning-struck," on account of his sudden selection in childhood by a virgin priestess after the death of his predecessor. Possessed by the lake goddess at the Pura Ulun Danu temple complex, the priestess in a trance chooses each high priest, who is treated with immense respect. No matter his caste, Sanglingan is superior to all other Balinese priests, so esteemed is the water over which he has been awarded divine authority.

That the high priest, along with other priests stationed at water temples lower down the volcano, oversees Bali's impressive irrigation system must explain this unusual status. For only Dewi Danu guarantees the island's water supply: she is incarnate herself in this life-giving element, sharing her own goodness among the *subaks*, the village irrigation societies which oversee the cultivation of the island's terraced paddy fields. Without the cooperation of the lake goddess and the rice goddess, the Balinese people would starve. Their proper propitiation is literally a matter of life and death.

The rice goddess Dewi Sri is utterly chthonic, possibly because she displaced a dying-and-rising plant goddess during the early Majapahit period. For the Balinese, Dewi Sri represents everything that is good and beautiful, making her the most widely worshipped deity on the island. Similar to certain deities of ancient West Asia, the original plant goddess Dewi Melanting spent half the year above the ground and half the year below. In Sumer, the earliest civilization from which records survive, we are aware of an agricultural dimension to the stark contrast between life in the world and death in the underworld.

At Uruk, a Sumerian city that flourished around 3000 BC in what is now southern Iraq, a ceremony during the New Year celebrated the start of another agricultural cycle when the ruler impersonated the holy shepherd Dumuzi and a high priestess Inanna, the goddess of fertility. Their sacred marriage was believed to ensure the city's safety and prosperity. The Sumerian myth behind this annual rite for the growth of plants, animals, and people is quite explicit about the endless contest being waged between renewal and destruction, between life and death.

Unwilling to accept the absolute nature of death, Inanna journeyed to

An ornamental gateway at the Pura Ulan Danu, the chief temple of the
water goddess Dewi Danu

"the land of no return" so as to challenge her sister goddess Ereshkigal, "the queen of the underworld." At each of its seven gates, Inanna was obliged to shed a garment or ornament until she stood naked before Ereshkigal. After hanging lifeless on a stake for three days, the water god Enki sent two sexless beings to revive Inanna with the "food and water of life." But after her miraculous recovery, the goddess could not shake off a ghastly escort of demons as she wandered from city to city. They refused to depart unless a substitute was found. So Inanna returned home to Uruk, took offense in finding her husband Dumuzi enjoying himself at a feast, and let the demons take him away to Ereshkigal's domain. Thereafter Dumuzi's fate was spending half the year in the land of the living, the other half with the dead.

This earliest known example of a dying-and-rising deity throws light on Dewi Sri's own death. Unlike Inanna though, the Balinese rice goddess achieved no resurrection following her death and burial. Other gods had killed Dewi Sri so as to prevent her from being raped by a

A shrine dedicated to Dewi Sri, the indigenous Balinese rice goddess

lustful Shiva. Once beneath the ground, plants grew from the corpse of Dewi Sri, sticky rice from her breasts and ordinary rice from her eyes. A remorseful Shiva is then believed to have given these plants to the Balinese for their food.

The sheer fertility of Bali's volcanic soil may be an explanation for the permanent disappearance of Dewi Sri underground. Without the obvious seasonal changes experienced in ancient Sumer, the Balinese would have had less anxiety over the yields of their paddy fields. Dewi Sri did not need to return to the world in anthropomorphic form: everywhere sprouting rice signaled her continued fertility underground. And the presence of shrines dedicated to the rice goddess in almost every field ensures her complete satisfaction. The most striking aspect of the Balinese countryside is the ever-present paddy field, a patch of land invariably covered by water. With the aid of Dewi Danu and Dewi Sri, therefore, farmers are able to harvest vast quantities of rice. Before any planting is done, a village priest always leads a delegation of farmers to the ultimate source of water, Lake Batur, where gifts are offered in the temple complex and a small amount of water is taken from the lake. This holy water then stays in the village temple for the duration of the rice crop's growing cycle.

While offerings are carefully placed on field shrines for Dewi Sri, other gifts are offered to the unfriendly spirits lurking underground. These *bhuta-kala*, or "earth demons," receive their offerings near the shrines reserved for the goddess, but they are placed on the surface of the ground itself. This is intended to divert their attention from what the farmers desire to protect, in this case the rice crop. Outside houses and shops, small offerings perform the same function: along with plated palm leaves, they may include a few grains of rice, flower petals, even a coin or two, plus arak, an extremely strong rice wine. The demons are so greedy that they devour any kind of offering. When a rice crop fails, villagers say that the *bhuta-kala* are dissatisfied.

The disastrous introduction of continuous cropping during the 1970s, when farmers were forced to abandon traditional methods at the insistence of Jakarta, only served to strengthen Balinese belief in the value of a ritual approach to Dewi Sri's boundless generosity. Chaos in water scheduling and terrible outbreaks of pests almost caused a famine. Through a patent disregard for the traditional contribution made by the priesthood to an ecologically viable system of rice cultivation, Bali endured a decade of exceptionally poor harvests. Nobody really appreciated then the effectiveness of the *subaks*, whose members were used to working closely with priests devoted to the service of Dewi Danu.

It was more than fortunate for the Balinese that a percipient American anthropologist named Stephen Lansing grasped how the careful coordination of rice planting always played a key role in keeping pests down. His brilliant analysis of the situation in *Priests and Programmers: Technologies of Power in the Engineered Landscape of Bali*, which he published in 1991, came as an absolute revelation because it demonstrated the critical importance of temples in water management. Lansing was at first interested in Balinese religion, but he soon realized how totally interlinked were the geological, ecological, social, and religious aspects of this unusual island. As he later reflected, water temples had been previously overlooked by anthropologists because they seemed unimportant in comparison with the great temple complexes. But by synchronizing the flooding of rice paddies, pests were reduced to the benefit of all farmers throughout the regular procession of natural cycles, the seasons of growth and change. "When Balinese society sees itself reflected in a humanized nature, a natural world transformed by the efforts of previous generations," Lansing concluded, "it sees a pattern of interlocking cycles that mimic these cycles of nature."

SACRED SITES

Places of worship in Bali are everywhere, ranging from modest family and field shrines through village and water temples to elaborate aristocratic shrines and temple complexes sponsored by royalty near palaces and large towns. Because a Balinese temple is never considered to be a deity's permanent residence, with a highly revered cult statue, but rather an attractive place to which invisible gods and goddesses can be invited to visit, the number of sacred sites are countless. In the 1950s a visiting anthropologist calculated that there were 20,000 temples, but this is far too low a total: it is now thought that well over half a million places of worship exist. Most of the larger temples have two or three open courtyards surrounded by a low wall, each courtyard leading into the next through a stone gateway, and with a number of pavilions and shrines, the majority covered with thatch, some with a single roof but others with as many as a eleven thatched roofs rising high into the sky. There are no inner sanctums,

A temporary rice store on the edge of a paddy field

no covered areas reserved for special rites. During festivals the gods manifest their presence on special chairs, or cloth-covered thrones, raised high above the level of a temple courtyard: these sacred places are topped with white parasols as a protection from the sun.

The landscape itself is spiritual, with so many locations favored by deities that hardly anywhere can be said to lack divine significance. Villages, fields, hillsides, even uncultivated ground, are so permeated by supernatural influences that the Balinese never feel themselves separate from the invisible realm; and just by raising their eyes towards the chain of volcanoes which forms the backbone of Bali, they are reminded of the abode of well-disposed spiritual powers. Towering Gunung Agung is a constant reference point for belief, the very center of Balinese religion and the equivalent of Meru, the Hindu cosmic mountain.

Yet Gunung Agung stands for much more than Mount Meru, despite being the home of the imported Hindu deities, for the good reason that the Balinese have from earliest times regarded the summits of volcanoes as the dwelling place of their own deified ancestors. Being closest to living people, the honored dead are the first point of spiritual contact and their cult, conducted daily through rituals at garden shrines, acts as a vital link between the visible and invisible worlds in Bali. Cremation rites are indeed looked upon as a guarantee of release for the spirit of the deceased as well as its safe transfer to the spiritual realm, where senior family members become *dewa yang*, or "family gods."

Deities belonging to the Hindu pantheon, which were imported to Bali following the Majapahit conquest of 1343, have acquired definite Balinese characteristics but they still seem remote in contrast to the indigenous spirits who wield power over everyday life. Rather the great Hindu gods, the creator Brahma, the savior Vishnu, and Shiva the destroyer feature in myths about the formation of the universe. Yet their divine attributes have undergone a degree of change: instead of Agni, the original Hindu fire god, Brahma has taken over this function, while Vishnu, Wishnu to the Balinese, has become a god of waters, fertility, and the underworld. Vishnu is still imagined to ride upon the golden sunbird Garuda, but sometimes his companion is none other than Dewi Sri, the slaughtered rice goddess. Perhaps the most startling transformation has happened to Shiva, in Balinese Siwa, who is sometimes described as a bearded hermit called Batara Guru, or "the supreme teacher."

The ancient rivalry of Brahma, Vishnu, and Shiva, however, has not been entirely forgotten. According to the Balinese creation myth, Batara Guru quarreled with Brahma for the privilege of making human beings. When Brahma admitted that he did not know how to do this, Batara Guru was allowed to try first. So he made four clay figures and he gave them life. Seeing how Batara Guru had made people, Brahma did the same and remarked upon the easiness of the task. Annoyed by this slight, Batara Guru deluged Brahma's figures with rain and caused them to disintegrate. When the downpour stopped, Brahma tried again but this time he baked his creation. On seeing these new figures, Batara Guru boasted that he would eat excrement if Brahma was able to give the baked people life, but Brahma succeeded in doing so and demanded that Batara Guru make good his boast. Even more annoyed than ever, Batara Guru took some clay and made living dogs which thereafter sniffed excrement.

The unruliness of Shiva is a constant theme in Balinese mythology, the demon Kala being regarded as his troublesome son. Although he has to some extent been tamed, Kala still incorporates in his fearsome character all the evil of the indigenous demons. It should perhaps be noted that the Balinese hold no prejudice against dogs, and immediately after independence in 1949 they protested vehemently when officials sent from Jakarta ordered the shooting of pigs and dogs, both "unclean" animals in the eyes of these Muslim administrators.

One reason for Balinese protection of their dogs is a firm conviction that these animals possess second sight. A howling dog is said to have penetrated *niskala* and recognized the presence of a malignant spirit. Even temples welcome dogs. A *kuluk pengigeng*, or "guardian dog," is usually found sleeping in the shade of an outer temple courtyard. From a local household the dog turns up each day and is rewarded with food at lunchtime. Its primary role is the judgment of offerings made by worshippers at the temple. Because of an ability to penetrate the unseen realm, such a dog knows when a gift is unsatisfactory and as a result it will bark and jump about to the embarrassment of those who have brought the inadequate offering.

Not to be outdone by the indigenous deities of Bali, the Hindu gods now claim to have made the island a veritable paradise. One myth tells how Bali was once flat and barren with no hills, let alone mountains. When Java fell to Islam, these disgusted Hindu deities abandoned the

Javanese and moved eastward where they remodeled Bali's landscape, by throwing up the great volcanoes that provide the rich volcanic soil and the plentiful supply of water so necessary for successful rice cultivation. More likely of course is an alternative version of their arrival. It says the dispossessed Hindu gods were enticed across the narrow channel separating Java from Bali by a kingdom sympathetic to Hinduism, since King Kapakisan had already established at the Pura Besakih temple complex on Gunung Agung a place of worship worthy of the *batara*, or "high gods."

Part Two

AN HISTORICAL PERSPECTIVE

The Saraswati festival procession at Ubud

Chapter Four

EARLY BALI

"This desperate attack of the Balinese Grandees, who chose death, could not but arouse admiration for their proud heroism."

H. H. van Kol on the 1906 Badung *puputan*

The close relationship between Bali and Java goes back much further than 1343, the year in which the Javanese state of Majapahit subdued the Balinese, once and for all. Even though present-day Balinese regard this conquest as the most decisive event in their history, the cultural debt they owe to Java can be traced to 1284 and the accession of Kertanagara, the charismatic ruler of Singhasari, then a rising east Javanese power.

Not only did Kertanagara first bring Bali into Java's cultural orbit by briefly annexing the island, but even more he set the pattern for kingship in Java and consequently Bali, once a vassal ruler was installed by Majapahit. For King Kertanagara took royal authority to an extreme. Previously Java's Indian-influenced dynasties had aspired to divine authority and individual kings were looked upon as incarnations of the Hindu gods, but during Kertanagara's reign the pinnacle of the realm became the royal court rather than a temple complex. This fundamental shift in religious outlook must account for the unprecedented powers attributed to King Kertanagara, whose high-handed actions were to draw the Mongols into Indonesian politics.

Kertanagara claimed to have been initiated into secret Tantric rites that gave him control over demonic forces. Trance, alcohol, and sexual exercise (a practice then common to Hinduism as well as Buddhism) were said to sustain this unusual spiritual ascendancy. In a colossal statue, Kertanagara's highly syncretic worldview even led to his own depiction as the Buddha. For in the king's person it was believed that the essences of every religion now resided, an awesome strength Kertanagara was going to need in dealing with the Mongols after he gratuitously insulted their envoys in 1289. Refusing to send a member of the royal family as a hostage to the Mongol court at Beijing, Kertanagara felt secure enough to tattoo the faces of Kublai Khan's ambassadors and send them back in disgrace. Expanding Singhasari's influence into Sumatra, where Palembang was attacked in 1272, the Malayan peninsula, Borneo, and Bali may have been part of Kertanagara's strategy to form a grand alliance against the Mongols.

Inheriting the political role of the Chinese emperors, Kublai Khan resented the growth of Kertanagara's authority in maritime Southeast Asia, a reaction that would have been strengthened by the complaints he received from small tributary states in the Indonesian archipelago, who were fearful of the aggressive policy being adopted by Singhasari. So often did their tribute-bearing envoys raise this concern that in 1292 Kublai

A scene from the *Sutasoma* tale, painted on the ceiling of the audience chamber at the Klungkung palace

Khan dispatched a fleet of 1,000 ships to humble Kertanagara. Having overcome the eastern Javanese navy and landed near Surabaya, the Mongol expeditionary force advanced on Ketanagara's capital, unaware that the troublesome king was already a casualty of a local conflict. Incredible though it seems, Kertanagara's son-in-law, Raden Vijaya, persuaded the commander of the expedition to punish those who had killed Kertanagara and restore the situation. Thus Raden Vijaya ascended the throne of the new state of Majapahit, allowing the Mongols to carry away vast quantities of booty without becoming involved in a costly guerrilla war.

Opinion has always been divided about Kertanagara. In the *Nagarakertagama*, an epic poem composed by the Buddhist monk Prapanca under the patronage of Majapahit's kings, the story does not commence with the establishment of Majapahit but with the reign of Kertanagara. According to Prapanca, the Singhasari monarch was a serene and compassionate ruler. The fifteenth-century *Pararaton*, on the other hand, portrays him as nothing more than a drunkard and womanizer. Perhaps Kertanagara's greatest triumph was to be declared a *jina*, a Javanese term reserved for someone who has achieved enlightenment. In the *Sutasoma*, a fifteenth-century tale of a Buddhist prince, the king actually appears as a divine incarnation: he is described as having "the jewel mind and wise body" of an utterly perfect man. If Kertanagara were not included as the teacher Prince Sutosoma, the tale would be yet another account of gods and mythical kings locked in a timeless struggle between good and evil. That the young prince was a *jina* himself only serves to enhance the impression of the Singhasari monarch's supreme accomplishment: an understanding of the scriptures that disclosed ultimate truth. As Prapanca insisted in the *Nagarakertagama*, Kertanagara followed the path of a faultless Buddhist.

After the Majapahit takeover of Bali, the fame of Kertanagara spread widely among the Balinese. At the royal palace of Klungkung, for instance, scenes from the *Sutasoma* are painted on the ceiling of the audience chamber. Even though they have been restored on several occasions, the most recent repainting following the 1908 Dutch assault on the palace, their faithfulness to the traditional style of *wayang* painting is a testimony to eastern Javanese influence on Bali. Figures closely resemble the shadow puppets which had captivated audiences in Java for centuries. With the transfer of Indianized literary and visual traditions from Java to Bali under

Majapahit rule, it comes as no surprise that Ketut Kresna Kapakisan was accorded divine honors. This Majapahit-sponsored king was the youngest son of Danghyang Kapakisan, a priest whose advice was greatly valued by Gajah Mada, Majapahit's powerful chief minister. Preparations for Ketut Kresna Kapakisan's duties as a vassal ruler included a change of caste status, from brahmin to warrior. The unequivocal backing of Gajah Mada smoothed the way for his assumption of power in 1352, and the chief minister never had cause to regret his choice of ruler for Bali.

King Kapakisan set up his court at Samprangan, near the modern town of Gianyar in central Bali. But the general focus for the Balinese nobility was less Samprangan, where the first palace was built, than Gelgel; because the descendants of Kapakisan moved their court to this southern town before the end of the fourteenth century. A war of succession undermined Majapahit's strength in the early 1400s, when Malacca was beginning to develop its role as the chief entrepôt for Southeast Asian trade. Arguably the new Ming dynasty, established after the expulsion of the Mongols from China in 1368, marked a turning point in the fortunes of Majahahit, since its Chinese emperors looked to the Straits of Malacca as the main artery of east-west commerce, and not Java. The fledgling state of Malacca was therefore protected from Thai and Indonesian interference by the great Ming admiral Zheng He, who made use of a temporary naval base at Malacca during his ocean voyages. A tributary mission to China in 1405 was rewarded by Emperor Yongle with official recognition of Malacca's independence.

Three years later the ruler of Brunei was accorded a special honor when he died in China. So pleased was the emperor with this "southern king" who came to present tribute in person, that he was splendidly received at court, expensively buried, and his infant son accompanied home by a Chinese commissioner with instructions to assist the prince during his minority. Today the statuary lining the approach to the royal tomb can still be seen near Nanjing.

Stable foreign relations were a serious matter for Emperor Yongle, whose title means "perpetual happiness." Concerned to restore Chinese suzerainty in the "southern oceans," this emperor had dispatched the grand eunuch Zheng He on his first seaborne expedition in 1405. By the time Yongle died in 1424, these voyages had caused the authority of the Son of Heaven, as the Chinese emperor was known, to be acknowledged by courts as far away as India, Arabia, and Africa, even Egypt sending an ambassador to China. In 1415 the sultan of Malindi sent an embassy with exotic gifts, among them a giraffe for the imperial park. At the palace entrance in Nanjing, Yongle personally received the animal, along with a "celestial horse" and "celestial stag." The giraffe was looked upon as "a symbol of perfect virtue, perfect government, and perfect harmony in the Empire and the Universe." To mark the emperor's appreciation the ambassadors were conducted all the way back on the fifth voyage of 1417–19.

Another factor in Majapahit's decline was undoubtedly Islam. Parameswara, the founder of Malacca, was a Hindu-Buddhist king but he encouraged Muslim traders to use his port-city. The nodal location of Malacca was fully appreciated by Emperor Yongle, who gave Paramesvara a war junk to protect his capital from seaborne attack. And it made no difference to the Chinese emperor that shortly afterwards Malacca adopted the Muslim faith, then being spread by the permanent residence of Indian merchants in the Indonesian archipelago. Admiral Zheng He was, after all, a Muslim too. How very different Chinese tolerance was from the religious fanaticism of the Portuguese, whose sense of national identity had been forged through a long struggle against Muslim states in Iberia. When Alfonso de Albuquerque, the second Portuguese viceroy in Asia, took Malacca by storm in 1511, he told his followers that its capture would destroy Islam locally, bankrupt Cairo and Mecca, besides obliging the Venetians to buy spices in Lisbon: a truly wonderful mixture of spiritual and financial gain.

The Annals of Semarang even credit Chinese Muslims with introducing Islam, although this may be no more than a memory of Zheng He's great fleet calling at Javanese ports. For modern Samarang continues to celebrate at the Sam Po Kong temple the admiral's personal faith. The fact that this major Javanese city, situated on the northern coast of the island, was already Muslim is an indication of the pressure being applied to Hindu Majapahit. When its last king was defeated and killed in 1527, a wave of refugees moved to Bali. They included nobles, priests, and craftsmen so that new craft centers still in operation today sprang up with goldsmiths at Celuk, painters at Kamasan, and metallurgists at Klungkung. The most influential refugee was Danghyang Nirartha, a priestly adviser who joined the Balinese court at Gelgel.

From the record of Zheng He's seven seaborne expeditions between 1405 and 1433 we know how at Surabaya, a large port on the northern coast of Java, the Chinese fleet sometimes anchored for four months, waiting for a favorable monsoon wind for the homeward voyage in July. From Surabaya the admiral went by boat upriver to Majapahit, where he discovered Chinese copper coins were in use as currency. He also met Chinese merchants who had taken up residence there. This came as no surprise to Zheng He because Gresik, another port near Surabaya, had been founded by a southern Chinese who had sent tribute to Emperor Yongle in 1411. Despite no mention in the record of Zheng He's voyages of any visit to Bali, it seems improbable that smaller Chinese ships were not sent to both the nearby islands of Madura and Bali during the fleet's stay at Surabaya. The Balinese themselves believe that contact between Bali and China is longstanding.

An instance of such early contact was the Chinese wife of King Sri Jaya Pangus, who married a merchant's daughter at Singaraja two centuries before the Majapahit conquest. In spite of matrimonial difficulties arising from the queen's inability to provide Sri Jaya Pangus with a son and heir, and the unhelpful intervention of the lake goddess Dewi Danu, the royal couple became at the end of their troubled lives the indigenous god and goddess of prosperity: their remote temple at Baliankang, situated to the north of Lake Batur, preserves a real sense of this unusual transformation. It meant that Lakshmi, the Hindu goddess of good fortune, was never imported to Bali.

GRANDEUR AND DECLINE

The sixteenth century was Bali's golden age. Stimulated by the influx of Javanese refugees fleeing Muslim domination in Java, the reign of Waturrenggong witnessed political, economic, and cultural progress unmatched before or afterwards. Balinese arms gained a foothold in eastern Java and captured the islands of Lombok and Sumbawa; farmers extended the area under rice cultivation, so that improved harvests were able to feed a growing population; and, last but not least, there was a cultural renaissance that fused the rather staid Majapahit traditions with the island's own more informal approach to art and architecture, music, and drama. This spontaneity has never been lost, something which makes the culture of Bali appear so fresh and exciting now.

Pura Besakih, Bali's most important place of worship

King Waturrenggong retained cosmic responsibility for the island's welfare, with his court defined as the magical-political center of the universe. Here and at the Pura Besakih temple complex, located on the southern slope of Gunung Agung, elaborate rituals were performed to maintain the divine link. In this role Waturrenggong was assisted by Danghyang Nirartha, who raised the cult of the Hindu god Shiva to prominence.

Bali's golden age flickered during the reign of Waturrenggong's eldest son, Radja Bekung, and went out under his grandson, Anom Pamayan, who was obliged to abdicate. Military reverses in eastern Java, Sumbawa, and Lombok were compounded by bitter court intrigue, so in 1710 a royal cousin concluded that Gelgel was cursed and moved the court to Klungkung, a few miles to the north. There the new king assumed the title of Dewa Agung, or "supreme one," yet it was little compensation for the leakage of power to noble families, who soon set up kingdoms of their own. Although King Waturrenggong's authority had extended well beyond the shores of Bali, the island was now a patchwork of tiny states: Karangasem, Badung, Mengwi, Gianyar, Tabanan, Buleleng, Bangli, Jembrana, and of course Klungkung, whose rivalry and quarrels preoccupied the Balinese people.

The Dewi Agung's court at Klungkung still symbolized royal Hindu grandeur, but never again would one ruler exercise political authority over the island as a whole. Bali's other rulers were in effect rivals of the Dewi Agung, whose authority within his own diminished territory was often thwarted by determined villagers and priests belonging to progressively autonomous foundations. But a positive outcome of the breakup of a united Balinese kingdom was the expansion of cultural activity as each king tried to outshine his competitors in the fields of music, dance-drama, and the visual arts. Of all the kingdoms, Mengwi in western Bali was the most forceful until it overreached itself in 1891: then an alliance among its threatened neighbors brought defeat and partition.

Now Mengwi is a quiet town, visited by tourists wishing to see the

The soaring *meru* at the Pura Taman Ayun in Mengwi

renowned Pura Taman Ayun, the ancestral temple of the Mengwi royal family, which has a moated layout to recall the cosmic sea surrounding the Hindu world. Upon this vast expanse of water, Vishnu slumbers on the cosmic serpent Ananta between his incarnations. Given the sudden overthrow of the Mengwi kingdom, it is not a little ironic that its royal family should have relied on this savior god as their trusted guardian. The root of Vishnu's name, *vish*, means "to pervade," and he is regarded as the all-pervading presence in the universe, whose power is manifested through *avataras*, or "descents," in which a part of his divine essence is incarnated in human or animal forms. An avatar appears whenever evil threatens the Earth. It was as the hero Rama that Vishnu overcame the terrible demon Ravana in the island of Sri Lanka. But in Bali the god never came to the aid of Mengwi, even though today the local people remain loyal to the descendants of the defeated king and still cherish the shrines established for royal ancestor worship.

ENTER THE DUTCH

It was in this Bali of tiny, warlike kingdoms that the Dutch began to assert themselves. Although the Dutch had ejected with ease the Portuguese from the Indonesian archipelago, with the exception of the Lesser Sunda Islands and a part of Timor, Holland was not the power it had been before the nineteenth century. French domination had led in 1806 to the imposition of Napoleon's younger brother Louis as king. But Louis knew that his Dutch subjects would suffer most of all from the embargo that Napoleon hoped would cripple Britain's trade with Europe, and rather than enforce it in 1810 he went into voluntary exile. This act of defiance infuriated Napoleon and delighted the emperor's critics, but it did not improve the international trading opportunities of Dutch merchants, already cut off from their colonies by the Royal Navy. So strong were the British at sea that by 1811 France and its allies possessed no overseas territories at all.

With the return of peace in Europe after Napoleon's exile to St. Helena in 1815, the Royal Navy remained the largest navy in the world. Unchallenged, Britain could thus dictate the shape of maritime Southeast Asia. Thinking of the balance of European power, the Dutch were allowed to reoccupy their holdings in the Indonesian archipelago, although it was agreed that Holland would cede Malacca and recognize the British claim to Singapore for an undertaking that London would never enter into any

Cornelis de Houtman's fleet, which arrived at Bali in 1597

treaties with rulers south of the Straits of Malacca. Because the British government always preferred to have weak European countries as its colonial neighbors, it opposed neither the Dutch conquest of Aceh, the last independent sultanate in northern Sumatra, nor the Spanish conquest of the Sulu sultanate in the southern Philippines. In the 1880s a request from Sulu for assistance against Spain was turned down flat in London: Lord Granville, the foreign secretary at the time, advised the sultan to pray instead. The advice was not misplaced as a Dominican friar in Manila had just preached a crusade aimed at the Muslim inhabitants of the sultanate. The British were happy for the Spaniards and the Dutch to tidy up the last corners of independent Southeast Asia, but no other European country had permission to intrude.

So Holland got a free hand in its dealings with the Balinese. First contacts had taken place in the sixteenth century as Dutch privateers began to arrive in search of easy fortunes. In 1597, three ships commanded by Cornelis de Houtman reached Bali, their crews by then reduced from 249 to 89 men. Scurvy, accidents, mutiny, and pirates had taken their toll. Landing at Kuta in southern Bali, de Houtman spent several days hunting before he visited the royal court at Gelgel. No satisfactory agreement could be reached over trade, because the Balinese had too few products that were in demand at Amsterdam. Scoundrel though de Houtman undoubtedly was in his relations with the peoples he encountered in the Indonesian archipelago, Bali worked its charm on him to the extent he called the island Jonck Hollandt, "Young Holland." And two of his men jumped ship, apparently entranced by the beauty of the Balinese women. Despite the failure to establish viable commercial arrangements with Bali, de Houtman's account of his voyage excited Dutch merchants keen to dominate the spice trade. According to de Houtman, the king of Bali was "a good-natured fat man who had two hundred wives, drove in a chariot pulled by two white buffaloes and owned fifty dwarves."

Now began a period known in Holland as the *wilde vaart*, or "unregulated voyages," during which Dutch captains scrambled for a share of Indonesia's spices. Such were the profits gained by even the most incompetent masters that in 1602 competing merchant companies merged to form the United East India Company, which soon set up its headquarters on the present-day site of Jakarta. When Governor-General Jan Pieterszoon Coen informed the directors of the company of its occupation, he was instructed to call the new settlement Batavia, an ancient name for the Netherlands. Not only was Batavia a focal point for trade; it was also a military base in the struggle against Portuguese and Spanish traders already active in maritime Southeast Asia. But the

A sixteenth-century Dutch view of the king of Bali

51

establishment of a fortified outpost in western Java was to have unexpected consequences for the Dutch, once the steady extension of its influence throughout the Indonesian archipelago laid the foundation of a colonial empire, which by 1908 included the island of Bali.

The Dutch East India Company always had great hopes for Bali, a promise that was not to be fulfilled. As a Hindu kingdom, it was expected in 1633 that the Balinese would be willing allies against Mataram, then a powerful sultanate in central Java. Its aggressive ruler, Sultan Agung, had besieged Batavia in 1628 as well as 1629, but without a navy he was unable to stop its resupply by sea. The Dutch request for a military alliance fell on deaf ears for the good reason that Balinese foreign policy was never dictated by religion. Except for occasional exchanges of letters and gifts, this remained the tenor of Balinese-Dutch relations until the nineteenth century. Apart from slaves, Bali lacked useful resources for the Dutch East India Company.

Throughout the era of their supremacy in the Indonesian archipelago, the sole motive of the Dutch was to extract as much advantage as they could in their commercial relations with local peoples. Java was the first island to bear the brunt of this pressure, because Batavia needed plenty of rice for itself, its ships, and its growing number of outposts. Hardly surprising then was the rise of Mataram as Batavia's main antagonist. Situated in the rich agricultural region of central Java, Mataram began to emerge in the 1590s around the modern city of Yogyakarta, where an early ruler is credited with its forcible conversion to Islam. Despite finding himself unable to overcome Batavia, Sultan Agung remained uncompromising in his treatment of Dutch prisoners, shipwrecked sailors, and company officials alike. Only those who embraced the Muslim faith had any freedom to move around: most of those who converted took Javanese women as wives.

These Dutchmen would never be allowed to return to Holland, because race was always an unbridgeable gulf between the Dutch and the Indonesians. Settlers who married local women could never go home, other than in exceptional circumstances. The ban was then extended to men who used female slaves as concubines, but this did not stop them from chasing good-looking Indonesians because so few Dutch women came to live in Southeast Asia. More relaxed was the attitude of the Portuguese and the Spaniards, at least until Catholic missionaries arrived in force. At Malacca, St. Francis Xavier was shocked by the moral laxity: one of the Portuguese residents had 23 concubines. Yet in persuading them to marry one of their partners Xavier imposed a definite color bar. "When a woman was dark in color and ugly-featured, he employed all his eloquence to separate his host from her. He was even ready, if necessary, to find him a more suitable mate." Many Portuguese did not share this racial prejudice, but there were others who did, so the offspring from such marriages often found themselves poorly treated. As the Portuguese viceroy Antonio de Mello de Castro lamented in 1664, "our decay in these parts is entirely due to treating the natives thereof as if they were slaves or worse than Moors."

Batavia's request for an alliance against Mataram rulers would not have impressed Balinese rulers who were well aware of Dutch ruthlessness elsewhere in the Indonesian archipelago, which was most dramatically exposed in 1621 by the extermination of the entire population of the tiny Banda group of islands. Tiring of annual trade negotiations with the Bandanese over the purchase of nutmeg and mace, Governor-General Jan Pieterszoon Coen ordered a massacre of the islanders and their replacement with Dutch colonists and slave labor. The Dutch were always content to leave the institution of slavery alone: it is estimated that 8,000 Balinese slaves worked in seventeenth-century Batavia out of a total slave population of 15,000.

So infuriated was Governor-General Johannes van den Bosch in the 1830s by the abolition of slavery during the period the British took over control of the Dutch East Indies, in order to deny the territory to the French, that he called the decision a prime example of the "perverted liberalism" of Raffles. To restore a degree of subjection, Johannes van den Bosch introduced the *cultuurstelsel*, or "culture system," through which Javanese farmers had to devote one-fifth of their labor or sixty-six days a year to the cultivation of export crops for the Dutch colonial authorities. Profit was once again the order of the day as an impoverished Holland attempted to recover financially from Napoleon.

Appointed to administer Java during the Napoleonic War, Thomas Stanford Raffles had sent troops against the Balinese kings of Buleleng and Karangasem in 1814 in an attempt to end the slave trade. They submitted but the trade continued nonetheless. After 1816 the restored Dutch colonial authorities tried to get the Balinese kings to accept Batavia's suzerainty without any success. But these rulers were willing to provide soldiers for the Dutch colonial army in return for payment, and these military slaves proved valuable enough to persuade Batavia to leave Bali alone for a couple of decades.

But two factors had convinced the Dutch by 1840 that Bali must be brought under Batavia's direct influence: Balinese piracy and the plundering of shipwrecks, plus the growing interest of other European powers in the island. Bali's international trade had increased remarkably and, in particular, with the energetic British colony of Singapore. Its free-port status was yet another legacy of Raffles, who in 1819 had convinced the sultan of Johore about the advantage of an English East India Company trading post on the island. Unwilling to make any tax concession itself, Batavia could only watch with envy the growth of Singapore's trading links with islands in the Indonesian archipelago not yet firmly under its control.

At last in 1841 a Dutch ambassador managed to get the Balinese kings of Badung, Klungkung, Karangasem, and Buleleng to sign treaties recognizing the authority of Batavia. It was not the intention of the colonial authorities to administer Bali immediately, but the treaties created a legal basis for the exclusion of any other European power. Although the Dutch would have preferred a single treaty with the Dewa Agung at Klungkung, the fractured nature of political authority in the island ruled out such a straightforward arrangement. In spite of the Balinese kings thinking at the time that they had not given away any of their power, the treaties did severely limit their ability to maneuver in a future crisis.

A thorn in the side of the Dutch was Mads Johann Lange, a Danish trader based in the southern Balinese port of Kuta. From Hong Kong the enterprising Dane had sailed to Lombok and Bali, in search of commercial opportunities. Earlier Lange worked for Jardine Matheson, one of whose founders James Matheson did so much to foment hostilities between Britain and China. The First Opium War of 1840–42 suited the business partners William Jardine and James Matheson because it prevented the Chinese authorities from banning their sale of Indian-grown opium. Unable to acquire sufficient silver to sustain an unfavorable balance of payments involved in the China trade, caused by massive purchases of tea, the English East India Company had deliberately stimulated the production of opium in India. Except for a single year, 1782, when its own vessels sold the drug in Guangzhou through an acute shortage of bullion, the English East India Company was careful to leave opium sales to private traders. This policy did not fool Beijing and in 1839 a special commissioner was sent to southern China with orders to stamp out the whole sordid business.

The First Opium War, which resulted from this action, humiliated the Chinese empire and led to the cession of Hong Kong as a British sovereign base. With his personal experience of the opium trade, Lange saw no problem in importing the drug to Bali, where at Kuta his activities easily surpassed a Dutch trading post already in the town. His house, factory, and warehouses were constructed on land belonging to the king of Badung. Both the royal courts of Badung and Klungkung valued Lange's advice, but the Dane showed respect to every Balinese ruler, traveling around the island on horseback to visit their courts. This consideration for local etiquette paid handsome dividends since Lange obtained slaves at knock-down prices and sold them to slave traders in Kuta at an enormous profit. Using his contacts in Hong Kong, Lange also became a major importer of Chinese copper coins, which were used as currency in Bali. He bought these coins at the rate of 1,400 to a Singapore dollar and sold them in Bali at the rate of 700 to 1, realizing a tidy 100 percent profit on every transaction.

It was the decision in 1145 of the Song emperor Gao Zong to encourage commercial contacts with Southeast Asia which first caused a massive outflow of Chinese coins. So worried did China become about this drain of currency that barter trade was tried instead: silks, embroideries, and porcelain were offered in return for spices. But Chinese coinage remained the preferred medium of exchange in Bali. So valued were these coins that they were attributed magical powers and widely used to adorn sacred objects, including textiles. Today Balinese painted wall hangings are often suspended from Chinese coins, since the holes in their centers allow the insertion of string. And they are also woven into ritual fabric in the belief that they provide an extra defense against demonic interference.

Pragmatism marked Lange's overall approach to business life: to please the Balinese he took a local wife, who gave him two sons, and to please the Chinese merchants with whom he cooperated, he married one of their daughters, who gave birth to a daughter of his own. Yet Lange's trading operation was not destined to last. Steamships had begun to replace sailing ships and Kuta was unsuitable for these new vessels. Lange remained in business until 1859, when he announced his return to Denmark. Before he could embark, however, he fell ill after dining with a prince at Denpasar, and died, it was believed, of poison. As one contemporary said: "There was more of the bold Viking than the prudent trader in his nature... He delighted in overcoming all difficulties save those of commercial life."

With the passing of Lange, the Balinese kings were deprived of a worldly adviser at the very moment the island was vulnerable. As a result of Dutch military activity in 1846, 1848, and 1849, Batavia gained control over northern Bali, where Singaraja was developed as a port for steamships. It soon eclipsed Kuta as the center of the opium trade. Buleleng was indeed the first kingdom to come under colonial rule in 1854. To its south, Jembrana was reduced to the same status in the following year and, from 1860 onwards, a Dutch official stationed at Singaraja administered the whole of northern and western Bali, according to orders received from Batavia.

Yet it took another forty-six years for the Dutch to achieve complete mastery of the island, an advance facilitated as much by squabbles between the remaining independent kings as the application of modern weaponry. The territorial ambitions of Mengwi were at the center of this internecine conflict, although its ultimate origin lay in an attempt by Klungkung to subdue all of southern Bali. The Dewa Agung intrigued with the rulers of Badung and Tabanan, both of whom had territorial disputes with Mengwi, and in 1891 he ordered the chief minister of Mengwi to present himself at Klungkung and explain the reasons for his reluctance to adjust borders. Fearing for his own safety, this minister refused to obey the order, which was the signal for troops from Badung, Bangli, and Tabanan to open hostilities. Soldiers from Klungkung also joined the invasion. Hemmed in by enemies, the king of Mengwi left his palace in a sedan-chair and, at the nearby village of Mengwitani, he drove a dagger through his heart rather than become a prisoner.

Two of his closest followers managed to get away and at Karangasem they reported what had happened to King Gusti Gede Djelantik, who was a relative of the Mengwi royal family. Once he realized how the ambitions of the Dewa Agung stood behind these events, Gusti Gede Djelantik lost all patience with Klungkung. Already appointed a *stedehouder* (local ruler) by the Dutch, the Karangasem king as a high colonial official was in a position to influence Batavia's treatment of the Dewa Agung, who seems to have had no inkling of the coming onrush of colonialism himself. The attitudes of the Dutch authorities at Batavia were steadily hardening towards the Indonesians, whom they saw in the main as uncooperative colonial subjects. This frustration was aggravated by the continued resistance of Aceh, a sultanate in northern Sumatra. To deal with the stubborn Acehnese, harsh policies were recommended by L. W. C. van Berg, a noted specialist on foreign affairs. He said that the Aceh should be settled by Amboinese, preferably ex-colonial servicemen in fortified villages. They would gradually take over from the "degenerate" Acehnese "in the same way that savages withdrawal from the spreading of civilization…and die out."

A pretext for a similarly harsh line to be adopted in Bali came in 1904, when the king of Badung was accused of tolerating the looting of a shipwreck off Sanur. Despite the lack of a proper investigation, which would have disclosed how the Chinese-owned schooner was deliberately run aground in order to demand excessive compensation and how men were sent to guard the ship as soon as its wreck was reported to the royal court in Denpasar, the local Dutch officials demanded a large payment from the king of Badung. It was as flimsy as the excuse used in 1856 by Britain to justify the start of the Second Opium War.

Then a Chinese-owned coastal vessel no longer registered in Hong Kong was boarded at Guangzhou by Chinese harbor police in pursuit of pirates: the British consul regarded the incident as "an insult of a very grave nature" to the flag that the schooner had then no right to display, to the delight of British traders who welcomed an opportunity for treaty revision. That the schooner was rigged with batten sails and had flown no flag, so that it appeared to be a local vessel, cut no ice at all in London. Riding on a wave of popular enthusiasm for his gunboat policy, Lord Palmerston was only too pleased to have an excuse to resort to arms. Only an unquestioned belief in the civilizing value of commerce can explain how a country such as Britain could, on one side of the globe, try to block the African slave trade while, on the other, insist that massive quantities of opium were exported to China.

It seemed enough that the Sulawesi-based schooner wrecked off Sanur was actually entitled to sail under the Dutch flag to justify an armed response from Batavia, once Badung refused to accept any financial liability. Five warships duly arrived at Sanur with 3,000 colonial troops in late 1906. Naval gunfire had already reduced most of Denpasar to a ruin before the attackers were confronted by gaily dressed men, women, and children simply armed with swords and spears. Unflinchingly, these Balinese people marched into a hail of shells and bullets, while others stabbed each other or died by their own hands. This well-publicized Dutch encounter with *puputan*, or "until the last," caused an outcry of protest in Holland without doing anything to prevent a second mass suicide two years later at Klungkung.

Seeking to impose its opium monopoly in Bali, as elsewhere in the Dutch East Indies, Batavia stirred up trouble the length of the island. Only in Karangasem was Gusti Gede Djelantik able to maintain order himself. Clashes with Dutch colonial forces near Klungkung were construed as outright rebellion by the Dewa Agung, who recklessly decided on a last-ditch stand for Balinese independence. Prior to building defenses at Klungkung, the Dewa Agung convened a meeting of all the Balinese rulers so as to urge joint resistance to the Dutch. At the gathering, Gusti Gede Djelantik smashed an egg against a rock to show the futility of an armed confrontation with Batavia. He urged negotiations but the Dewa Agung would not listen. In 1908 the scene was therefore set for a repeat of the Denpasar massacre, except that the number who died in the Klungkung *puputan* was 300 compared with 1,800 during the first one. The king of Bangli, who had lent support to the Dewa Agung, wisely capitulated. The *puputan* on April 28, 1908, at Klungkung inaugurated the colonial period in Bali's history, which would last until 1949.

Chapter Five

COLONIAL BALI

"In the Dutch East Indies… the prevailing colonial atmosphere created an invisible barrier between colonizers and colonized. Although never expressed verbally, it was apparent in many areas of social behavior. It was very subtle, ranging from suppressed disdain to polite avoidance of intimate personal contact."

Prince Made Djelantik of Karangasem

The island of Lombok, to the east of Bali, had already been subdued by the time Balinese independence was destroyed in 1908 at Klungkung. The tangled relationship between Bali and Lombok unraveled during the 1890s, when the Muslim population of Lombok rose against their Balinese masters. Although Karangasem was closely associated with Lombok, and indeed its overlord, the Hindu ruler of the island had chosen to acknowledge Batavia in 1843. He subsequently showed himself more than willing to agree to its demands, but the Dutch constantly sought an excuse for imposing direct rule over Lombok. A desire to control opium smuggling and slavery meant that the Muslim uprising was a godsend for Batavia, and a blockade was followed in 1894 by a full-scale invasion. The last stand of the Balinese ruler's followers ended in a *puputan* that received little notice in comparison with the later ones at Denpasar and Klungkung. Besides enlisting the rebellious Lombok Muslims, the Dutch colonial authorities got the king of Karangasem, Gusti Gede Djelantik, on their side.

The ageing ruler of Lombok died in Batavia a year after his disposition. Unlike Bali, where the Dutch eventually restored all the kingdoms in 1938, Lombok remained under direct colonial rule, not least because its Muslim inhabitants were unwilling to accept a Hindu king again. No member of the Lombok royal family was ever allowed to return to the island.

Appreciating how the Dutch annexation of Lombok, and the loss of territory there, had left Karangasem as a weak Balinese kingdom, Gusti

Gede Djelantik ceded his state to Batavia in return for an acknowledgment of his continued role as regent. Lineage has always been a preoccupation of the Balinese nobility and so becoming a *stedehouder*, a highly esteemed rank in the colonial hierarchy, Gusti Gede Djelantik ensured the continuity of his own family's exulted position. As a ruler, he could now be certain that his relations would be able to maintain the integrity of their lineage without any difficulty. They were, after all, still royalty. In central Bali the kingdom of Gianyar followed Karangasem's example in 1900, largely because its existence was then under threat from dissident nobles as well as from the ambitions of the Dewa Agung at Klungkung.

Elsewhere there was no appetite among Balinese kings for following the example set by Karangasem and Gianyar. But the shipwreck off Sanur in 1904, and the refusal of the Badung king to accept any blame for the looting of its cargo by his subjects, gave the Dutch a reason for conquering this kingdom two years afterward. Since the king of Tabanan had lent his support to Badung, he was overthrown as well. The destruction in 1906 of the Bandung court at Denpasar encouraged the Dutch to believe that the remaining independent rulers of Klungkung and Bangli would soon throw in the towel, but the Dewa Agung at Klungkung was too proud to admit that no hope of successful resistance now remained. Since Gusti Gede Djelantik could not convince him otherwise, Klungkung and Bangli drifted into the pointless war with the Dutch. Ashamed though many people in Holland were at the violent end to Balinese independence, Batavia had achieved what it always wanted: the acquisition of the entire island.

The last *puputan* at Klungkung, in which the line of Ketut Kresna Kapakisan was almost extinguished, marked the advent of full colonial rule. Yet its exploitive nature in the Dutch East Indies as a whole was already coming under intense scrutiny in Holland, where the publication of the anticolonial novel *Max Havelaar* in 1860 had revealed the harsh side of Dutch rule in Java. To the amazement of Holland, the Dutch East Indies had provided nineteen percent of all government revenue in the 1840s, a figure that grew to thirty-one percent over the next two decades, an entirely different situation to the Philippines, which the United States took from Spain in 1898. There American investment, according to President William McKinley, was intended to "educate the Filipinos, and uplift and civilize them."

Two views of early Batavia

Perhaps the oddest Western colonial venture in Southeast Asia was the American occupation of the Philippines. Just as Britain had not acquired an empire there by accident, but through intense competition with France, so the United States could not claim that its annexation of the Philippines occurred in a fit of absentmindedness. Although it suited President McKinley to portray the event as an unforeseen result of American intervention in the Spanish Caribbean, the truth is that he had already decided to advance his country's position in the Pacific by means of the acquisition of key islands.

American missionaries were soon disconcerted by the discovery that the Filipinos were already Christians, having been forcibly converted to Catholicism by Spain. Worse still there remained in the southern Philippines a sizeable Muslim population whose determination to resist conversion was by no means weakened by the ousting of the Spaniards. Most baffled of all were the Japanese, who regarded the American colony with a mixture of fascination and frustration. They wondered how the first people to escape from the clutches of European colonialism could presume to restrain Japan's own imperial ambitions while becoming Southeast Asian colonialists themselves.

McKinley's disingenuous notion of improving the lot of the Filipinos never entered the heads of colonial officials in the Dutch East Indies, despite a great deal of soul-searching in Holland itself. Eduard Dekker, the author of *Max Havelaar*, was fully aware of the colonial situation: he had worked in Java and seen the *cultuurstelsel* regime at first hand. He explained how

> the Government of the Dutch East Indies likes to write and tell its masters in the Motherland that everything is going well. The Residents like to report that to the Government. The Assistant Residents, who, in turn, receive hardly anything but favorable reports from the Controleurs, also prefer not to send anything disagreeable to the Residents. All this gives birth to an artificial optimism in official and written treatment of affairs, in contradiction not only to the truth but also to the personal opinion expressed by the optimists themselves when discussing those affairs orally, and—stranger still!—often in contradiction to the facts in their own written statements.

This devastating exposure of Batavia's self-serving and secretive rule, so concerned to hide the extent of its own oppression and corruption, became a powerful weapon in the hands of liberal politicians in Holland, who wanted to put an end to forced labor altogether. But these same liberals faced a dilemma because they wished to abolish *cultuurstelsel*, the system of compulsory labor imposed in the 1830s, without losing the profits that the Dutch government increasingly drew from the island of Java.

The Dutch East Indies could no longer be portrayed as a paradise on Earth and by the start of the twentieth century this had brought about a significant shift in colonial policy. Voices raised in favor of relief for the oppressed peoples of Java, who were at last deemed worthy of justice and social progress, led to the recruitment of a new breed of colonial officers. And they journeyed eastward with copies of *Max Havelaar* in their luggage. Even though the so-called ethical policy which emerged was only another species of colonial exploitation, the introduction of new enterprises, including the extraction of minerals and oil, raised living standards throughout the Dutch East Indies, gave good returns to investors and, most of all, satisfied anxious humanitarians.

At the very moment that Queen Wilhemina announced in 1901 an enquiry into welfare in Java, and thereby gave official approval to an ethical approach, Batavia was paradoxically in the middle of an aggressive forward policy aimed at the remaining independent parts of the Indonesian archipelago, as the assaults on Bandung and Klungkung were shortly to bear witness. At The Hague, former minister for foreign affairs Van Karnebek told the Dutch parliament how this new belligerence signaled the end of "an old tradition in the East Indies," whereby one sought to establish "contacts with the population and its leaders," and indeed to do so gradually. Such an approach, he said, was being replaced by "the rather simple method of armed force: it is a fact that the sword is drawn far more readily than it used to be, at the orders of the colonial administration."

An awareness of the precarious nature of Dutch rule in the Indonesian archipelago had always haunted Holland, but this fear was pushed into the background by a belief in the efficacy of ethical colonialism. Yet systematic subjugation and economic exploitation would create over the next half century exactly the conditions suited to a mass movement demanding Indonesian independence.

But Gusti Gede Djelantik's nephew, the Karangasem prince Made

Two crops exploited under the Dutch *cultuurstelsel* system: sugar and coffee

Djelantik, was certain that the ethical policy blunted in Bali the sharp edge of Dutch colonialism. In his remarkable autobiography, *The Birthmark: Memoirs of a Balinese Prince*, he even wondered whether his father, the successor of Gusti Gede Djelantik, at first

> realized the limitations of his power in Karangasem… [Because] the advisory role of the Dutch Government's representative… imposed on his sovereignty as Raja, the so-called Controleur, was executed in a most tactful manner. To all appearances Father could regard himself as a Raja, ruling over the Kingdom of Karangasem, and what was more relevant, the people of the Region, unaware of politics, saw him as the traditional monarch.

Later his father, Gusti Bagus Djelantik, admitted that he regarded these "initial years as his school years, since he had never had the opportunity to pursue formal education in any school." But "gradually he took over the initiatives from his Dutch advisor," ruling his people with justice and compassion. During his childhood and adolescence, Gusti Bagus Djelantik's education was provided in the palace by high priests who introduced him to the Hindu epics, the *Sutasoma,* and Balinese tales.

According to his son Made Djelantik, the Badung *puputan* of 1906 had a decisive effect on Dutch colonial attitudes. The mass suicide demonstrated an unexpected Balinese determination, with the result that Batavia "pledged to leave the social and political structure of Bali as much as possible in its traditional form as long as it did not contradict Dutch interests." This was the reason why Gusti Bagus Djelantik was recognized as the ruler of Karangasem and awarded the title of *stedehouder*, like his predecessor Gusti Gede Djelantik. The same semiautonomous arrangement was introduced in Gianyar, where a descendant of the former king was appointed as regent with a Dutch advisor.

But the remaining regions of Bali were directly administered by Dutch colonial administrators, who were supervised by the Resident of Bali and Lombok, from his headquarters in Singaraja. An Assistant Resident was stationed at Denpasar, since the location of Singaraja on the island's northern coast meant that its remoteness from populous southern Bali caused day-to-day decisions to be slow. Singaraja had been developed by the Dutch as a port capable of receiving steamships, not long after the annexation of the north Balinese kingdom of Buleleng, and so its choice as the center of colonial administration was inevitable.

Because there were so few Dutchmen available for service in Bali's colonial administration, not more than several hundred at most, the cooperation of the indigenous nobility was essential to the success of Dutch rule. The justification for placing the kingdoms of Badung and Tabanan in an unfavorable administrative position was the conviction that among the descendants of the former rulers who had survived the 1906 *puputan* there were no trustworthy figures. A consequence of this was that in the conquered kingdoms administrative most duties were undertaken by nonroyal members of the nobility.

In addition to the administrative districts run by these nobles, the Dutch colonial authorities drew the villages into the system of government. Each village was accepted as having two heads: on one hand, the *bandesa*, the old spiritual leader, and on the other hand, the *perbekel*, the new secular head. Whereas the *perbekel* was subordinate to district officials and expected to implement decisions ultimately taken by the Resident, the independent *bandesa*'s responsibilities lay entirely in the religious sphere, as he had to oversee temple ceremonies and sacrifices. The extent to which this extension of authority down to village level meshed with the Balinese way of life is evident in President Sukarno's own vision for the Republic of Indonesia. This Balinese-Javanese politician saw the basis of the new state as a vast collection of self-governing village communities.

Political considerations stood behind the Dutch espousal of village autonomy. By making the village the basic element in Balinese society, the colonial government attempted to protect villagers from overbearing nobles at district level as well as counterbalance the power of the regents, such as Gusti Bagus Djelantik. The acquiescence of this ruler was by no means a forgone conclusion in 1909, when at barely twenty-one years of age Gusti Bagus Djelantik came to the throne.

But it was fortunate for the colonial authorities that Gusti Bagus Djeltanik, whose title was Anak Agung Agung Anglurah Karangasem, stayed on as regent because his reign lasted the whole period of Dutch supremacy as well as the Japanese interregnum. And during this time he was widely recognized as an astute ruler and an enthusiastic advocate of Balinese culture. His response to the 1917 earthquake was typical: he called for the revitalization of Hinduism. Along with the regents of

Gianyar and Bangli, two other kingdoms which had ceded power to the Dutch, he convened meetings with prominent priests who agreed that the natural and social setbacks in Bali had arisen through the neglect of traditional religious obligations. The only solution was the restoration of the caste system, so that everyone knew how they should behave in a manner pleasing to the gods: the proper celebration of religious ceremonies, and the rebuilding of temples, in particular those whose fabric had been damaged by the earthquake. In the repair of temples, the regents were helped by the timely support of Dutch administrators, who financed building work from government funds.

What Gusti Bagus Djelantik really intended through his public sponsorship of culture was reclaiming the spiritual leadership of the Balinese kings. "Certainly the Netherlands–Indies Government is a just ruler," he told the Resident in the early 1920s, "but it is only a ruler in relation to material interests." The spiritual dimension belonged to the Balinese kings, whose main task was to encourage reverence for the gods and to ensure that cremation rites allowed the dead to gain an appropriate reincarnation. So pleased were the Dutch with this material-spiritual distinction that they permitted the heir to the throne of Klungkung to return seventeen years after the 1908 *puputan*. A child during the mass suicide, Dewa Agung Oka Geg never forgot the horror of that fateful event: his belated homecoming from exile in Lombok was celebrated in the reconstruction of the royal palace, whose architecture is so admired by visitors to Klungkung today.

Balinese kings were notorious for having many wives and Gusti Bagus Djelantik was no exception in that he married twelve women. During a period of high infant mortality, this spreading of the royal seed was a precautionary measure intended ensure the survival of a male heir. While some of these marriages were dictated by political considerations such as shoring up the king's authority in outlying territories, the decisive factor always remained the continuation of the dynasty since two of Gusti Bagus Djelantik's wives were returned to their families when they could not provide heirs. Yet this king never had more than three wives at the same time, and these queens lived in their own compounds within the palace. When he decided to favor one of his wives, the king would send a courtier to tell her to get prepared for his arrival. In all, Gusti Bagus Djelantik had thirty-five children, of whom sixteen were boys.

By 1929 the Dutch felt secure enough in Bali to let all the former kingdoms become semiautonomous and their rulers join a new deliberative forum called the Council of Kings. It met in Denpasar under the chairmanship of Gusti Bagus Djelantik from 1931 onward. Although the proposals of the Council had to be approved by the Resident before they could be formally adopted and put into effect, the return of quasi-royal authority was a welcome reassurance for the Balinese people as a whole. The favor shown to the regent of Karangasem arose from this kingdom's ready accommodation to Dutch rule, just as those rulers who belonged to royal families that had offered the least resistance to the colonial takeover were similarly indulged.

A 1930s travel poster

It was appropriately at the Pura Besakih temple complex in 1938 that the Dutch announced to the eight Balinese kings the full restoration of their royal authority. Worried about the possibility of a Japanese advance into maritime Southeast Asia, Batavia thought it wise to allow greater autonomy in Bali, where both the nobles and royal families had come to accept the inevitability of Dutch colonial rule following the *puputans* of 1906 and 1908.

But not every Balinese person was convinced about the advantages of a return to royal government, in part because the island's traditional isolation was no longer intact. The modern world now intruded in daily life: telephones, roads, motor transport, schools, hospitals, all pointed in a very different direction. Even Made Djelantik could see the contradictions troubling Bali on his return home from studying medicine abroad. "Discrimination between Dutch and Indonesian students was unknown in Holland," he reflected, but in Bali the old colonial attitudes prevailed as if nothing had changed.

The Second World War

This Karangasem prince, Gusti Bagus Djelantik's second son, had gone to Holland shortly before the outbreak of the Second World War, dodged the Gestapo, graduated as a doctor, married a Dutch girl, and after the surrender of Japan, he returned in 1946 to Bali and addressed large crowds at public meetings. The Dutch colonial authorities obviously hoped that Made Djelantik would be able to reconcile the Balinese to the post-war situation. At The Hague, a senior official told him that political conflict raged in Bali. "You know that your father was very much loved by his people," he said. "It is still so, but only by the older generation. There is trouble with the youngsters." When he added that "the hardliners in the old colonial army and among the politicians" intended to hold onto the Dutch East Indies at any price, Made Djelantik realized the Dutch government wanted him to persuade the younger Balinese generation to talk about constitutional change, rather than engage in a guerrilla warfare.

Having agreed to a six-week visit on the understanding that he could say whatever he liked, Made Djelantik returned home with his Dutch wife, who was warmly received at Karangasem by Gusti Bagus Djelantik and the royal family. At a thanksgiving ceremony for their safe arrival, Made Djelantik could not help reflecting how confusing it must have been for his wife: there was "an absence of solemnity in what was supposed to be a serious and holy business." The presence of "a blond Dutch girl" was far too exciting for his sisters not to flock about her all the time. After the couple were married in traditional Balinese style, which in Karangasem involved both Hindu and Buddhist high priests, the public speeches that were scheduled for Made Djelantik to deliver in Bali disappointed the Dutch, because he chose to talk mainly about health matters.

One new custom the returning prince noticed during the visit was how people along the roadside leading to the royal palace bowed low as they passed, a legacy of the recent Japanese occupation. An unsettling aspect of the Imperial Japanese Army's rule had been the arbitrariness of its repression. Failure to bow properly to a soldier was often enough to merit detention or death.

What Holland failed to grasp was how the brief Japanese triumph had changed Southeast Asia. Unlike the British, both the Dutch and the French refused to accept the stark realities of the post-war world, since restoring some kind of imperial presence in Indonesia and Vietnam was for them almost a psychological necessity following the German occupation of their countries. Neither France nor Holland possessed, however, the military strength to restore their colonial administrations once Japan surrendered. And the sudden end of hostilities resulting from the American dropping of atomic bombs on the Japanese cities of Hiroshima and Nagasaki also caught the British quite unprepared. There were just too many tasks for Allied Forces in August 1945: assisting the return of Holland as an imperial power could never be a priority, once the depth of Indonesian opposition was apparent.

The Dutch were so anxious to return to Java that they agreed to whatever arrangements might be required. The only troops immediately available belonged to the Royal Netherlands Indies Army, who hailed largely from the small island of Amboina. As these native soldiers had remained loyal to the Dutch, the Imperial Japanese Army made some 18,000 of them prisoners of war. In the absence of large numbers of Dutch troops, Britain found itself in the invidious position of being the advance guard of returning Western authority.

Because the Dutch were so militarily weak and British forces spread thin in Southeast Asia, London expected the Dutch to negotiate with the nationalists in Java as had happened successfully in British Burma. But it had not reckoned with Hubertus van Mook, the governor-general of the Dutch East Indies. He resented the lightness of the British touch, wrongly believing that Dutch domination could be easily restored by force. And he correctly guessed that the Labour government in London had no interest in assisting the Dutch, when decolonization was very much part of its own agenda. With Indian politicians demanding independence for their own country, the role of Indian servicemen had already become a deeply contentious issue, especially when they were involved in operations that might reinstate European colonial rule in Southeast Asia. No less exasperated was the British premier Clement Attlee, who was leading the decolonization program himself.

A more pressing reason for Attlee's impatience with the Dutch than Indian public opinion were the string of mutinies which occurred among Allied forces from India to Singapore. In Malaya, a refusal to parade led to a mass court martial in 1946, when 200 men of the Parachute Regiment were sent to prison. They had just returned from a tour of duty in Java. Despite their protest having a definite connection with poor conditions in camp, these long-serving soldiers were worried about finding themselves at a disadvantage in the job market or higher education, if they came back to Britain late. For Indian troops, the position was even more uncertain, once the prospect of the subcontinent's partition emerged. At the start of 1946, a full-scale mutiny had broken out in the Royal Indian Navy, involving ten naval bases and fifty-six ships. This mutiny began at a signals establishment in Bombay when its British commanding officer called a group of sailors "black bastards" and triggered a protest that spread the same day to signal stations as far away as Aden and Bahrain. The spontaneous disobedience was based upon accumulated grievances—poor accommodation and food, bad pay, and a perception of an uncaring naval leadership—but it quickly assumed a role in the Indian independence movement. Riots inspired by the mutinous sailors convulsed Bombay, as hundreds were killed or wounded in street battles. Even though order was restored to the city and a commission of inquiry largely vindicated the sailors' complaints about dismal conditions and racial harassment, the British were left with a big question mark hanging over the Royal Indian Navy's reliability.

Ignoring the British desire for a political settlement, Hubertus van Mook strung out talks with the nationalists established at Bandung in central Java until it was clear that they would have to secure Indonesian independence themselves. After the British withdrawal, the Dutch tried subdue the whole of Java as well as economically important areas in Sumatra, by diverting funds provided by the United States for post-war reconstruction in Europe. When this was unsuccessful, van Mook had no choice but reopen talks with "a terrorist so-called government." The Americans were never really interested in Indonesia, other than to demand that trucks supplied originally to the British and now being used by the Dutch should have the "US" stenciled on their sides painted out. Holland could never afford a protracted colonial war, so when at the United Nations the Soviet Union lent its support to the Indonesian cause, the Americans ditched the Dutch as swiftly as the British had done. Independence was now inevitable and, while the new nation was at first called diplomatically the Netherlands–Indonesian Union, nobody expected any mutual relationship to last.

Only the British succeeded in achieving a dignified retreat from empire, because Clement Attlee was exceptional among European leaders in appreciating how the Greater East Asia Co-Prosperity Sphere had rung down the curtain on colonialism. It is something of a paradox that Japan's own bid for empire caused the downfall of Western imperialism in Asia. But the nationalist aspirations stimulated by the short but spectacular Japanese thrust into Southeast Asia were to be beyond the capacity of the returning colonial powers. Euphemistic as the name of Japan's new empire was for conquered peoples, the Greater East Asia Co-Prosperity Sphere brought a sudden end to centuries of European domination. The granting of independence to India, Pakistan, and Burma in 1947 should have convinced the Dutch that the Indonesian archipelago would soon have to be relinquished as a colony too. It did not and so Bali unnecessarily suffered two more years of violence.

Unable to subdue China, the target of the Imperial Japanese Army since 1937, and short of strategic materials through an American embargo on the sale of metals and oil, Japan had signed in 1940 a treaty with Germany and Italy and then seized French, British, Dutch, and American colonies in Southeast Asia. After the Japanese surrender, Emperor Hirohito said that the topic of pre-war discussion in Tokyo was always oil. Western confidence and prestige plummeted with defeats as widespread as Hong Kong, Guam, the Philippines, Malaya, Singapore, Burma, and Indonesia.

The poor state of defenses in Malaya and Singapore was repeated everywhere, including the great American naval facility at Pearl Harbor in Hawaii, which succumbed in December 1941 to a surprise attack by the Imperial Japanese Navy. But American industry soon made good the destruction inflicted upon the US Pacific Fleet at anchor there, whereas the Japanese were unable to replace any of the aircraft carriers they lost shortly afterwards at the battle of Midway. As this shift in the balance of power was not immediately apparent, Southeast Asian peoples had no choice but obey their new Japanese masters.

The Second World War came to Bali in February 1942, when the Imperial Japanese Army assembled forces there and in Sumatra prior to an invasion of Java, the most populous island in the Dutch East Indies. In the dramatic thrust south, the length of each Japanese advance was about the range of their land-based aircraft. Thus aircraft from one captured base would support the attack on the next. If no such base was available, carrier-borne aircraft were employed. By the time the Japanese reached Bali, Denpasar airfield had already been so heavily bombed as to be unserviceable. At sea, a Dutch-led sortie in the Lombok Strait was inconclusive despite inflicting serious damage on a Japanese destroyer. A week later in the Java Sea, thirteen Allied warships were lost, among them the heavy cruiser HMS *Exeter* of River Plate fame. There, in 1939, this ship, in the company of two other cruisers, had obliged the German pocket battleship *Graf Spee* to scuttle itself off Montevideo. Despite its undoubted efficiency as a warship, the *Exeter* proved no match for the Japanese cruisers *Haguro* and *Nachi*, each with heavier guns and superior armor. They also had torpedo mounts inside their hulls, above their engine rooms. And with a speed almost equal to a destroyer, the *Haguro* and the *Nachi* could enter or avoid an engagement as circumstances dictated.

The two Japanese cruisers saved 714 officers and men from the *Exeter*'s crew. They were well treated by the Imperial Japanese Navy, perhaps as a consequence of its old relationship with the Royal Navy dating back to the Anglo-Japanese Alliance of 1902. Once on land though, they had to endure the same indifferent treatment as surrendered Allied soldiers. In just a few months, Japan had taken control of Southeast Asia, captured 250,000 troops, mostly Asians but including a British, an Australian, and an American division. Although this was achieved with modest numbers and few casualties, the Imperial Japanese Army was protected by a powerful naval shield, whose easy sweep across the southern seas disguised the fundamental weakness of the Japanese position. Admiral Yamamoto Isoroku, the author of the Imperial Japanese Navy's strike on Pearl Harbor, was under no illusions about the fate of his country in an extended contest with the United States. It was "like fighting the world," he said. "But it has been decided. So I will fight my best. Doubtless I will die on board the *Nagato.*" The admiral was mistaken about this, because in April 1943 he met his death not on his flagship but over Bougainville, when his plane was shot down after radio interception of a message giving details of a tour of inspection.

The collapse of the Dutch East Indies in early 1942 delighted almost all Indonesians, some of whom actually assaulted Dutch troops and civilians. The Imperial Japanese often had to rescue many of them, making their subsequent internment almost a relief. But Japanese ignorance of Indonesian ways thwarted Tokyo's desire to establish an anti-Western regime because Dutch knowledge was initially found to be essential in maintaining control. The Imperial Japanese Army was obliged to intern Dutch colonial officers so slowly that they were lulled into a false sense of security. While they did not greet the Japanese invaders with any enthusiasm, the Javanese in particular took undisguised pleasure in the downfall of the Dutch. One colonial officer stationed in Java wrote later how

> we had a general notion about the Javanese people. I quite understood
> they didn't exactly worship us, but that they harbored such a hatred for
> us as then appeared came as a surprise to me. I never thought it was so
> bad.

The ripple effect of the Javanese reaction soon reached Bali, although there was no violence against the few Dutch administrators there.

But if there was one welcome thing that Japan's New Order brought to the Indonesian archipelago, it was an end to the racial discrimination that had typified Dutch colonial relations. Apart from clubs reserved for Japanese military officers, there was no bar any longer to membership of any society on the basis of ethnicity. For the Indonesians, whom the Dutch preferred to go barefoot, this was a significant improvement. But it should be noted how Made Djelantik considered wearing shoes and socks a "torture" on formal occasions, when the colonial authorities expected Balinese royalty to dress up.

From the start of the occupation of Bali, the brutality of the Imperial Japanese Army was directed at the Balinese rather than their former colonial overlords. An exceptionally uncooperative religious leader in northern Bali was beaten and hung upside down for days. Balinese nobles were also singled out as a suitable target, since they had been prepared to cooperate with the Dutch colonial authorities. Yet it was not long before Balinese kings were seen by the Japanese as indispensable for the maintenance of orderly government. Once again the Balinese people watched the evolution of yet another colonial partnership, which would set the agenda for social change after Japan surrendered.

The replacement in royal courts of Dutch advisers with Japanese officials only served to underline this continuity, which was deeply resented once the tide of the war turned in favor of the Allies. Even though food requisitioning and compulsory labor caused outbreaks of famine, Bali did not suffer as much as Java, where nearly 2.5 million people died of starvation during 1944 when stockpiles of rice were being created by the Japanese for a prolonged conflict. But chronic inflation added to the overall problem as a flood of occupation currency soon resulted in the value of its notes being less than the paper on which they were printed. Shortages, profiteering, corruption, black markets, and early death typified the war years. A sole benefit were the efforts of an increasingly desperate Japan to enlist local support for the defense of the Indonesian archipelago against the return of the Dutch: in effect, they assisted the post-war revolution. In late 1944 Tokyo went so far as to promise the Dutch East Indies outright independence.

THE TRIUMPH OF NATIONALISM

One of the nationalist leaders by the name of Sukarno had anticipated this crisis. And he knew how to exploit the public platform that the Japanese gave him to blame the Dutch for Indonesia's woes. The size and excitement of the crowds of Javanese who came to hear him unsettled senior Japanese army officers, but they could find nothing to censor in Sukarno's reiteration of the declared aim of the Greater Asia Co-Prosperity Sphere: namely, returning Asia to the Asians. He told the Javanese that, custodian though Japan undoubtedly was of this freedom from Western colonialism, "the fate of our people is in our hands and not those of others." It was a clever line of argument because Sukarno drew upon the genuine desire of Indonesians to be rid of the Dutch and the rash claim of the Japanese to be their liberators. Although Japanese flags always decorated the rostrum provided for his public speeches, by the close of the Second World War Sukarno had managed to unite the various nationalist groups and raise the demand for independence to fever pitch.

Once Tokyo accepted that it was impossible to resist the Allies, Sukarno and other nationalist leaders were indeed asked to draft a constitution for an independent republic. The new state was to incorporate under a strong presidency not only the territories of the Dutch but those belonging to Britain in Malaya and Borneo as well. This wider geographical ambition sowed the seeds of future conflict between Malaysia and Indonesia in the mid-1960s. Then Sukarno's so-called Confrontation against the Federation of Malaysia was thwarted by the rapid deployment of Commonwealth forces, so that its failure to produce any political dividends for the Indonesian president undermined his own position, and led to an army coup in Jakarta.

Because in 1945, however, the Indonesian nationalists did not want independence as a gift from the Japanese, they unilaterally proclaimed the Republic of Indonesia on August 17, 1945. The main focus of opposition to a restoration of Dutch rule was the island of Java. Yet even Bali, to which the Dutch returned in 1946, was not prepared to go back to pre-war arrangements. Nationally inclined Balinese resisted the return of a colonial regime, even though the nobility in an attempt to safeguard their interests openly supported the Dutch. Faced with widespread opposition, Holland decided to replace a colony centrally administered from Batavia with a confederation of states, each having its own parliament. The Dutch hoped that this alternative to the single state being advocated by the republican rebels in Java would appeal to provincial interests, and to an extent it did. All the new states were in fact headed by Indonesian nobles. But the Dutch never overcame Javanese opposition to this semicolonial arrangement and the political experiment failed.

Pro-republican rebels in Bali were swiftly eliminated, a *puputan*-style last stand taking place at Marga in 1946. Less than a hundred Balinese fighters under the command of I Gusti Ngurah Rai were ambushed at this Tabanan village and subjected to bombing. Rather than surrender, they recklessly charged their attackers. Their heroism is remembered in Bali every November, while the island's airport as well as the university at Denpasar are named in honor of Ngurah Rai.

The new confederation of states, named the Negara Indonesia Serikat, was to remain under the Dutch crown but advice and guidance from ex-colonial officials would replace previous command and direction. Bali was placed in the State of East Indonesia, which had its capital at Makassar in southern Sulawesi. In order to ease this transition from outright colony to a semi-independent territory, Made Djelantik had been flown home for his six-week speaking tour. That he was deemed to have been insufficiently positive about continued Dutch involvement in Indonesian affairs explains his temporary exile from Bali. The doctor-prince was not allowed to practice medicine in the island before the Republic of Indonesia achieved its independence in 1949.

But Made Djelantik had been reassured by a message that he received from Ngurah Rai during his lecture tour. One evening this note was thrust into his hand:

> We remain brothers. Destroy this piece of paper, Ng. Rai. My dear friend, I fully approve of what you are doing. Please carry on with your mission. I will not follow your steps, because I have *vowed* that I will continue our armed struggle until my last drop of blood! Let us fight together each in his own way. Destroy his piece of paper, Ng. Rai.

Made Djelantik never met Ngurah Rai again. By the time he returned to Bali, the rebel leader had already been killed at Marga.

The establishment of a fully independent Indonesia was, among other things, used to dismantle any remaining colonial institutions and replace them in Bali with a locally elected parliament. An early casualty of the revolutionary fervor that swept across the Indonesian archipelago was the abolition of Balinese kingship. In Jakarta, the republican leaders disliked the cozy relationship which had existed between Dutch colonial officials and the various royal courts; they also thought that the Balinese people had been lukewarm in their support for the independence movement; but even worse, as Muslims, these new power-holders had no conception at all about the cultural role played by Balinese kings in a traditional Hindu society.

Gusti Bagus Djelantik "suffered not so much from material loss," Made Djelantik said, "as from a sense of powerlessness and humiliation." Only then did his doctor son learn how his father had sold a piece of land each year to pay the government taxes due from his tenants. All the king had asked of them was a supply of rice and coconut for the royal palace, besides contributions to the religious ceremonies held throughout the year in Karangasem. Under the Dutch government revenue derived from two sources: the opium monopoly and land taxes.

Chapter Six

MODERN BALI

"Driving into Denpasar for the first time after so many years, I was struck by a new phenomenon… On top of some of the big buildings people had built *merajan*. The sight of house temples in traditional Balinese style on top of cosmopolitan structures of concrete and glass evoked feelings of disturbing disharmony."

Dr. Made Djelantik

Inauspicious though the start of independence was for Balinese culture, with the sudden sweeping away of royal authority, traditional values were resilient enough to sustain Bali's unique character. And neither the bloodshed which accompanied the overthrow of President Sukano in 1965–66, nor the terrorist bombs specifically aimed at international tourists in 2002 and 2005, have had any lasting impact upon Bali's attractiveness. Visitor numbers rose year by year so that tourism now accounts for ten percent of the island's economy. Low-budget tourism, however, has had an unfortunate effect in parts of southern Bali, and especially at Kuta where discos, bars, and, cheap accommodation transformed a sleepy seaside town into "an ugly part of Bali," according to many Balinese people. Yet, on the whole, the island has weathered the storm of modern times rather well, and remains a cultural gem set in an idyllic landscape.

Given the range of economic and social issues confronting an independent Indonesia, following the defeat of Japan and the expulsion of the Dutch, it is hardly surprising that Western-style democratic government quickly foundered. Coming into existence on December 27, 1949, the new Republic of Indonesia inherited an incredible variety of social traditions stretching across a far-flung archipelago, many islands of which had no inkling of what modern democracy entailed. At village level there was a very strong tradition of self-determination but this did not easily translate into elections for representative government in Jakarta, the new name for Batavia.

A struggle for unity has indeed typified Indonesian independence, which many viewed as nothing more than an attempt at Javanese domination. It did not help that economic development was concentrated in Java, where the overwhelming majority of Indonesians lived. The city of Jakarta itself witnessed unprecedented growth, its population tripling between 1945 and 1961. Politicians soon discovered that a democratic constitution, however, was not enough to keep the Indonesian armed forces under control. The situation only worsened as President Sukarno exploited factional and regional differences to assume executive authority. In 1959, he replaced parliamentary democracy with "Guided Democracy" and wrapped himself in the trappings of power, much to the annoyance of Balinese politicians such as Ide Anak Agung Gde Agung, who preferred imprisonment to collaboration with Sukarno.

Sukarno's declaration of a guided democracy was the worst possible step taken by an Indonesian leader, because it set in motion a chain of events that led not only to his own fall from power, the deaths of over half a million people and a military coup, but even more it ended any real chance of democratic progress during the rest of the twentieth century. From 1957 to 1965 Sukarno's authoritarian conduct undermined the Republic of Indonesia's economy, placed enormous pressures on its society and excluded almost every citizen from legitimate political activity. It was a gift to General Suharto, the successor of Sukarno, since it allowed him to concentrate authority in the hands of the president once he had seized power himself.

Sukarno's own opportunity to acquire almost unlimited power arose from the turmoil of party politics, which had descended to a level of distrust that precluded any form of cabinet government. Muslim reformers and traditionalists split in acrimony, while only the communists gained any popular support. Founded in 1914, the Communist Party of Indonesia started life as a social democratic movement but changed its name to the Patai Komunis Indonesia in 1920, inspired by the success of the revolution in Russia. After a series of abortive uprisings, the party was driven underground by the Dutch colonial authorities and remained a shadowy force until the end of Dutch rule. At first opposed to Sukarno, the Communist Party of Indonesia became in the late 1950s so disillusioned with Moscow that it decided to align itself politically with the progressive aspects of "Guided Democracy." For its part, the Soviet Union would continue to fund the Indonesian armed forces right through the crisis of 1965–66 that witnessed the wholesale massacre of communists as well as the enforced retirement of Sukarno himself.

In Sumatra and Sulawesi, whose foreign earnings largely sustained Java, new political forces came to the fore as army officers forged unorthodox links with local groups as a means of financing their units and increasing their personal wealth. The United States had been clandestinely supporting such outer-island movements in an effort to counter Sukarno's leftist tendencies. American submarines ran military supplies to rebellious Indonesian troops in Sumatra and American aircraft assisted the Sulawesi insurrection. Neither rebel group prospered for long, but the armed forces had already demonstrated an ability for unilateral action.

The driving force behind the American policy of subversion was John Foster Dulles, a fiercely anticommunist secretary of state. Believing that Sukarno was turning leftward rather than using the support of the Indonesian communists to bolster his own political position, Dulles sanctioned covert operations in the Republic of Indonesia. As he told his closest aides:

> As a matter of general policies, don't tie yourself irrevocably to a policy of preserving the unity of Indonesia. The important thing is that we help Indonesia, to the extent they allow us, to resist any outside influence—especially Communism. The preservation of unification of a country can have danger. And I refer to China. The territorial integrity of China became a shibboleth. We finally got a territorially integrated China—for whose benefit? The Communists.

Simplistic though this explanation of the establishment of the People's Republic of China in 1949 undoubtedly was, Dulles had a point in warning about inflexible objectives. There was no tradition of representative democracy in the Indonesian archipelago, and the idea of a single, unified state was comparatively recent. It was better, he said, that the country should break up so as to eliminate "Communism in one place or another, and then in the end, if they so wish arrive back at a united Indonesia."

With the death of Dulles in 1959, after a two-and-a-half-year fight with cancer, Washington put aside its Cold War anxieties and decided it would be wiser to deal with Sukarno rather than continue the effort to unseat him. Even to the extent of being lukewarm about the Federation of Malaysia, until the British transferred troops from West Germany, thereby weakening the defense of Western Europe. Another reason for the change of US policy was a growing realization in Washington that the Indonesian armed forces were now the key element in the archipelago's politics, and the post-Sukarno era would be dominated by its senior commanders.

In spite of growing opposition to "Guided Democracy," Sukarno clung to power with the aid of the Communist Party of Indonesia and the Indonesian armed forces, an uneasy alliance that triple-digit inflation eventually ended in a bloody military coup in 1965. Sukarno's economic policies, centered upon improving health, education, and infrastructure, might have worked if he had not ploughed so much money into military adventures. Each year the rate of inflation soared to more impossible levels, which in turn put an immense strain on the international value of the *rupiah*, Indonesia's unit of currency. Only at the time of the East Asian monetary crisis in 1997–99 was the collapse of the currency more severe, when it lost over eighty percent in value. As a result of Sukarno's extravagance, the foreign currency reserves of the Republic of Indonesia had by 1965 ceased to exist.

During the final years of Sukarno's rule as an executive president, his fiery oratory was still capable of rousing huge crowds. He accused Malaysia of being a neocolonial stooge, but the swift buildup of Commonwealth land, sea, and air forces thwarted *Konfrontasi* (Confrontation), Sukarno's military challenge to the new Federation. In September 1963, the Indonesian president had announced that Indonesia would "gobble up Malaysia." Armed incursions did occur in Malaysia, and particularly in Sarawak, but since there was no clear military or political advantage for the Indonesian armed forces in fighting such a conflict, the border war was in late 1966 finally abandoned. This lack of enthusiasm came as a surprise to Britain, since it was known that Indonesia's military establishment numbered 412,000 men, with 350,000 in the army alone. Even its corps of paratroopers numbered 33,000 men, more than the whole of Malaysia's own armed forces. And these Indonesian soldiers were in possession of an impressive armory of Russian and American arms and equipment, including guided missiles.

The Communist Party of Indonesia's greatest political advance, but also its greatest tactical error, was what came to be known as "Unilateral Action," a wide-ranging campaign of land reform that worried the Indonesian armed forces. Seizures of land from 1963 onwards threatened the interests of large landowners, who included military men and, in eastern Java, scholarly Muslim families. As the majority of farmers owned less than a two acres, which was insufficient to grow food for a family, the campaign was not unpopular. Alongside the land redistribution program, however, the communists set up cells in the countryside so as to prepare for a more uncompromising agrarian revolution in the future. Unilateral action had most impact in Java and Bali, where there were deep divisions between landlords and tenants. Although opponents of land reform fought back with vigor, suggesting that support for the Communist Party of Indonesia was weaker than expected in many areas, Indonesian generals still had to tread carefully because Sukarno's charisma was far from threadbare.

CONSPIRACY AND BLOODBATH

Only with the sudden illness of Sukarno in August 1965 was there a chance of political change. But a month later, a group of air force officers with links to the Communist Party of Indonesia, in effect Sukarno's praetorian guard, launched what they called an action to protect the "Great Leader of the Revolution." Based at Halim Perdanakusuma airbase in east Jakarta, they set out to kill the country's seven most senior generals. Three were shot dead in their homes, three others were taken away for execution; their bodies were dumped in a disused well. A seventh general, the commander-in-chief Abdul Haris Nasution, managed to escape the assassins with minor wounds. His adjutant and his daughter, however, were killed in his stead. During these bloody events Sukarno was staying in the house belonging to his fifth wife, situated in west Jakarta, but afterwards he went to the airbase.

Too upset to take charge of the chaotic situation, Nasution left his immediate deputy Major-General Suharto to assume command. A relatively unknown military figure, Suharto swiftly took control of the armed forces and ended the coup. Despite rumors of his own involvement with the air force assassins, it seems more likely that he had been excluded from the death list in the mistaken belief that he was an apolitical figure. Shortly afterwards Suharto outlawed the Communist Party of Indonesia, and then authorized the slaughter of its members.

The orchestrated attack on communists soon became a catch-all for targeting anyone of the left. Sometimes anti-Chinese prejudice led to the indiscriminate killing of Indonesian Chinese residents as well. This even occurred in Bali, where the Chinese had long been welcome as settlers and indeed a Chinese merchant's daughter became the island's goddess of prosperity. Although Made Djelantik refused to allow killers into Denpasar hospital where he worked, there was nothing he could do to save a nephew who, as a local government servant, was wrongly accused of being an active supporter of Bagus Suteja's left-wing regime in Bali.

Skillful military propaganda claimed that, prior to the assassinations in Jakarta, naked women had performed a lascivious dance in front of the conspirators and indulged in an orgy after the murdered generals' genitals were severed and their eyes gouged out. The allegations of genital mutilation were bad enough, but in a socially conservative society such as Indonesia the naked dancing and group sex reinforced the view that communist attitudes and traditional values were utterly incompatible.

Muslim activists were ordered to *sikat*, literally "sweep clean," the country of all communist sympathizers, and a bloodbath duly ensued. During 1965 and 1966 as many as 500,000 people were killed with the approval of the armed forces, while over 1,500,000 went to prison. General Nasution told a huge student gathering in Jakarta that since the conspirators had "committed treason, they must be destroyed and quarantined from all activities." Sukarno's recovery of health made no difference at all, because Suharto steadily outmaneuvered the president and his followers until the general was fully in charge of the country. By early 1966 Sukarno had been forced to transfer much of his authority to Suharto, who ensured within another year that the "Great Leader of the Revolution" was powerless and subject to house arrest. Sukarno soon died a broken man.

In 1968 President Suharto introduced his own New Order, which would last until its popular overthrow in 1998. The stability that the New Order promised was welcomed abroad and many countries were willing to offer assistance in dealing with Indonesia's chronic debts. Really delighted with the change of regime, Washington justified the mass killings in terms of the Cold War as "the most historic turning point in Asia in a decade": entirely overlooked was the fact that Sukarno's deposition resulted from no more than a bloody military coup. Although the violence was at its worse in central and east Java, the killings spread to other islands including Bali. An estimated 80,000 Balinese were killed, roughly five percent of the island's population. The conflict in Bali reflected that of the republic at large, with the communists espousing the cause of the peasantry, and the landlords refusing to accept any redistribution of land holdings. Yet the catalyst of an already tense situation was the attempt of the Communist Party of Indonesia to sabotage a high-profile Hindu funeral at Klungkung. Outraged Balinese took a terrible revenge, dumping in the sea or mass graves thousands of victims.

The extent of the killings, which even today baffles the Balinese themselves, had much to do with the grip that local communists achieved over the island's administration following the abolition of kingship in 1950. With the gaining of independence from Holland, those Balinese in the strongest position politically were members of the anticolonial resistance. The most prominent was Bagus Suteja, a cryptocommunist leader who went on to become Bali's governor. A not atypical revolutionary, Bagus Suteja's enthusiasm for change even encompassed women's breasts, which he insisted should henceforth be covered up. Before the Second World War, travel posters had displayed bare bosoms as one of Bali's more exotic attractions. The Dutch colonial authorities had tried and failed to achieve a cover-up, as indeed had the nationalists during the 1930s, but it was the puritanism of Bagus Suteja that finally carried the day.

Governor Bagus Suteja had been educated in Singaraja and initially he enjoyed the confidence of the returning Dutch, who appointed him to an administrative post in 1946, but he was soon imprisoned for his republican sympathies. With the establishment of the Republic of Indonesia, Bagus Suteja skillfully prevented Balinese rulers from exercising any power by getting rid of the Council of Kings. In spite of losing an election shortly afterwards, President Sukarno intervened and appointed Bagus Suteja as governor anyway. In 1959 yet another presidential intervention was required, since the unpopular governor heavily lost a second election.

Plagues of mice and rats during the early 1960s were interpreted by the Balinese as signs of trouble ahead, although the most obvious omen was the sudden eruption of Gunung Agung in 1963. Not only did this unexpected event disrupt the Eka Dasa Rudra ceremony at the Pura

Besakih temple complex, but it killed 2,000 people and destroyed enough paddy fields in Klungkung and Karangasem to start a famine. Over 75,000 Balinese were obliged to move to less affected areas, crowds of refugees pouring into Denpasar and Singaraja. Many Balinese saw the eruption as a definite sign of cosmic imbalance and spiritual impurity. In this context, the abortive communist coup in Jakarta seemed its inevitable climax, and an expression of all that was alien to Balinese culture.

Held at the most sacred temple site in Bali, the Eka Dasa Rudra ceremony represented a centennial purification of the island. Its real purpose was to placate Shiva, to contain the violent side of his character as Rudra, "the howler." For the great Hindu god is also Bhairava, "the joyous devourer," who haunts cemeteries and places of cremation, wearing serpents round his head and skulls for a necklace, attended by a host of demons. The elaborate ceremony was staged in 1963 at the insistence of Bagus Suteja, despite the date being several years in front of the prescribed one. Desperate to present himself as a Balinese traditionalist, the determined governor had overruled senior priests who warned of the gods' anger should the ceremony go ahead as he had ordered. Yet Bagus Suteja's overriding desire to appear as a true Balinese was bound to fail, when his own closest associates publicly condemned caste, the very foundation of society in Bali. It was one thing to push aside royalty, quite another to end the social distinctions which had shaped the Balinese way of life from the fourteenth century onwards.

At the same time, villagers were urged to challenge feudal landowners and great efforts were being made by communist activists to get village officials on their side. These activities badly split village communities because they were seen as an assault on traditional Balinese values. Bagus Suteja did not dare to attack the Hindu religion outright, but the general drift of his policies could not be disguised for ever. Just before the Jakarta coup brought General Suharto to power, this fundamental clash in outlooks became obvious at Klungkung, where the Communist Party of Indonesia mobilized its Balinese members to disrupt the funeral of Dewa Agung Oka Geg. The passing of this senior king was deeply mourned by traditionalists throughout Bali, because he had done much to preserve the island's culture after independence. So conversant was Oka Geg with religious ritual that he was able to advise priests, and indeed probe their understanding of key texts. His cremation on an eleven-tiered tower was therefore looked upon as a fitting tribute to a respected man.

Just before the funeral procession left the royal palace at Klungkung, the communists were only stopped from rushing in and desecrating the pier by the timely arrival of the military. Even then, they violently clashed with mourners before dispersing. When news of Suharto's seizure of power became known in Bali, along with the anti-communist purge which the general initiated in Java shortly afterwards, the time seemed right for a traditionalist revenge. Communists as well as suspected communists were hunted down and slain indiscriminately. Between October 1965 and February 1966 blood was shed all over Bali, as old scores and new insults were swiftly avenged. Everyone who had a grievance settled it then.

Although Indonesian forces soon arrived from Java, they were confronted by an unusual state of affairs. As one commander put it: "In Java we had to egg on the people to kill communists. In Bali we had to restrain them." But this did not mean that the Indonesian army gave no assistance at all to the death squads, who roamed the island in pursuit of fugitives. Military vehicles were used to transport these squads from village to village and for gathering communists together for mass executions. People with only the most tenuous connections to the Communist Party of Indonesia would sit in their houses as bands of young killers went by, shaking with fear that the bands would stop at their door. Even though communists dressed in white were led to the killing fields and executed *puputan*-style, they were denied Balinese cremation rites and instead thrown into mass graves. Other victims were either tossed casually into rivers or dumped in the sea. Although the fate of Bagus Suteja remains unknown, he was last seen being driven away in an army jeep. His wife and children, however, were left unharmed.

The mass slaughter of 1965–66 in Bali was a social convulsion as powerful as a volcanic eruption and, at least to the outside world, an event of totally unprecedented and baffling proportions. How was it that the peaceful and friendly Balinese could suddenly resort to such a level of violence? Theories about Indonesian ferocity, the Southeast Asian tendency to run amok, hardly fits the bill; because the sheer number of "amokers" points rather to a group response to a perceived threat directed at Balinese culture. The hapless Bagus Suteja may have disliked bare breasts during his governorship, but he was never as extreme as some of his fellow communists who condemned traditional Bali as nothing more than a cultural anachronism. Perhaps the governor had come to appreciate how the island's way of life rested essentially upon the village community.

It was this fundamental feature of Bali's culture, according to Made Djelantik, that triggered "the mass hysteria which exploded after a series of events that for many years had caused despair, suppressed anger, and frustrations." He adds that "within the Balinese community there was a strong belief that the Communists had made the earth 'unclean' with their propaganda against religion throughout the previous years." As a result, "the Balinese accepted the horrible killings as acts of purification... and believed that these happenings were manifestations of transcendental forces."

Convenient though it may appear to describe the outburst of violence in 1965–66 as taking place "according to the will of the gods," this does constitute the Balinese view of the terrible event. Discounted is the desire of the Indonesian generals to gain control of the country, once they despaired of democracy, guided or otherwise. The Balinese simply say that their island's troubles happened to coincide with those of Java. If President Suharto's regime went on to become no better than Sukarno's government, before it fell in 1998 amid cries of "corruption," "cronyism," and "nepotism," this has little influence on such a point of view. All that Bali hopes for is a future without any more catastrophes, now the gods seem to be appeased. Island-wide purification ceremonies, immediately after the killings, were the means by which this was apparently achieved. In addition, the Eka Dasa Rudra celebration was celebrated in 1979 at the correct date.

TOURISM AND DEVELOPMENT

Under Suharto's New Order the island of Bali was chosen for tourist development. Indonesia' first Five-Year Plan (1969–74) specifically stressed the importance of international tourism as a factor in the country's economic advancement. Although Sukarno had encouraged Indonesians to visit Bali, supported Balinese artists and dance troupes, and exploited the island's cultural heritage to impress international guests, he was no enthusiast for large-scale tourism. His visceral hatred of Europeans as well as Americans slowed the growth of Indonesia's tourist industry and it was not until after his deposition that it could get properly into gear.

Sukarno's spirit is believed to linger in this guesthouse at Pura Tirtha Empul

Sukarno's settled dislike of the United States dated from 1957, when Washington decided to back army officers trying to usurp power in Sumatra and Sulawesi. A reluctant Britain then agreed to a US task force basing itself in Singapore for this covert operation, despite few Singaporeans having any sympathy for Indonesia's rebellious colonels. So incensed was Sukarno by the abortive intervention, a CIA report tells us, that the Indonesian president "transferred the full fury of his anti-Dutch complex to the United States and Britain." It did not, of course, please Sukarno that six years later the British created the Federation of Malaysia by combining an already independent Malaya with Singapore, Sarawak, and North Borneo in a single state.

The lukewarm attitude of the Indonesian armed forces towards Confrontation, as Sukarno termed his challenge to the Federation of Malaysia, probably doomed the military operation from the start. Yet the highly permeable 995-mile border between Indonesia and the Borneo states of Sarawak and Sabah, the new name for North Borneo, would have offered the Indonesian army a real chance of success. As it was, the jungle became the scene of cross-border conflict and counter-insurgency operations for over three years. Once Indonesia called off this war in 1966, the British knew that Malaysia had solved the problems they faced as the last Western colonial power in Southeast Asia, with the exception of Portugal still stubbornly occupying East Timor.

Even before the official ending of Confrontation in September 1966, there were signs that Suharto would seek better relations with the West. The Foreign Office in London said that the "needless suffering" of the anti-communist purge which the general had sanctioned was "deeply regrettable," but it had at least served to "reduce the already dwindling pressure on British and Commonwealth troops defending Malaysia." Crocodile tears perhaps, but by not turning the 1965–66 bloodbath into a major international issue Britain secured Indonesia's acceptance of the Federation of Malaysia. Yet the British never lent their support to Suharto's regime to the same extent as the Americans, who were even willing to overlook the Indonesian army's rape of East Timor. Not until the East Timorese bishop, Carlos Filipe Ximenes Belo, received in 1996 the Nobel Peace Prize would Washington acknowledge the dreadful plight of the East Timorese.

The Nobel Prize citation did not mince its words. The world was told how "in 1975, Indonesia took control of East Timor and began systematically oppressing the people. In the years that followed it has been estimated that one-third of the population of East Timor lost their lives due to epidemics, war, and terror." This bad publicity obliged the United States to join an international force which, finally in 1999, ended Indonesia's brutal annexation of East Timor.

With the new emphasis placed by Suharto upon international tourism in the early 1970s, most Balinese were eager to participate in its development. Possibly their pre-Second World War experience of tourists, when very rich visitors stayed in the famous Bali Hotel at Denpasar, inclined them to welcome an increase in tourist numbers. But there was still a degree of anxiety over the preservation of the island's character, until a report prepared by a French consultancy on behalf of the Balinese provincial government reassured the traditionalists. What seems to have persuaded them was the report's chief recommendation that hotels should be concentrated in southern Bali, close to Ngurah Rai airport.

A modern hotel in the traditional style near the beach

Another factor that saved Bali from being overrun by foreign visitors, besides the remoteness of its location, was the arrival of Indonesian vacations. Heavy taxes imposed on Indonesian tourists leaving the country prompted many families to vacation within the republic. Weekend flights from Jakarta to Ngurah Rai airport were soon fully booked, turning the southernmost part of Bali into a prime destination for wealthy Indonesians. During the 1970s there were equal numbers of foreigners and locals visiting the Island of the Gods, as tourist brochures then described Bali.

The promotion of Bali as a cultural paradise is understandable, although its beaches were also being discovered as equally appealing as its many temples. Plush beach hotels opened to cater for tourists who preferred sunshine and sand, the lower end of this market finding its focus at Kuta, on the southwestern edge of the island. In the 1970s backpackers first put this town on the tourist map, with lodging houses and cheap hotels throwing wide open their doors for business. Even if the flood of foreigners transformed Kuta in ways that failed to please all Balinese, so far it has avoided the worst excesses of Thai tourist resorts such as Phuket and Pattaya. How long this lasts in an era of cut-price package vacations remains to be seen.

In 1992, a total of 2.5 million tourists spent their holidays in Bali. This influx had a profound effect on the economy, not only in terms of the spending power suddenly introduced to the island by these visitors but even more by the range of their expectations about what constitutes a good vacation. Apart from stimulating agriculture, especially in the production of meat, fruit, and vegetables for hotels and restaurants, tourist interest in handicrafts and cloth led to an upsurge in activity that astonished even the Balinese. A growing trade in garments now contributes more than sixty percent to the export value of Bali. Fashionable cloth and finished clothes are exported to Indonesia's large cities and to overseas markets as well.

Besides purchasing handicrafts and clothes, tourists wanted to see performances of Balinese dance-drama, famous since Walter Spies and Beryl de Zoete published their informative study entitled *Dance and Drama in Bali*, just before the Second World War. Bali had at last progressed in Western eyes beyond the bare-breasted dancing girls and the malevolent witches who had previously come to typify the essence of the island's culture.

The distinctive quality of Balinese dance was brought home to Made Djelantik by his young daughter Trisna, after she performed at the Albert Hall in 1951. The leader of the Sadler's Wells Ballet was so impressed by her movements and gestures that he invited her to watch rehearsals, presumably to see whether Trisna would be tempted to learn ballet. But she told her Dutch mother that she would "miss something in it. It is," she said, "too much physical exercise." Later Made Djelantik realized that this nine-year-old had put her finger on "the essential difference between the mechanical perfection of Western ballet and the transcendental quality of even the simplest Balinese dance."

Not every performance of dance-drama in present-day Bali is necessarily of such a high standard, yet there is always a sense of another dimension of meaning, an insight into a culture that defies ready analysis. What Balinese dance-drama possesses, Made Djelankit believes, is "*taksu*, the magic of the spiritual force, behind the dance movements." It was this realization of the fundamental strength of traditional dance that determined the Balinese people not to allow their rich culture to sink to the level of folklore entertainment staged in tourist hotels.

Tourist entertainment at a hotel

Yet there are still deep-seated worries over their island's future, and not all of these concerns are about culture. Tourism has brought with it problems of rising prices, pollution, and criminality, especially in and around Kuta, with several high-profile drug smuggling cases reported in recent years. Outside investment also impacts on the physical landscape as houses and hotels have spread beyond the area originally designated for tourist development, and even invaded paddy fields. Planning restrictions were conveniently forgotten during the late 1980s and the early 1990s when Suharto's family and friends became involved in major projects, either directly themselves or through taking a percentage from international hotel chains. Worse still, it was considered fashionable for wealthy Jakarta residents to own second homes in Bali, to the extent that the island was ruefully called a colony of Java. The overthrow of Suharto in 1999 put a temporary stop to speculation, without really devising a plan for sustainable tourism.

Then Bali seemed an island of peace in comparison with the riots and violence in Jakarta's streets, as the opponents of Suharto physically dismantled his New Order. Yet this calm was rudely shattered by terrorist bombs in Kuta, where 199 people were killed in 2002, and another twenty people three years later in a second bombing. Most of the victims were Australian tourists, for whom Kuta had become a tropical equivalent of Benidorm. Perhaps for the first time the ordinary backpacker realized that Bali was part of the Republic of Indonesia, whose majority religion was Islam. For the Balinese, nevertheless, the advent of Muslim extremism on their island was truly shocking. They could not understand how a suicide bomber could walk into a Kuta bar and blow himself and others to smithereens.

Although Balinese priests conducted ceremonies on Kuta beach to appease the spirits of those who died in the explosions, there remains a lingering doubt over the effectiveness of the exorcism they carried out there. Taxi drivers report how ghosts still frequent the seafront, as the lights and engines of their empty vehicles are often switched on when they are parked. For this reason there is a marked reluctance on the part of taxis to hang around Kuta after dark. The mischievous spirits are thought to be the foreigners who were killed in 2002 and 2005.

The bombings were seen by many Balinese as part of a wider threat from Islam. It was noticed how Bali only became a target after Javanese people took up residence and the arrival of workers from neighboring islands, who were attracted by the building boom. As manual laborers from Lombok and eastern Java hailed from conservative Muslim areas, there was a strong feeling among the Balinese that a fifth column might be in the process of emerging. At the start of the twenty-first century, great hopes were centered on Megawati Sukarnoputri when she became president. She was Sukarno's daughter and had spent a great deal of time in the island, staying with her Balinese grandmother and learning to dance in traditional fashion. Singled out as a political opponent of Suharto, she had required Balinese vigilante protection during more than one visit. Yet Megawati Sukarnoputri turned out to be a profound disappointment to the Balinese, since she combined a casualness as regards her presidential duties with an Emelda Marcos-like enthusiasm for shopping in Singapore. Her shopping sprees never approached the excess of the Philippine first lady, but Megawati Sukarnoputri's neglect of Bali deeply hurt the islanders.

It was in fact her two predecessors, the aeronautical engineer Bacharuddin Jusuf Habibie and the half-blind cleric Abdurrahman Wahid, who gave Bali the enhanced political and economic freedom which the island so badly needed, through their program of regional autonomy. And decentralization continued under the former general Susilo Bambang Yudhoyono, the first Indonesian president to be directly elected in 2004. His initial term of office was immediately marked by a tremendous natural disaster, when an earthquake off Sumatra produced a tsunami which overwhelmed the Acehnese coastline, killing nearly 100,000 people. Interesting though are Susilo Bambang Yudhoyono's own reflections on his difficult presidency, because he said that one of the most serious challenges he faced was not the natural catastrophe but a threat from an ill-disposed sorcerer. In 2009 the president claimed he was under constant attack from "revolving clouds," an event that caused a law to be hurriedly passed in Jakarta banning the use of black magic to injure or kill people. But it is unlikely that any of Bali's witches were ever deterred by the new legislation.

As Susilo Bambang Yudhoyono was stepping down after a second presidential term in late 2014, there was apprehension in Bali about the direction politics in Jakarta might take in future. An attempt to end direct presidential elections then was viewed by the Balinese as a move designed to return power to the political power brokers in the capital, where hard-line Muslim groups were already causing trouble over the inauguration of

Basuki Ahok Tjahaja Purnama as Jakarta's governor. The Islam Defenders Front accused Ahok of insensitivity to issues of ethnicity and religion. The fact that the new governor was a Christian of Chinese descent seems to have been the reason for the opposition: an overwhelmingly Muslim city could not be run by a non-Muslim. Reminiscent of the intolerance shown in Bali by administrators sent from Jakarta immediately after the foundation of the Republic of Indonesia, this dispute also reminded the Balinese of the difficulties they had encountered in persuading the national government that they possessed a legitimate religion of their own, and not just a bundle of superstitious beliefs. Only Ida Sanghyang Widi Wasa's position at the head of the Balinese pantheon obliged the Ministry of Religion in Jakarta to accept that Bali had a recognizable faith.

Part Three

A TOUR OF THE ISLAND

Ida Sanghayang Widhi Wasa presides over the Pura Agung Jagatnatha temple

Chapter Seven

SOUTH BALI

"The king, seeing his cause was lost, told his followers that to defend the palace was hopeless, but anyone who wished could follow him into a *puputan*, a 'fight to the end'. The only honorable thing left for him was to die a dignified death, rather than be exiled like the Raja of Lombok, to die away from Bali, and without the proper rituals of cremation."

Miguel Covarrubias

The place where this massacre took place is the Taman Puputan, or "*puputan* park," a large grassy open space in the middle of modern Denpasar. Here, in 1906, nearly 2000 men, women, and children were mown down by Dutch machine guns. The town had already been shelled from warships anchored off Sanur as well as by field artillery during a Dutch expeditionary force's advance on the capital of Badung.

Because the king of Badung, Ida Tjokorda Ngurah Jambe, had refused to pay compensation for a schooner that was wrecked and looted on the coral reefs at Sanur, Batavia chose to invade south Bali and impose a colonial regime upon its inhabitants. The dispute was a convenient excuse to get rid of another independent Balinese kingdom. But the Dutch soldiers sent to overcome Badung were astonished at the sight of the king, his family, his courtiers, and his guards marching calmly towards them across Taman Puputan. Armed with no more than spears and daggers, and dressed in white as befitted such a solemn occasion, these people ignored the order to halt and instead rushed at the Dutch. After a first volley failed to stop them, machine guns opened fire with devastating effect. But this did not end the Badung attack, because the king's brother, a twelve-year-old boy who could hardly carry his spear, led yet another group forward. When they again refused to stop, they were all shot down too.

The conquest of Badung attracted worldwide attention. Dutch reporters who accompanied the expedition witnessed what to Europeans was an incomprehensible event. They were baffled not only by Balinese indifference to bullets but even more by the self-immolation of the king's wives and daughters, who stabbed themselves over the dead king's body. When the horrified Dutch troops ceased firing, the surviving women threw handfuls of gold coins, yelling that it was payment for killing them. The loss of a single Dutchmen reveals just how one-sided the *puputan* really was.

Although an unshakeable belief in reincarnation stood behind the decision to choose death rather than surrender, the necessity of this mass sacrifice at Denpasar shocked the Balinese as much as the Dutch. It was almost the last attempt to stem colonial encroachment in Bali. Just how determined Batavia was to annex the island became immediately obvious in the treatment of Tabanan, whose ruler had lent support to Badung in the dispute over the schooner. The king of Tabanan offered to surrender on condition that he be allowed to retain his title and have the same rights as the rulers of Karangasem and Gianyar. When this was refused and he was told to expect deportation to the island of Lombok, the king and his heir killed themselves.

The Dutch parliamentarian H. H. van Kol was so dissatisfied with the official version of events that he conducted his own investigation. Batavia's blatant disregard for international law struck him forcibly one night when he wandered through Denpasar,

> along the paths where crowds of men, women, the elderly, and children (people like ourselves), had faced death with heads held high, where corpses had been stacked in layers—as I saw in my mind's eye "this dreadful mess of smashed bones and limbs torn to pieces, dragged through the dirt": at that moment I decided—whatever may happen— to do my duty in the name of Christianity and Humanity.

And it did not take van Kol long to establish that the schooner was deliberately run aground so that the owner could lodge an inflated claim for compensation. Equally telling was the discovery that the king of Badung had nothing to do with the shipwreck and had in fact dispatched guards to protect its cargo from looters as soon as he learned about it. That Batavia had already sent a military surveyor to map south Bali was all that van Kol needed to brand the destruction of Badung as a deliberate example of imperialist opportunism.

Today the Badung massacre is commemorated annually in September, when Denpasar stages a reenactment at Taman Puputan. *Baris*, the dance of warriors, is performed in the city, which has a festive atmosphere through the setting up of food stalls in a people's market. The heroic stand against Dutch colonialism is not forgotten, but the good-natured Balinese are unable to allow sadness to spoil any social occasion for very long.

Next to Taman Puputan are two important buildings: the Pura Agung Jagatnatha and the Museum Bali. Both should be seen during a visit to Denpasar. The former temple is dedicated to Ida Sanghyang Widi Wasa, the supreme Balinese deity, in whom all the ordering and disordering tendencies of the cosmos are resolved. The equivalent of the Hindu concept of *brahman*, the holy power that resides in every part of the universe, Sanghyang Widi Wasa embraces creation, preservation, destruction, and of course, renewal. Built in 1953, the Pura Agung Jagatnatha can be seen as Bali's state temple, an unequivocal expression of divine unity. Although the Balinese had always looked upon Sanghyang Widi Wasa as the all-embracing divinity, it was politically expedient immediately after independence to demonstrate how the island's religion was more than a rag-bag of unrelated superstitious beliefs.

Despite the moderation of Indonesia's first minister of religious affairs, who incidentally was the father of Abdurrahman Wahid, the fourth president of the Republic, there were Muslim officials in Jakarta entirely unsympathetic to Balinese religion. They could see nothing that approached their own conviction in the unity of Allah. The Republic of Indonesia's constitution guarantees freedom of worship, but access to government funds for religious purposes was denied to Bali until the position of Sanghyang Widi Wasa had been fully clarified. Even then, Jakarta's recognition of Balinese religious beliefs was hardly wholehearted.

To underline the legitimacy which Sanghyang Widi Wasa's universal role confers on Balinese religion, a regular cycle of festivities is celebrated in the Pura Agung Jagatnatha. These are held every fifteen days according to the waxing and waning of the moon. And two women are permanently employed by the government to prepare offerings for these events, a singular arrangement since women living in the locality usually undertake this task when an *odalan*, or "temple festival," takes place. High above the main courtyard of the Pura Agung Jagatnatha, on a white pagoda, a golden image of Sanghyang Widi Wasa blithely surveys the scene.

Preparing offerings at the Pura Agung Jagatnatha temple

The name Denpasar, which means "a temple to the north of the market," does not refer to the Pura Agung Jagatnatha, but it is a reminder of how central religious ceremonies have always been here as elsewhere in Bali. This is transparent in the exhibits on display in the Museum Bali, which is next door to the temple. In four separate pavilions can be found examples of Balinese craftsmanship which date from prehistoric times until the present day. Carved stone sarcophagi, widely used for secondary burial prior to the arrival of Hinduism; clay containers in the shape of friendly spirits, serving as bowls or candle holders; grotesque wooden carvings of giants, gods and goddesses, even a drunken Dutch soldier; female statuettes clothed in Chinese coins, whose magical power is still respected; the inevitable Rangda, threatening as ever with her lolling tongue in search of human blood; fertility symbols including a huge phallus decorated with human figures; *krises* (daggers) that once belonged to kings and nobles; beautiful textiles and painted fabrics; Barong the good lion and other figures in dance-drama; a collection of masks for *topeng* and *wayang wong*

A goddess covered with Chinese coins in the Museum Bali

performances; and *cili* symbols, the intricate decorations prepared for the worship of the rice goddess Dewi Sri. All these exhibits, along with statuary in the courtyards, make Museum Bali an excellent place to begin a tour of the island.

To the north of Taman Puputan, on a very busy road, is located the Bali Hotel, the very first accommodation to be built for foreign tourists. In the 1920s the novelty of its glass windows and tiled roof caused a sensation among the inhabitants of Denpasar. By the Second World War, however, a steady flow of rich visitors meant that the hotel was a familiar feature in the city, whose population was then around 25,000. Motor cars were virtually unknown before the 1950s, when the total number of vehicles in Bali had still not reached 2,000. Now Denpasar has a traffic problem which is only eased by two million mopeds: these tiny motorbikes often carry two or three passengers, sometimes four when children travel with their parents. They dash through lines of buses, trucks, and cars without apparent concern, or accidents. For Bali is no island of lotus-eaters, the indolent Lotophagi whom Odysseus encountered on his epic voyage home from the Trojan War. Landing on their island, some of his men tasted the lotus plant and only wanted to stay there for ever, eating the fruit in blissful ignorance. Odysseus had to have them dragged back to his ship by force. Such laziness is not a part of the Balinese character. On the contrary Bali is filled with busy people, an aspect of the island's life that goes some way to explain the crowded scenes in many contemporary paintings.

Although in 1930 the Mexican traveler Miguel Covarrubias and his wife Rose soon left the Bali Hotel and moved into a pavilion constructed with typical Balinese materials of wood, mud, and thatch, others were happy to remain hotel guests. Covarrubias was keen to encounter the real Bali and this accounts for their brief stay, but Charlie Chaplin preferred Western-style luxury and Balinese entertainment laid on by local dancers, something that continues to satisfy tourists in better-class hotels today. It cost Chaplin $7.50 a night then.

Disconcerting as the bustle of Denpasar may appear to a newcomer, the city is worth patient investigation. Besides open-air markets selling every kind of tropical fruit and vegetable, there are streets in which textiles, clothes, handicrafts, and jewelery can be purchased at reasonable prices, although an indifference to the desired article or determined bargaining is always a wise precaution. The Balinese are honest traders but they do not see it as their duty to stop a customer throwing money away.

After these exciting transactions in the center of Denpasar, visitors can enjoy two other cultural institutions on the edge of the city: the Sekolah Tinggi Seni Indonesia and the Taman Werdi Budaya. The first one is the Indonesia Institute of Arts, where schoolchildren study traditional dance, music and art. Here gamelan ensembles practice and accompany young dancers. Near the institute is the Taman Werdi Budaya, or Cultural Development Park, more simply known as the Arts Center. Set among gardens with lotus ponds, the Arts Center features paintings, carvings, puppetry, silverwork, textiles, and dance costumes. The annual Balinese festival of dance and music is held here, a celebration of the island's cultural heritage that Colin McPhee did so much to encourage. This Canadian-born composer not only brought gamelan music to the attention of the outside world, but during the 1930s he urged the Balinese to treasure their own unique musical traditions. An early discovery of McPhee was that dance is inseparable from music, and he sought throughout his stay in Bali to sponsor this remarkable symbiosis by helping young musicians and dancers to develop their talents. A children's gamelan category in the annual Balinese festival is a legacy of McPhee's tireless efforts.

Of the various temples in Denpasar, the Pura Mutering Jagat Dalem Sidakarya is esteemed for the quality of its holy water. Located in the southern part of the city, this temple is sought out by people in need of its purifying effect. The temple's name means "the work can be done," an undoubted reference to the satisfaction of worshippers who go there. So widespread is the use of the holy water prepared by priests and priestesses that Balinese beliefs have been termed Agama Tirtha, or "holy water religion."

During the month-long Eka Dasa Rudra ceremony, which is held once every hundred years at the Pura Besakih temple complex in order to purify the entire island, holy water is taken there from this temple. Holy water also comes from Mount Semeru in Java, Mount Rinjani in Lombok, and even from the Ganges in India. This last source is intended to remind Shiva about his role as Ganga-dhara, "the upholder of the Ganges." Once this river flowed in heaven, only washing the sky. As a result, the world became so filled with the ashes of the dead that there seemed no way of cleansing it. To solve the problem, the sage Bhagiratha brought the Ganges out of the sky. But such were the dimensions of the sacred river that its flow would have caused devastation on Earth had not Shiva intervened and let its full force pour over his head, where the water was able to meander amid his matted locks and compose itself in seven smoothly flowing tributaries.

Even though this myth has connections with regularly recurring phenomena, like the torrential rainstorms of the monsoon or the rush of rivers when charged with melted snow, Hindu belief in Shiva's decisive action shows how the god is more than Rudra, "the Howler." Yet the Eka Dasa Rudra is still an exorcism, a festival aimed at taming the wildness in Shiva's makeup. Once appeased, Rudra can be relied upon to protect Bali for another century. The Eka Dasa Rudra held in 1963, at the insistence of the island's communist governor Bagus Suteja, was overshadowed by Gunung Agung's unexpected eruption. A second centenary ceremony held in 1979, however, restored Balinese confidence because according to the high priests this was the correct date for this important event.

East of Denpasar is the coastal town of Sanur, where the wreck of a schooner in 1904 started the chain of events that led to the Badung *puputan* two years later. Coral reefs surrounding south Bali make navigation hazardous anyway, but there is probably no better place than Sanur for a deliberate shipwreck. So plentiful is the coral off the town that the Pura Segara, a temple dedicated to the sea god Baruna, is constructed with a mixture of stone and coral. Balinese ambivalence about the sea explains the cautious approach to Baruna, who can either help or hinder sailors as the mood takes him. As long as nothing is said to offend the sea god, then a safe passage is usual, especially after an animal sacrifice has occurred. Each year fishing villages drop into the waves live cows, weighed down with heavy stones. The Pura Segara suggests that Baruna's cult goes back to pre-Majapahit times, since the pyramidal shape of its coral offering tables are not repeated in other temples. Here perhaps is a rare survival of prehistoric Balinese rituals.

Close to the Pura Segara is the Museum Le Mayeur, once the seaside home of a Belgian artist by the name of Adrien-Jean Le Mayeur de Merpres. On his arrival in 1933, he was fifty-two years old and only intended to stay on the island for a few months. But Le Mayeur was so enchanted by its natural beauty that he decided to stay for the rest of his life. He had met the fifteen-year-old Ni Nyoman Pollok, a renowned *legong*

A carved doorway at the Museum Le Mayeur

dancer; she became his wife and his muse. In their exotic residence, now the Museum Le Mayeur, there are paintings of Ni Pollok as well as a fetching photograph of her dancing. Unfortunately the salt-laden air has not been kind to the paintings in spite of protective glass, but the house itself is well worth a visit, if only to appreciate the paradise that Le Mayeur created for Ni Pollok and himself. It was, he said, an ideal location for "an Impressionist. There are three things in life that I love: beauty, sunlight, and silence. Now tell me where to find these things in a more perfect state than in Bali?" After Le Mayeur died of cancer in 1958, Ni Pollok married an Italian doctor who was expelled from the Republic of Indonesia shortly afterward. She lived alone in Sanur until her own death at the age of seventy in 1985.

Not far from the Museum Le Mayeur stands the Grand Bali Beach Hotel, the first of five modern hotels built by President Sukarno out of Japanese war reparations. The early history of this particular hotel is notorious for supernatural happenings. Staff suffered fits caused by malignant spirits while furniture moved on its own at night. It was believed that they were the result of the hotel's construction on an old cemetery. Although the hotel burned down in 1993, it was rebuilt to the same height as before, which was higher than a coconut tree. This limitation had just been introduced to preserve the character of Bali. Sanur's antiquity as a port is confirmed by a second temple, the Pura Belanjong, located at the southern end of the town. It boasts a stone pillar with an inscription in Balinese and Sanskrit, dating from the start of the tenth century. This royal edict indicates how Sanur was already a flourishing center for trade over a millennium ago.

Benoa bay separates the mainland of south Bali from Bukit Badung, or "Badung Hill," a raised limestone peninsula with sparse vegetation. Getting to Bukit Badung is now much easier than it was, since a new bridge cuts across the middle of the bay. Previously vehicles had to pass through Kuta, a rather tacky coastal town in comparison with Sanur. The road from Kuta traverses a narrow neck of land to Bukit Badung.

NUSA PENIDA AND BUKIT BADUNG

Considered a part of Klungkung rather than south Bali, the nearby island of Nusa Penida is only a short ferry ride from Benoa harbour, now Bali's main seaport. Originally a penal colony for the kingdom of Klungkung,

Ni Pollok, Le Mayeur's wife and muse

the inhabitants of present-day Nusa Penida make a living through fishing and seaweed farming. As arid as Bukit Badung, the tiny island has tried to supplement its economy through the encouragement of snorkelers and divers. While they can explore coral reefs in crystal clear water, sun-lovers are able to enjoy quiet sandy beaches. The sea around the island is comparatively free of sea snakes, unlike the deeper channel between eastern Bali and Lombok. The Balinese never seek to kill these multicolored creatures because they are moody Baruna's boon companions. Whereas on land black-and-white snakes are also left alone through their connection with indigenous deities, green and black snakes are readily killed. A black and white snake appearing in a Balinese family compound is usually interpreted as the visit of an ancestor.

Nusa Penida is not cultural Bali at its best. There are a couple of interesting village temples, one of which is dedicated not surprisingly to the sea god, and the sacred cave of Goa Giri Putri, near Suwana on the island's eastern coast. The Goa Giri Putri, or "cave of the mountain princess," belongs to Parvati, an aspect of the great Hindu goddess Devi. Parvati means "she who dwells in the mountains," an appropriate name for a mate of Shiva, who prefers to live at the summit of Gunung Agung.

As one of the consorts of Shiva, Parvati bore a child necessary for the preservation of the world. Through great austerities the demon Taraka had been granted by the creator god Brahma the boon of being invincible to any creature except the offspring of Shiva. As Shiva was then an ascetic, the gods had to find a goddess capable of exciting him sexually. It cost Kama, the equivalent of the Greek love god Eros, his body to rouse Shiva from his meditations. As soon as he realized that one of Kama's flower-arrows had disturbed him, Shiva reduced the love god to cinders with a burst of fire from his third eye. Yet Kama had managed to interest Shiva in Parvati, much to the relief of the gods.

But soon these deities became fearful of the unborn child, whose powers were going to be more formidable than the demon Taraka. So much so that they interrupted Shiva and Parvati's love-making, with the result that Shiva spilled his seed outside the goddess. Passed from container to container, because of its fiery nature, the divine substance at last produced in the Ganges the war god Karttikeya, who found his way home from the river. By defeating Taraka with his irresistible bow, twelve-handed and twelve-eyed Karttikeya rescued the world.

Dusk at Pura Luhur Uluwatu on Bukit Badung

Guides with pressure lamps wait at a small temple near the mouth of Gao Giri Putri, so as to assist visitors in exploring the large limestone cave. Shrines dot the interior whose roof rises in places to a height of fifty feet. Cut off though Nusa Penida is from the rest of Bali, its reputation as a stronghold of black magic is well known. Not only are the inhabitants themselves expert in the magic arts, but the island is the fabled home of the arch conjuror Ratu Gede Mas Mecaling. Throughout mainland Bali priests conduct special ceremonies to keep people safe from his devious wiles.

Opposite the entrance to Benoa bay is a long and narrow sandy spit called Tanjung Benoa, whose tip comprises a fishing village with a Chinese temple. It must have served as a place of worship for merchants from China when their junks put in here. Frequented now by Balinese fishermen seeking good catches, the tiny temple is in excellent condition. Where the spit joins Bukit Badung proper stands Nusa Dua, a complex of hotels, shops, restaurants, and sports facilities; it was constructed during the 1980s on land deemed unsuitable for agriculture.

The rest of Bukit Badung boasts a single interesting temple: the Pura Luhur Uluwatu at the western end of the peninsula. Standing high upon a promontory, the temple affords breathtaking views across the sea to the island of Java during daylight hours, while at dusk the sunset is quite magical. It is a pity that Pura Tanah Lot, another coastal temple in western Bali, has been as over-promoted as Pura Luhur Uluwati: only the beauty of their natural settings compensates for the flood of cars that bring tourists late each afternoon.

Two Javanese figures are connected with Pura Luhur Uluwatu. The first is Empu Kuturan, who arrived in the tenth century and proclaimed a Buddhist–Hindu gospel. At this period Hinduism and Buddhism had become so intertwined that it became impossible to separate their characteristics. The syncretic tendency continued down to the reign of Kertanagara 200 years later, when this ruler of the eastern Javanese kingdom of Singhasari was thought to combine in his person of essences of both Buddhism and Hinduism. Although Kertanagara briefly annexed Bali, the intervention of the Mongols gave the island another century of independence. It was the successor kingdom to Singhasari, the maritime empire of Majapahit, that brought Bali firmly under eastern Javanese control in 1343, but the full impact of its religious outlook was not felt until the arrival of Danghyang Nirartha around 1537.

Balinese tradition holds that the caste system was rudimentary before Danghyang Nirartha gained the ear of King Waturrenggong at Gegel. Appointed as the court's religious advisor, this ultra-orthodox priest made certain that the worship of Shiva took center stage in Bali, even though Waturrenggong was actually regarded as an incarnation of the preserver god Vishnu. In reaction to the triumph of Islam in eastern Bali, where Majapahit had just succumbed to Muslim arms, the refugee priest was determined to convert Bali into the last redoubt of Hinduism in the Indonesian archipelago. In this aim Danghyang Nirartha succeeded, but only through reaching a compromise with existing Balinese beliefs. Though he ensured that his candidates took over the major temples in the island, village priests were left to continue with the worship of indigenous deities.

Dangyang Nirartha journeyed all over Bali, building temples and shrines. It was at Pura Luhur Uluwatu, however, that he achieved *moksa*, complete enlightenment and liberation from the endless round of rebirth. Because of this event, only the king of Badung, in whose realm Bukit Badung stood, could worship there. The last king regularly visited Pura Luhur Uluwatu right up to his death in the 1906 *puputan*. Constructed largely with coral, a more durable building material than soft volcanic rock, the temple is better preserved than many older buildings. The exact date of its foundation is hard to determine; though the layout and decoration points to the sixteenth or seventeenth century, there would have been a place of worship on this spectacular site from much earlier times. Unusual is the presence of guardian statues in the form of the elephant god Ganesa, although he is one of Shiva's sons. After his father in a towering rage had torn off his head, Parvati prevailed on Shiva to restore Ganesa and he replaced the head with an elephant's, the first that came to hand.

Given that Ganesa, the counterpart of the Greek god Hermes, also removes obstacles and vouchsafes wisdom, it is not likely that the elephant god was thought to have aided Danghyang Nirartha's achievement of enlightenment. This may be the reason for Ganesa's statues flanking the temple's inner and outer gateways. Several shrines are dedicated to Danghyang Nirartha, including the three-tiered *meru* in the temple's inner court, on the cliff edge. This is supposed to be the spot where *moksa* occurred.

From Pura Luhur Uluwatu the road to Kuta passes Ngurah Rai airport at Tuban. It is named after the rebel leader I Gusti Ngurah Rai, who died in a miniature *puputan* at Marga in 1946. Then he led his remaining followers in a reckless charge against surrounding Dutch troops. Despite his own aristocratic background, Ngurah Rai had no sympathy with either the rulers or their noble supporters, for whom the restoration of Dutch colonial rule seemed the only way to guarantee their traditional positions in Balinese society. As far as he was concerned, the way forward for Bali after the Second World War was as part of an Indonesian republic.

Kuta, Legian, and Seminyak form a seaside conurbation that that improves as one moves northwards, in part because the buildings there do not reach the beach. At least one hotel in Seminyak tries to protect the seashore to the extent of guarding turtles. It puts up fences on the beach where turtle eggs are buried in the sand, places the hatchlings in protective tanks, and then releases them into the sea when they are strong enough to swim. The Balinese greatly appreciate this, because their island is believed to rest on the back of the gigantic turtle Bedawang as well as two *nagas*, the Hindu name for cosmic snakes. Once a turtle was sacrificed in the outer courtyard of a temple during a festival, but now a pig has to satisfy the demons instead. Cluttered and crowded as Kuta is, the town possesses one redeeming feature in the Fei Long Chinese restaurant, whose cuisine is a match for the best in China itself.

Chapter Eight

NORTH AND WEST BALI

"The land, with everything that grows on it, the water that flows through it, the rock it holds in its womb, belongs without exception or limitation to the invisible gods and spirits who inhabit it."

A nineteenth-century Dutch visitor

The nearest temple of note at Tanah Lot is situated due west of south Bali. Formerly belonging to Mengwi, the kingdom which was dismembered in the early 1890s, it is now located in Tabanan. Stretching as far north as Lake Bratan, Tabanan is a wonderful combination of coast, valleys, hills, and mountains, its terraced paddy fields a constant reminder of the historical basis of Bali's prosperity. Rice has made this part of the island very rich.

Again Danghyang Nirartha, the energetic Javanese priest who came to Bali during the sixteenth century, is responsible for Pura Tanah Lot, the so-called "sea temple of the Earth." Built on a rocky islet just offshore, the temple is reminiscent of a Chinese painting, an effect only spoiled by the congregation of souvenir shops that have followed the flood of tourists visiting the temple site. Along with Pura Lutur Uluwatu, another clifftop temple associated with Danghyang Nirartha, Pura Tanah Lot is the place most visited by foreigners. Even the need to shore up the eroded base of the islet with concrete has not reduced their number, despite the ugliness of the reinforcement.

Only with great difficulty was the temple founded by Danghyang Nirartha. A local guru deeply resented the priest's claim to speak on behalf of Hinduism and a magical contest ensued. To show just how powerful was his own magic, Danghyang Nirartha moved the rock upon which Pura Tanah Lot was built into the sea and turned his scarf into sacred snakes. These poisonous guardians took up residence in caves at the base of the rock, from where they are said to still ward off evil influences. His triumph here caused Danghyang Nirartha to be called Padanda Sakti Wau Rauh, or "the just arrived magic-powerful high priest."

Pura Tanah Lot, perhaps the most popular temple with tourists

The Tabanan king Gusti Ngurah Agung, who inherited much of the land formerly belonging to Mengwi, did not enjoy these acquisitions for very long. Caught up in the 1906 conflict between Badung and the Dutch, he could not avoid the wrath of Batavia afterwards. Approaching the senior Dutch official in Bali, Gusti Ngurah Agung changed his golden umbrella for a green one in sign of submission, but this public gesture was pointedly ignored and, in despair, the king of Tabanan cut his own throat while his son was poisoned with an overdose of opium. Thus the kingdom of Tabanan, along with Badung, fell into Dutch hands.

Yet Gusti Ngurah Agung's family continued as unofficial leaders among their ex-subjects. Their palaces were used for dance-drama performances and members of the royal family still presided over major temple ceremonies. When in 1938 the Dutch colonial authorities decided to restore all the Balinese kingdoms, with as much autonomy as it was thought wise to permit, Cokorda Ngurah Ketut discovered as the king of Tabanan that he was one of the least powerful rulers. Whereas

Karangasem, Bangli, and Gianyar were left alone by the Dutch, the northern and western kingdoms of Buleleng, Jembrana, and Tabanan had been placed under direct colonial rule and their royal families had lost land from their private estates. Moreover, these royal families were beset by internal rivalries, as there were many claimants to the three thrones. In Badung the restored ruler was chosen from a branch of the royal family which had not participated in the *puputan* at Denpasar.

Backed by Dutch military power, the restored kings were able to enjoy the income raised in their kingdoms, after the colonial administration had levied its own taxes on land and the sale of opium. This situation remained undisturbed until February 1942, when Japan took control of Bali. Once the tide of the Second World War turned against the Japanese, however, Balinese rulers were under great pressure from the Imperial Japanese Army in terms of food production and unpaid labor. The king of Gianyar was actually exiled to Lombok for showing insufficient enthusiasm for the Greater East Asia Co-Prosperity Sphere, the name by which Japan's newly acquired empire was known.

In Tabanan, King Cokorda Ngurah Ketut ruled as best he could but the kingdom was a shadow of its former self. Something of this past glory is visible today north of Tanah Lot at Krambitan, where the Puri Agung, or "great palace," and the Puri Anyar, or "new palace," evoke the past authority of Tabanan kings. Their seventeenth-century buildings are home for Cokorda Ngurah Ketut's descendants, besides providing an income through doubling up as a guesthouse and restaurant.

To their north is the town of Tabanan, a bustling commercial centerand the location of the Museum Subak. Now recognized by UNESCO as a world cultural heritage, the *subak* system of irrigation really needs to be understood in order to appreciate how hard the Balinese people have toiled to perfect its operation. According to a museum brochure, the exhibits celebrate Tri Hita Karana, "the harmonious relations" that must underlie the *subaks*, or "irrigation societies." These relationships are with the gods, with *subak* members and with the environment. A typically Balinese socio-religious approach to agriculture, the *subak* system began its development during the pre-Majapahit period through an association of farmers and priests that guaranteed the distribution of water where and whenever it was required. Only now has it been realized how ecologically sound the irrigation system really is.

The Museum Subak reveals how it works, the effort needed to maintain its complicated network of tunnels and channels, and demonstrates the continued importance of rice in Bali's economy. An interesting exhibit is a model of a traditional farm compound, with its separate buildings carefully positioned within a protecting wall. Pride of place is naturally given to the granary, the *lumbung*, whose raised floor protects harvested rice from vermin. Here is stored the precious gift of two indigenous goddesses: the rice goddess Dewi Sri as well as the water goddess Dewi Danu.

East of Tabanan is the quiet town of Mengwi, once the capital of a kingdom of the same name. No longer dignified as an administrative region like Tabanan, Mengwi is still visited because of the Pura Taman Ayun, or "water garden." Here the gods are venerated as well as deified former kings. Most visitors are impressed by the soaring *merus*, the thatched towers dedicated to various Balinese deities. They line one side of the island at the center of this remarkable temple. It was built in the mid-eighteenth century and restored in 1937. Even though some Balinese think that the moat around the temple island has a connection with the *subaks*, through ensuring the harmonious circulation of water from the mountains to the paddy fields, to the rivers draining into the sea and then back to the mountains in rain clouds, the reference is in fact to the cosmic ocean that surrounds the Hindu world.

North of Tabanan are the rice-growing terraces that have made the area so wealthy. They culminate at Jatiluwih, whose name means "a beautiful place." High in the Tabanan hills, this village's terraced paddy fields stretch in every direction as far as the eye can see, affording the most spectacular views. Here yellow, white, black, and sticky varieties of rice are all grown. With local Balinese rice farmers are able to harvest two crops a year, but with imported strains they can manage three crops. At the moment Bali produces enough to feed itself, but with a growing population, increased visitor numbers, and the loss of paddy fields around urban centers, the island may have to start importing rice in the not too distant future.

Backtracking from Jatiluwih to the main Tabanan-Singaraja road, two places of interest may be visited. The first is the hot spring at Yeh Panas, where a small temple is dedicated to the local water spirits. During the Japanese occupation, Yeh Panas was a popular resort for members of the

Rice terraces at Jatiluwih

Imperial Japanese Army: now this thermal spring is divided between a hotel spa and a public bathing pool. The other place of interest is the memorial at Marga for those Balinese who fell in 1946 fighting the Dutch under the command of I Gusti Ngurah Rai. Their suicidal last stand was reminiscent of the Badung *puputan* forty years earlier.

Since the balance of power had dramatically changed in the Indonesian archipelago following the Japanese surrender, Holland tried to save its colonial possessions through a federation of states linked to the Dutch crown. Bali was placed in the Negara Indonesia Timoer, the state of East Indonesia. But this federal arrangement failed to satisfy the Indonesian nationalists in Java, the stronghold of resistance to the Dutch; nor did it appeal to Balinese in sympathy with republican ideals. So Ngurah Rai and others fought on. Although they did not live to see the establishment of the Republic of Indonesia in late 1949, their sacrifice is remembered in Bali in a solemn ceremony every November.

The main road north to Singaraja climbs through hilly countryside before twisting and turning to reach Lake Bratan, situated amid extinct volcanoes. As they are much older than either Gunung Agung or Gunung Batur, erosion has greatly reduced their height and allowed forests to climb their flanks. Lake Bratan itself is surrounded by densely forested hillsides topped with clouds. Occupying the ancient crater of Gunung Catur, the lake is 3,937 feet above sea level, a lower height than Lake Batur, Bali's largest freshwater reservoir.

Along with two smaller lakes to its west, Lake Bratan is the source of the springs that sustain farms in both Tabanan and Buleleng. But in Buleleng dry-land methods of cultivation predominate because the chain of mountains in which Lake Bratan lies is a watershed, with less rain falling to its north. During the so-called Javanese monsoon, however, torrential downpours soak the whole area but, from May until October, there is often a prolonged drought. When rainfall is heavy Lake Bratan can overflow and submerge Pura Ulun Danu Bratan, the island temple dedicated to the water goddess Dewi Danu. In 2014 a drought in Java and Bali had the opposite effect, stranding this iconic island temple and a

Pura Ulun Danu Bratan, high and dry in the 2014 drought

smaller one belonging to the rice goddess Dewi Sri on a mudbank.

Rather like Pura Tanah Lot on the coast, the popularity of Pura Ulun Danu Bratan has led to an unsightly sprawl of shops and restaurants along the adjacent shore. The temple itself is guarded by large statues of frogs, creatures believed to be close to divinity. The Balinese are convinced that they can never be reincarnated as a frog, and they are duty bound to protect these amphibians from snakes.

Villagers living near Lake Bratan incline more to Buddhism than Hinduism, and so a stupa can be seen on the lake-shore. Six miles from Singaraja at Banjar, there is even the Brahma Arama Vihara, a recently built Thai-style Buddhist monastery. Once an independent principality run by a priestly family, Banjar put up stout resistance to the Dutch, but by 1849 the whole of north Bali was under intense pressure from Dutch military power. That year a decisive battle between the Balinese and the invaders was fought at Jagaraga, a village to the east of Singaraja. A Balinese force of some 15,000 men, of whom 2,000 were armed with rifles and the others with spears, was smashed by a Dutch expeditionary force equipped with field artillery. Whereas Dutch casualties in the battle were 33 dead and 148 wounded, the Balinese lost thousands.

Military operations then switched to the south of the island where defeat threatened Klungkung and Karangasem, until the death of the Dutch general in charge of the expeditionary force and the ravages of tropical diseases amongst his troops led to a stalemate, which Mads Lange ingeniously converted into a peace agreement. Somehow this resourceful Danish merchant succeeded in temporarily preserving the Balinese kingdoms, but the adjustments made to their territories only served to encourage conflict between them. By the mid-1850s, the Dutch had a firm grip over most of northern and western Bali, and half a century later they ruled the entire island.

The Pura Dalem at Jagaraga celebrates the destructive side of Shiva, an appropriate dedication in view of the bloody battle that took place there. Yet the bas-reliefs inside the temple are not without a sense of humor, since they depict an armed bandit holding up two Europeans driving in a car, an airplane crashing into the waves, and a Dutch steamer being attacked by a sea monster. A similar interest in contemporary events is visible at the Pura Meduwe Karang at Kubutambahan, less than three miles north of Jagaraga. There the early Dutch artist W. O. J. Nieuwenkamp has been carved, peddling along on his bicycle. Nieuwenkamp traveled everywhere in Bali at the start of the twentieth century, sketching whatever he encountered.

Close to Lake Bratan are two other mountain lakes. The largest, Lake Buyan, is almost the same size as Lake Bratan but the other, Lake Tamblingan, is much smaller. One of the most unspoiled areas in Bali, Lake Tamblingan has rainforest right down to its water's edge, where monkeys and exotic birds can be observed moving among the trees. The hillsides of Bali abound with monkeys, although there are specific places where large numbers congregate in so-called monkey forests. These may be explained by the local supply of food: offerings made in temples and shrines account for half the monkeys' diet, in spite of stiff competition with dogs for the rice, peanuts, and fruit they contain. Monkeys usually get the better of dogs, but not human beings when they dare to eat rice stalks or grub for sweet potatoes in village gardens. Because the Balinese place such importance on harmonious relations, like the Tri Hita Karana philosophy we met earlier in the Museum Subak at Tabanan, there is no attempt to keep the monkey population under control.

For Tri Hita Karana, or "the three ways of ensuring the welfare" of Bali, assumes that balance and unity is the natural condition of the universe, as indeed it is for the individual. So every prayer and offering in a Balinese temple or shrine aims to maintain a creative harmony between the forces of good and evil. Male-female, good-bad, life-death; these are the opposites that need to be kept in constant equilibrium. Tooth-filing is a prime example of this quest for balance, since the reduction of the top six front teeth is believed to curb animality. That monkeys in particular have sharp canines and incisors must explain the ambiguous position of Hanuman, since he was never embraced by the Balinese as a deity. Unlike in India, he remains an immortal animal.

SINGARAJA AND WEST

While the road down to Singaraja, the chief settlement on Bali's northern coast, has an impressive array of hairpin bends, the regularity of its own streets is a reminder that, from the imposition of Dutch rule until 1953, the town acted as the administrative center of the island. Even before the Dutch arrived, Singaraja was already a busy port whose inhabitants hailed from Java, Arabia, and China. The presence of a Chinese temple near the waterfront underlines the town's involvement with long-distance commerce, while several mosques meet the spiritual needs of traders from other Indonesian islands. A cosmopolitan atmosphere still prevails in Singaraja, although the island's political and commercial center of gravity has of course now shifted southward. Benoa harbor and the Ngurah Rai airport ensure Denpasar's present-day dominance, but the northern port resonates in Balinese folklore and myth. The marriage of an early king of Singaraja and a Chinese merchant's daughter is a case in point: it produced Bali's very own god and goddess of wealth.

Perhaps Singaraja's antiquity is best expressed in the Gedong Kirtya, a library founded by the Dutch in 1928 for the preservation of Balinese *lontar* manuscripts. These are specially cut palm leaves inscribed with a stylus and then rubbed with blackening in order to make the script legible. Because of their availability, palm leaves were used for writing purposes throughout maritime Southeast Asia, their only shortcoming a tendency to disintegrate in humid conditions. Some of the works in the library are therefore relatively recent copies of older manuscripts. Also preserved in the Gedong Kirtya are several tenth-century royal edicts inscribed on sheets of bronze.

The coastal road westward from Singaraja is much quieter than its equivalent in the south, for the good reason that Javanese lorries headed for Lombok follow the shorter southern route from the port of Gilimanuk. There are no towns of any size on the northern coast until this ferry link with Java is reached, although the village of Pulaki deserves a visit. Its two small temples are connected with Danghyang Nirartha, whose youngest daughter was raped and left for dead in what is now the Taman Nasional Bali Barat, the West Bali national park. She had wandered off and fell victim to a couple of woodcutters near Pulaki. According to Balinese legend, so enraged was Danghyang Nirartha by this violation that he purified the girl and transformed her into the goddess Dewi Melanting. The association of the priest's daughter with the original Balinese plant goddess must recall the annual death and resurrection of this deity, just as the rape has an obvious parallel in Shiva's uncontrollable lust for the rice goddess Dewi Sri. The other gods killed and buried Dewi Sri in order to keep her inviolate.

Apart from raising his wronged daughter to the status of a goddess and establishing her cult at the Pura Melanting, Danghyang Nirartha also

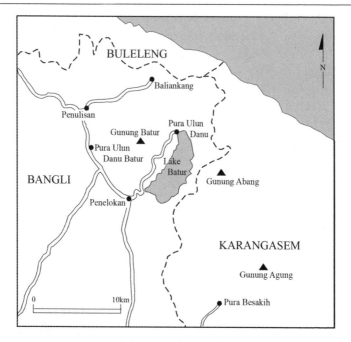

Lake Batur and surroundings

deified the girl's distressed mother. Local villagers relate how the Javanese priest cursed the men responsible for the crime and made them the invisible servants of his wife at the Pura Pulaki. Even now they still roam Pulaki, causing dogs to suddenly howl.

The West Bali national park is vast. Established in 1984, its forested hills, mountains, coast, and offshore reefs are among the last remaining untouched areas in the island. Within its borders is Gunung Prapat Agung, the extinct volcano that was so revered by the prehistoric inhabitants of Gilimanuk; they looked upon the volcano's summit as the abode of their gods and their deified ancestors. In Gilimanuk, the Museum Situs Purbakala has items that were excavated in the early settlement, which is at least 4,000 years old.

Modern Gilimanuk is a nondescript town marked only by a monumental archway, the so-called gateway to Bali, which stretches across the main road like similar structures erected by Saddam Hussein in

Baghdad. Instead of giant hands holding crossed swords, though, the Gilimanuk gateway comprises four cosmic serpents facing in the cardinal directions, their entwined tails supporting in the center the throne of Ida Sanghyang Widi Wasa, Bali's supreme deity.

During the prehistoric period Gilimanuk was a tiny island, and not the peninsula from which a ferry service now connects Bali with Java. The southern coastal road which takes vehicles eastward through Jembrana is always busy. Quite often it does not seem to be running through Bali at all, since many Javanese settlers live here and their mosques give the landscape a non-Hindu feel. Even Perancuk, the place where Danghyang Nirartha first landed in Bali, is dominated not by a temple but a mosque.

Quite different from Jembrana is the northern part of the island, to the east of Singaraja. Turning off the coastal road at Kubutambahan, the site of the fascinating Pura Meduwe Karang, a whole series of twists and turns leads to Bali's most active volcano, Gunung Batur. Many tourists come to see this volcano and its crater lake because there are restaurants

One of Bali's oldest temples, the Pura Tegeh Koripan preserves pre-Hindu rock worship

with good views of both these natural features.

Before reaching Gunung Batur though, there is an impressive temple at Penulisan. Dedicated to Shiva, the eleventh-century Pura Tegeh Koripan is the highest temple in the whole of Bali, situated near the summit of the extinct volcano Gunung Penulisan. On a clear day it is possible to see from the temple the island's northern and eastern coastline. Pura Tegeh Koripan is actually a hilltop complex of five temples, whose original foundation certainly precedes the triumph of the Hindu faith. Ancient rock worship is transparent in altars displaying carved figures and even unhewn rock. Near the highest temple there is also a very early shrine composed of wood and thatch. The 300 steps that have to be climbed in order to reach Pura Tegeh Koripan from the village square at Penulisan deter many visitors, with the result that its tranquil atmosphere is a delightful change from more popular temples.

Even more unvisited is the remote temple founded for the worship of the Balinese god and goddess of wealth at Baliankang. The Pura Penataran Agung is reached via a number of country roads, leading northeast from Penulisan. This is dry upland country without any *subak* irrigation. Cisterns are used to store monsoon rain, but dry-farming methods are necessary to grow citrus fruit, vegetables, and coffee. Here is one of the sources of *luwat* coffee, whose seeds have passed through the bodies of wild civet cats. Along Bali's busier roads there are advertisements for this unusual drink, but without the frankness of its Chinese name. In Malaysia, it is simply called *maoshi kafei*, or "cat-shit coffee."

At Baliankang access to the Pura Penataran Agung again involves much climbing, since the temple is situated on the far side of a deep ravine. Steps go down to a footbridge over a gushing stream and then up to the large temple compound, which stands on a dry ledge of land. The temple's usual visitors are Balinese worshippers who come to seek better luck in their lives. It is firmly believed that the temple's god and goddess are capable of bestowing good fortune.

According to Balinese tradition, these deities were originally King Sri Jaya Pangus of Singaraja and his wife Kang Ching Wie, the daughter of a prominent Chinese merchant. After many years of unsuccessfully trying for a son and heir, the king decided to set sail in the hope that a sea journey would rejuvenate him. But after a storm, Sri Jaya Pangus was stranded on an enchanted island full of beautiful plants and animals. Uncertain of his

The remote Pura Penataran Agung and its temple dog

Worshippers on their way to the Pura Penataran Agung in search of prosperity

future, the king succumbed to the charms of the lake goddess Dewi Danu and forgot all about the purpose of the voyage. Eventually Queen Kang Ching Wei tracked him down only to discover that her husband was living with Dewi Danu, who had given birth to a child. Initial conflict between Sri Jaya Pangus and Kang Ching Wei was, however, quickly resolved through the strength of their love for each other, and even Dewi Danu acknowledged the depth of their affection. Not only did she protect them from demonic attack, but finally rewarded their constancy by turning the loving couple into divinities.

Services conducted in Pura Penataran Agung, where Sri Jaya Pangus and Kang Ching Wei may have achieved complete enlightenment at the end of their lives, always seek to ensure the prosperity of an individual or a family. It is telling that Kang Ching Wei should have become Bali's indigenous goddess of wealth: her father and fellow Chinese traders had evidently made Singaraja a wealthy port. Shrines dedicated to Kang Ching Wei are still treated with great respect in Balinese marketplaces and the

Pura Ulun Danu Batur is a complex of over one hundred shrines

homes of shopkeepers today. If the Chinese merchant's daughter can be said to represent the wealth that can be derived from commerce, then the lake goddess must point to the regular profits that come from successful cultivation.

The subject of a favorite puppet show, the story of Sri Jaya Pangus and Kang Ching Wei's complicated marriage is treasured by the Balinese. Effigies of the divine king and queen are paraded through villages and towns on several occasions each year, since they are believed to ward off bad luck as well as evil spirits. The economic significance of early trade with China is also made perfectly clear at Pura Ulun Danu Batur, the great temple which faces Gunung Batur. Inside one of its courtyards stands a Chinese temple.

Another temple dedicated to Dewi Danu is located at the northern end of Lake Batur. Its high priest oversees the distribution of water for the irrigation system, and *subak* members visit this temple every year. They are in awe of the high priest who is always dressed in white and wears his hair long. As custodian of the crater lake, his responsibility for Bali's greatest expanse of fresh water is immense. How great the lake's storage capacity is remains a matter of speculation: though its dimensions are four miles long and one mile wide, for religious reasons its depth has never been plumbed. Yet as one *subak* member put it, Lake Batur is "the origin of water and the priest holds all of it in his hands."

Chapter Nine

CENTRAL AND EAST BALI

"At the supreme temple of Besakih, under the auspices of the colonial government, the spirits of the ancestors witnessed the consecration of the Balinese kings."

The 1938 restoration of Balinese kingship

In central and western Bali are concentrated the places of greatest cultural interest. Gianyar, Bangli, Klungkung, and Karangasem all possess impressive temples as well as creative villages, but Ubud in Gianyar is Bali's cultural hub. Because of the enlightened outlook of the town's ruling family in the early twentieth century, Ubud and its neighboring villages have developed into the acknowledged center of Balinese arts and crafts, music, and drama. To be expected, then, is the reverence shown there to Saraswati, the Hindu goddess of learning. In the 1950s the local artist and architect I Gusti Nyoman Lempad was commissioned to build a temple for the goddess in the town's center.

Saraswati, whose name means "rich in waters," was originally a river goddess in India. From the *Rig Veda*, India's oldest collection of hymns, it is clear that rituals were performed on the banks of the Saraswati River, which enjoyed a sacred status similar to the Ganges in present-day Hinduism. But the connection of the goddess with a specific river steadily decreased as the Indo-Aryans spread across the subcontinent. She acquired instead an association with speech, becoming the goddess of eloquence and learning. "She who goes from the mountain to the sea," one text proclaims, is transformed into "a pool of wisdom." Depicted as a graceful woman sitting on a lotus, with two or eight arms, Saraswati usually has near her a lute and a book.

Each October the town of Ubud stages a week-long festival in honor of Saraswati: it features impressive processions, religious services, dance-drama, exhibitions of painting and sculpture, even an international gathering of authors. This tradition stems from the support given to painters and sculptors by Tjokorda Gede Agung Sukawati, then the ruler

131

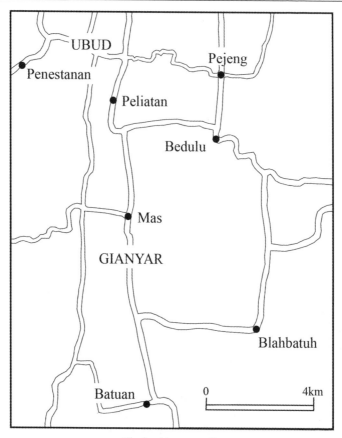

Ubud and its surroundings

of Ubud, and his brother Tjokorda Raka Sukawati. These enlightened princes were assisted by two European artists, Walter Spies and Johan Rudolf Bonnet. Whereas Spies fell foul of the Dutch colonial authorities and was arrested in 1939, Bonnet lived without difficulty in Bali until 1943, when the Japanese deported him to an internment camp in Sulawesi. Spies was already dead by this date, the ship on which the Dutch sent him to Sri Lanka having been sunk by Japanese aircraft. Although Bonnet returned to Bali after the surrender of Japan, he was himself obliged to leave Indonesia in 1957 when he refused to sell one of his paintings to President Sukarno.

Both Spies and Bonnet were primarily concerned introducing Western aesthetic ideas to local artists: Arie Smit, another European painter living in the nearby village of Penestanan, was not. Smit encouraged two promising village boys to become painters without trying to influence their work at all. The thrust of the Ubud-based artistic movement resulted in the foundation of the Museum Puri Lukisan, which no visitor can afford to miss. Nowhere else on the island is it possible to get such an insight into twentieth-century Balinese art than at the so-called "palace museum of painting."

I Gusti Nyoman Lempad was a key member of the artistic group that collected around Spies and Bonnet. His mastery of line was facilitated by Spies' introduction of paper to Ubud artists. And it was Nyoman Lempad who most of all drew the attention of Western visitors. The artist's relationship with the Ubud royal family was not necessarily an easy one,

A beautifully carved doorway at I Gusti Nyoman Lempad's house in Ubud

since the rules governing such relations were very rigid in spite of Dutch domination of Balinese society. That Nyoman Lempad lived next door to the palace, and was involved in its renovation, made little difference: he was still no more than a subject. Yet the artist's genius secured his independence and his beautiful house and garden reveal how confident he became in later life. In 1978 Nyoman Lempad died, well over one hundred years of age.

Opposite Nyoman Lempad's house is Ubud market, located at a crossroads in the center of the town. Much easier to negotiate than the streets and marketplaces at Denpasar, Ubud market remains a challenge for the casual stroller because every stallholder is convinced that his or her wares deserve to be purchased. Handicrafts, shoes, textiles, and clothing are the chief items on sale, but souvenirs especially produced for tourists can be examined too. Not far away on Jalan Suweta is another surprising feature of Ubud, a restaurant specializing in *babi guling*, or "roast suckling pig." This dish is a favorite of the Balinese, whose cuisine readily encompasses pork as well as beef. There are no holy cows in Bali, nor any sympathy for the animal taboos of Muslim residents.

In and around Ubud other art galleries and museums exist besides the Museum Puri Lukisan. Just up the road from Nyoman Lempad's house is the Seniwati Gallery of Art, which sells work by Indonesian women artists. A mile or so along the same road is the Neka Art Museum, whose collection of paintings rivals that of the Museum Puri Lukisan. It was founded in 1976 by Suteja Neka, a connoisseur of Indonesian art. What makes the Neka Art Museum famous is undoubtedly the large number of Arie Smit's works on display, since they capture the essence of Bali.

At Penestanan, a village to the west of Ubud, Arie Smit used to have his studio. It was here that Smit, a close friend of fellow Dutchman Bonnet, inaugurated the so-called Young Artists school, which places emphasis on color and decoration. Smit said he invited village boys to use his studio in order to help them "make paintings they could sell to buy land," but that he did not try to influence the style of their work, only the subject of village life. When in 2014 we visited Penestanan, the sole Young Artist still painting was I Ketut Soki, one of whose smaller works we purchased. Almost seventy years old, Ketut Soki's gratitude for Arie Smit's encouragement was palpable, and the freshness and vigor of his compositions are a tribute to the Dutchman's realization that within this

"Young Artist" painter I Ketut Soki in his studio at Penestanan

village boy was an important artist. Visitors to Penestanan should not be put off by the gaudy paintings displayed on the ground floor of the house in which Ketut Soki lives: his charming paintings are only to be seen in his studio, on the first floor.

Less interesting is the Blanco Renaissance Museum, the studio-home of the Spanish artist Antonio Blanco, who died in 1999. It is located near the bridge over the Campuhan ravine. South of Ubud, at Pengosekan village is the Agung Rai Museum of Art. Its permanent collection comprises Balinese and Indonesian paintings, while temporary exhibitions tend to attract large numbers of visitors. Close by, Peliatan is well known for its own paintings and woodcarving. But the village's greatest fame remains the *legong* dance, because during the 1950s a group of its girls went to Paris and New York, taking both cities by storm. Today this musical tradition is continued in one of the few all-women gamelan orchestras.

East of Peliatan is Pejeng, once the capital of Bali's earliest kingdom. History crowds round this prosperous village, which boasts two important sites. The first is the Museum Purbakala, whose exhibits feature an amazing range of prehistoric artifacts. Most viewed are the turtle-shaped stone sarcophagi, a singular Balinese method of secondary burial prior to the introduction of Hinduism from Java. The changeover to cremation under the influence of this new faith made the carving of an expensive sarcophagus redundant, but the surviving examples created for the benefit of wealthy families underline the Balinese preoccupation with turtles. Even though Hindu cosmic snakes were later placed beneath the island to assist the giant turtle Bedawang in keeping it raised above the waves, every Balinese knows it is Bedawang's strong back that acts as the island's true foundation.

The second site to be visited in Pejeng is the Pura Penataran Sasih, whose name refers to the moon's surface. It is believed that a part of this planet crashed here in the form of the great bronze drum presently housed in the temple. The earplug of the moon goddess is one suggestion for the five-foot drum, the largest example of casting in the Southeast Asian Bronze Age. The decorative star on its front, surrounded by wavy bands in a double spiral pattern, is characteristic of Dong Son design. The north Vietnamese settlement of Dong Son is the site where such ritual drums were first excavated. But the Pejeng drum is of Balinese manufacture. On its sides are handles and intense-looking faces; they are among the earliest representations of the human face in the Indonesian archipelago. The damaged drum is never moved from its tower in the Pura Penataran Sasih, but smaller drums are wheeled at the front of religious processions.

Although the Pura Kebo Edan, or "crazy buffalo temple," celebrates the exploits of the champion giant Kebo Iwo in Pejeng, his chief place of worship is in Blahbatuh, farther south. In the Pura Gaduh is a large stone head of the legendary giant, who served the last Balinese king before the Majapahit conquest. Kebo Iwo was the champion of King Bedaulu, the ruler with the head of a wild boar and the body of a man. Yet neither the king's magical powers nor his champion's muscular strength were sufficient to stop the eastern Javanese minister, Gajah Mada, from taking control of Bali. Either Kebo Iwo fell in battle or was buried alive. One version of the legend says how Gaja Mada tricked the giant into believing he could find him a mate. As no Balinese woman could match his size, Gajah Mada had a huge female puppet constructed with a warrior hidden inside. So pleased was Kebo Iwo that he was trapped in a well that he dug with his bare hands for his new bride. Gajah Mada is said to have ordered his soldiers to fill in

The legendary giant Kebo Iwo at the Pura Gaduh temple in Blahbatuh

the hole, while the giant was still working at the bottom.

The sequel to the burial tale is the curse that a dying Kebo Iwo is supposed to have uttered. He swore that he would return as a giant white buffalo and subjugate Java for 300 years. Some Indonesians hold that the curse came true in the shape of Dutch colonial rule. Pura Gaduh means "noisy temple," a reference to the tumult of battle: Balinese people who go there to ask for a share of Kebo Iwo's strength. Should tourists find the stone head in the temple smaller than they expect, they can view a much bigger statue of the giant a short distance away.

On the outskirts of Blahbatuh a company, the Puti Ayu, makes some of the finest *ikat* cloth in Bali. The process is very time consuming, but finished articles in silk or cotton are quite exquisite, the finest designs arising from the smallest number of dyed threads. Not far distant are other craft centers such as Celuk, where goldsmiths turn out beautiful jewelry; Mas, the premier place for woodcarving; and Batuan, the home of a distinctive school of painting that evolved during the 1930s.

Using mainly black or dark green colors, Batuan painters fill their compositions with busy scenes from everyday life: villages, ceremonies, and of course the spirit world. They are particularly fascinated with darkness and the invisible forms of demonic power around them. The tourist market for paintings made a huge difference to the lives of Balinese artists. Spies and Bonnet worked hard to promote their work, an effort the Dutch colonial authorities did much to help by setting up the Museum Bali in Denpasar. A wider awareness of Bali's cultural heritage was bound to benefit the island as well as its increasing number of visitors.

Closer to Pejeng is the enigmatic Goa Gajah, or "elephant cave." Similar to the rock-cut shrines farther north at Gunung Kawi, Goa Gajah possesses an aura of unreality and mystery. Probably carved at the end of the tenth century, this hermitage may have been intended for Hindu priests, since Bali was coming under increased eastern Javanese influence

The Goa Gajah or "elephant cave"

at the time. If Goa Gajah was commissioned by King Udayana, then his Javanese queen would have urged him to undertake the cave's construction. Like Gunung Kawi, the cave is approached by a long flight of steps that end in a valley furnished with pools. The colossal head above the entrance of the cave would have been carved to frighten away malignant spirits in the same manner as stone figures guard doorways now. The cave's musty interior has little to show other than Ganesa, the elephant-headed son of Shiva.

The long walk down 276 steps from the village of Tampaksiring to Gunung Kawi is made tolerable by the splendid sight of terraced rice fields spread out below, and the refreshing coconut milk available from stalls discreetly perched next to the stone stairway. At the very bottom of the valley is a temple dedicated appropriately to the rice goddess Dewi Sri, but the nine stupa-like shrines higher up its side are the really interesting sight. They were completed around 1080 for King Anak Wungsu and his wives. A tenth shrine, to the west, is reached by a short walk along the sides of several paddy fields. Unlike anything else in Bali, these rock-cut shrines were probably used for the ashes of the royal dead. Without any written documents to explain their purpose, it can only be presumed that Anak Wungsu was attempting to start some kind of cult.

Just north of Tampaksiring is the sacred spring temple of Pura Tirtha Empul. The Balinese believe that Indra created the spring in order to refresh his exhausted troops, who had been worn out fighting a demon king. The story must owe something to Indra's defeat of Vritra, a drought-causing serpent which had swallowed the cosmic waters and lay in coils on the mountains. With his thunderbolt, the sky god split open the stomach of Vritra, releasing the waters, generating life, and liberating the dawn. This victory of a sky god over an enormous serpent, the embodiment of mother earth, is a very old myth. For the Greeks it was the jealous earth goddess Hera, the consort of sky god Zeus, who sent her snake attendants to kill Heracles, the child of a clandestine affair between Zeus and the mortal woman Alcmene. The infant hero strangled the snakes in his cot, but Hera's relentless animosity drove Heracles to such a state of madness that he finally murdered his own family. To expiate this dreadful crime he undertook the famous twelve labors.

Next to Pura Tirtha Empul stands a luxurious government rest house, a favorite place of residence for President Sukarno during his tours of Bali.

Offerings being prepared at Pura Dasar in Gelgel

Today the Balinese are certain that his spirit lingers there. When President Suharto, the general who overthrew Sukarno, came to the rest house, all kinds of strange things are said to have happened.

The last temple to see in this part of Bali is Pura Kehen, a place of worship since the twelfth century. An enormous banyan tree shades the temple's first courtyard, where the walls are inlaid with pieces of Chinese porcelain. The second and upper court has a stone *padmasana*, or "lotus throne," for Brahma, Vishnu, and Shiva. Even more impressively carved are the fierce elephants guarding the temple's front entrance. The Pura Kehen is located about a mile outside Bangli town.

TEMPLES AND PALACES

By taking the main road south from Bangli, and then turning west at

Peteluan, two historic towns are reached: Gelel and Klungkung. The former was the capital of Bali from the fourteenth to the eighteenth century, when the court moved to Klungkung. The establishment of royal authority in both these towns was fraught with danger. The death of the first Majapahit-sponsored king, Ketut Kresna Kapakisan, left Bali in confusion because his eldest son proved quite incapable of ruling with wisdom. Described as a cuckold and a fop, he could neither inspire the Balinese nobility nor ensure that his court at Samprangan acted as the island's cosmic center. This worrisome vacuum prompted leading nobles to install at Gelgel one of Kapakisan's younger sons as king instead. He was Dewa Ketut Ngulesir, who restored confidence in the dynasty, thanks to the guidance the new ruler received from Shiva. It was upon the more secure foundation of kingship laid at Gelgel that Waturrenggong, his son and successor, inaugurated Bali's golden age.

The move to Klungkung in 1710 was also the result of dynastic difficulty. A restive nobility increasingly made the court at Gelgel seem politically irrelevant, although the cosmic implications of a weakened ruler were not lost on the Balinese people. At last, a descendant of Kapakisan reclaimed cosmic leadership at Klungkung, a town also known as Semarapura. Although the new king, Ida I Dewa Agung Jambe, styled himself the Dewa Agung, or "supreme one," Bali's disintegration into separate kingdoms and principalities could no longer be stopped. An empire that in its golden age had extended from eastern Java to Sumbawa was, in the eighteenth and nineteenth centuries, steadily reduced to a patchwork of squabbling powers. It was into such a divided Bali that the Dutch, driven by economic interests, began to assert themselves.

Virtually a suburb of Klungkung today, Gelgel has one of Bali's most important temples in the Pura Dasar, which is dedicated to Sanghyang Widi Wasa. Perhaps this dedication to the supreme Balinese deity, the summation of all divine power in the island, explains the reason for the temple's popularity with the *sudra* caste, who form the overwhelming majority of the population. So crowded are its festivals that the inhabitants of Gelgel spend a great deal of time in preparing for them. Local women virtually mass-produce offerings while their menfolk build the bamboo altars on which they are displayed.

While Gelgel was still the royal capital, its artistic needs were met by the most traditional school of Balinese painting at the nearby village of

The audience chamber at the Klungkung palace

Kamasan. King Waturrengong in particular commissioned paintings for his palace and the many temples that he patronized. His example was copied by nobles across Bali, making Kamasan in the process rich and famous. Even now its artists receive orders from both Balinese and foreign collectors. Its foremost painter is I Nyoman Mandra, whose studio warmly welcomes visitors.

At the Klungkung palace, Kamasan painters decorated in the *wayang* style the ceiling of Bale Kambang, the audience chamber of the Dewa Agung, the supreme Balinese king. It is indeed the main feature of the palace's Taman Gili, or "moated garden," but the court also met in the Bale Kerta Gosa, or "pavilion of peace and prosperity." Standing to the right of the main entrance, it has exquisite examples of Kamasan artists' work on its ceiling too. Whereas scenes from the *Mahabharata* form the subject of the paintings in the Bale Kerta Gosa, and especially the hero-warrior Bhima's quest for the souls of his dead parents, those depicted in the Bale Kambang are all drawn from the *Sutasoma*.

That Bhima had to battle terrible demons appealed to the Balinese, as indeed did the story of the Javanese prince Sutasoma, whose attainment of wisdom seemed to epitomize ideal kingship. So calm was Sutasoma that he even converted to nonviolence the demons and wild animals that threatened to devour him. As one incredulous demon asks the prince, "How could I possibly be defeated by you?" Essentially an explanation of the strength inherent in complete enlightenment, the fifteenth-century Javanese *Sutasoma* revolves around the spiritual authority of kingship when a ruler behaves according to the dictates of the Buddhist scriptures. As the teacher of Sutasoma is none other than Kertanagara, the charismatic king of Singhasari, this only serves to underscore the point. Diminished though his political authority was at Klungkung, the Dewa Agung could always gaze at Bale Kambang's painted ceiling and console himself with his own position in the cosmic order.

The Dutch attack on Klungkung in 1908 punctured any such bubbles of comfort that may have sustained Ida I Dewa Agung Jambe. Trouble between Klungkung and the Dutch arose from the imposition of an opium monopoly. Before Batavia introduced this island-wide restriction, the drug could be freely bought in any Balinese marketplace. For rulers with harbors the import of opium from Singapore provided a useful source of taxation. Ever seeking to profit from their relations with the peoples of the Indonesian archipelago, though, the Dutch saw the income from the sale of opium in Bali as a compensation for the lack of revenue the island generated in comparison with Java and Sumatra. But the new arrangement was opposed by the Agung Dewa's subjects: the Dutch opium store at Gelgel was burned down and its Javanese manager killed. Then a Dutch military patrol sent to investigate the disturbance also suffered casualties.

So it was deemed time to teach the Dewa Agung a lesson and a Dutch battalion marched on Klungkung. Having placed their artillery outside the palace, these soldiers were baffled by the apparent absence of resistance. Despite nearly a hundred residents of Gelgel dying in clashes with Dutch forces, there was no popular support for Ida I Dewa Agung Jambe. When he eventually emerged from the front gate of the palace with a long spear in his hand, it became obvious that a repeat of the 1906 Badung *puputan* was about to happen. Followed by his relatives and his faithful followers, the king walked into the Dutch line of fire. A modern painting in a newer part of the Klungkung palace shows these people falling victim to machine-gun bullets, although a salvo of shells actually started the massacre.

Proceeding westward into Karangasem, the first place worthy of a visit is the Bali Aga village of Tenganan, located in the foothills of Gunung Agung. It is reached by leaving the coast road between Sengkidu and Candidasa. Once the haunt of Western anthropologists, Tenganan is now a favorite with busloads of tourists, who are impressed by its layout: spacious family compounds line straight streets that crisscross the village. Even though they comprise a mere two percent of the population, the Bali Aga have kept their pre-Majapahit social system and beliefs intact. Their distinctive lifestyle was already apparent before 1343, the year in which the eastern Javanese overran Bali, because edicts issued by earlier Balinese kings refer to the Bali Aga as a separately administered people.

Since the Bali Aga took no interest in Hinduism, their caste-free society is the envy of modern Balinese who think the structure of the island's social system should be thoroughly overhauled. In Tenganan, as in the Bali Aga villages around Lake Batur, a council of elders is responsible for law and order while priests oversee religious observances and mediate between the seen and unseen worlds. A village assembly of married men advises the council of elders, meeting regularly at the *wantilan*, or "communal hall," in the middle of the village. The Bali Aga believe in reincarnation along with the rest of the Balinese people, but they do not practice cremation. Like the prehistoric inhabitants of Gilimanuk, at the extreme end of western Bali, the dead are placed face down in open graves covered by bamboo lattices. Older burials sometimes end with the removal of skulls, which are cleaned and stored on a stone platform nearby.

Of the coastal settlements of Karangasem the most attractive is the sleepy fishing village of Amed. Looking out to sea are views of Lombok while those inland are of Gunung Agung. The village remains an oasis of tranquility because its inhabitants put up the most determined opposition when the Balinese provincial government tried to introduce a ferry link to Lombok from here. Besides some excellent restaurants, Amed offers close to its black pebble beach the opportunity to fish from outriggers or snorkel among coral reefs. Farther up the coast at Tulamben there is good diving around an American ship, torpedoed by the Imperial Japanese Navy in early 1942. Shockwaves from the 1963 eruption of Gunung Agung broke the wreck in half.

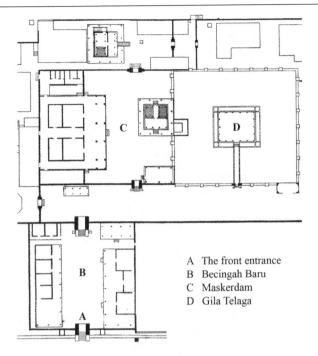

A The front entrance
B Becingah Baru
C Maskerdam
D Gila Telaga

The Puri Agung Karangasem

Some 2,000 people were killed by the unexpected eruption, and 75,000 others lost their homes and livelihoods because they could not cultivate lava-covered soil. The eruption lasted for over four months and then for another six months ash rained down on the surrounding countryside. Now Gunung Agung rarely emits smoke, although the volcano was reduced in height by nearly 1,150 feet.

The Karangasem royal family were at the Pura Besakih temple complex for the Eka Dasa Rudra festival when the eruption began. In his autobiography *The Birthmark*, Made Djelantik provides a vivid description of the event and its aftermath. According to this prince-doctor, "thick smoke was blowing high up from the crater and terrible rumblings were heard from below the earth mixed with a cacophony of metallic sounds like that from hundreds of blacksmiths working in a large forge." The family home at Amlapura, the capital of Karangasem, is well away from the volcano and suffered no damage. The Puri Agung Karangasem is still

145

A ceremonial gateway at the Karangasem palace in Amlapura

exactly as Gusti Gede Djelantik built the palace at the end of the nineteenth century. King, regent, and *stedehouder*, this far-sighted ruler understood how opposing the Dutch was pointless and the best policy for all entailed the preservation of Balinese culture.

Although the Djelantiks were regarded with considerable disdain after the establishment of the Republic of Indonesia for their pro-Dutch attitude, they did act as the chief guardians of Balinese ways during the colonial period. And the last effective king, Gusti Bagus Djelantik, may not have been far wrong in predicting that the new republic would be no less than Javanese domination. Its first two presidents, Sukarno and Suharto, certainly behaved as if Jakarta was Batavia reborn, with the same entitlement to dictate policy for every island in the Indonesian archipelago.

The Puri Agung Karangasem reveals how a Balinese palace was expected to function. It has three principal courtyards. In Becingah Baru, the outer one just inside the main entrance, there was accommodation for invited guests. The king would have received visitors in a second and inner courtyard that is entered through a monumental doorway, guarded by fierce statues to ward off evil influences. Named Maskerdam, the Balinese name for Amsterdam, this section of the palace speaks of the friendly coexistence between the kingdom of Karangasem and the Dutch colonial authorities. Its striking feature is the Gila Telaga, or "island pavilion," in the middle of a small pond. A raised building adjacent to the pavilion was used for ceremonial purposes. Divided into subsections, the third and innermost courtyard, housed the royal family. King Anglurah Ketut Karangsem had ten wives, from whom descended sixteen sons, nineteen daughters, and ninety grandchildren.

As the Pura Besakih temple complex is located in Karangasem, it was held in high esteem by the Djelantik family. The complex has always been used by other Balinese royalty, and in particular the Dewa Agung of Klungkung, whose family are still involved with its management. Now thirty temples and hundreds of shrines act as a powerful magnet for Balinese worshippers, although the Pura Penataran Agung is the prime destination because it contains a magnificent *padmasana tiga,* or "triple lotus throne," dedicated to Sanghyang Widi Wasa, manifest here as Brahma, Shiva, and Vishnu, the great Hindu gods. This particular throne dates from the eighteenth century, long after the Javanese priest

Danghyang Nirartha started the custom of setting them up inside Balinese temples.

Visiting Pura Besakih on the southern slope of Gunung Agung can be trying, because the complex of temples stands at the top of a steep incline on which four-wheeled traffic is forbidden. Only a lift on the back of a moped offers weary legs any relief. A resolute tourist will be rewarded by the experience of a visit, but Pura Besakih really deserves better transport arrangements.

Part Four

BALINESE CULTURE

A Balinese woman offering flowers at a garden shrine

Chapter Ten

BALINESE RELIGION AND BELIEFS

"If a witch is killed during the course of a night, the human body of this malignant spirit, back in bed, will die without any apparent cause."

A Balinese belief

In the fourteenth century the Majapahit conquest brought Hinduism to Bali, a transfer of faith that was significantly deepened 200 years afterward through the arrival of refugees fleeing the triumph of Islam in eastern Java. Because this influx included large numbers of priests it was hardly surprising how the island came to be seen as more than a sanctuary. Once the Hindu gods themselves were believed to have joined the eastward migration and taken up residence on Gunung Agung, the volcanic home of the island's indigenous deities, Bali was transformed into a cosmos. It had become, after all, the abode of the gods and goddesses who originated in ancient India.

Some knowledge of the characters of these powerful deities is necessary in order to understand the ease with which Hinduism meshed with the Austronesian outlook of the Balinese people. On their remarkable island, what the modern visitor sees is *sekala*, colorful ceremonies, ritual and dance-drama. What is not seen is the occult, *niskala*, the underlying magic which propels the dancer as well as the witch. For Bali's imaginative dimension, its unique atmosphere, derives from the unseen.

The Balinese world is permeated by magical power, because nothing is considered to be inanimate and wholly devoid of any ability to exert influence over other things, something which Westerners often miss. Even cars, buses, trucks, and motorcycles are treated with profound respect, just as wells and pumps receive daily offerings.

Since misfortune in Bali is always assumed to result from bad behavior, there is an urgent need to ensure proper ritual observances take place, to the extent that they shape the whole of daily life. Such a point of view, however, corresponds with the basic Hindu concept of maintaining a balance between opposing forces, of a cosmological equilibrium essential for the preservation of universal order.

Characteristically Hindu is the interdependence of both sets of immortals: the gods and the demons. During one of Vishnu's descents to Earth, in his incarnation as the tortoise Kurma, the sole purpose of the savior deity is to restore this relationship. As the elixir of immortality was lost in the deluge, neither the gods nor the demons could long survive without this miraculous drink and so the world order was under threat. Kurma acts as a support for a mountain around which, in a tug of war, the gods and the demons pull a serpentine rope in order to churn the cosmic ocean, and thereby obtain *soma*. Originally the fermented juice of a milky climbing plant, *soma* was offered in libations to the gods and drunk by brahmins. Its exhilarating quality delighted both, and it was not long before the beverage was attributed incredible powers. As the tortoise Kurma, Vishnu's objective is not to destroy the demons but, on the contrary, to ensure they remain the necessary opponents of the gods. Their perpetual antagonism, a balance of forces that gives the universe its dynamic, greatly appealed to the Balinese, whose own spirit-haunted island had to be reordered by their semidivine kings from time to time.

According to one Hindu tradition, it was Prajapati, whose name means "lord of creatures," who first created gods and demons alike and did not bother to distinguish between them. Early texts indeed stress the similarity of the two groups, though an attempt is occasionally made to describe their characteristics. "The gods took refuge in the day, the demons in the night," we are told. "They were of equal strength, and one could not easily distinguish between them. But the gods were afraid of night, darkness and death." Before the appearance of *soma*, the gods and the demons seem to have lived in harmony: competition for the miraculous drink, however, set them at odds with each other and the failure of the demons to secure a regular supply meant that the gods could kill them. In the *Mahabharata*, the world's second-longest poem, the Indian hero Arjuna reflects how the gods won their places in heaven by slaying "their kinsmen, the demons." Such is the way of the universe, the *Mahabharata* confirms, because "brothers kill brothers for the sake of a kingdom. Even the gods, knowing dharma well, killed the demons."

Yet Arjuna remains uneasy on the eve of the climactic battle on the Kurukshetra plain, near modern Delhi, since he realizes how the fighting will destroy whole families. Caught up in the conflict between the

Balinese demons

Pandavas and the Kauravas, the epic struggle related in the *Mahabharata* that fascinated both the Javanese and the Balinese, a reluctant Arjuna is only strengthened by Vishnu himself. Incarnated as Krishna, the god agrees to act as charioteer for his friend Arjuna, and it is to this Pandava prince that he reveals his true identity just before hostilities commence. What prompted this revelation and Krishna's sermon known as the *Bhagavadgita*, the "Song of the Blessed Lord," was the faltering of Arjuna. Seeing how overwhelmed he was with compassion and sadness, Krishna consoled Arjuna and said:

> The wise grieve neither for the dead nor the living. There never was a time I was not, nor you, nor these princes were not; there never will be a time when we shall cease to be... Only the hero is unmoved by circumstance, accepting pleasure and pain with equanimity, he alone achieves immortality.

But Arjuna was still unconvinced by Krishna's words about the spirit being "indestructible, immortal, unchanging," and so the god went on to explain the absolute necessity of the performance of duty. As a warrior, Arjuna has no choice but fight because his path to enlightenment was through action, not contemplation. "It is better," Krishna assured him, "to do your duty badly than to do that of another well."

To underline the truth of what he said, Krishna allowed Arjuna to glimpse his divine nature, which in comparison "a thousand suns would be a faint reflection of the Supreme Lord." Reassured by Krishna, returned to his human form, Arjuna expresses relief—"I am myself again"—and possibly like Peter, James, and John, after the transfiguration of Jesus, he begins to forget the avatar's divinity and take comfort in his outward appearance. Beneath the acceptance of war as endemic in ancient India were two beliefs: reincarnation and immutable class distinctions. Except for leaving society altogether and seeking self-knowledge as a hermit in the solitude of the forest, one's life was decreed at birth. His status as a warrior left Arjuna with no other possibility than slaying the enemy on the battlefield, an action that amounted to nothing at all in the context of the endless cycle of death and rebirth, not to mention the immortality of the spirit.

Dharma, often translated as "duty," is in fact the governing principle of the universe. Because Hinduism looks upon the universe as an ordered whole in which each person, each animal, indeed each object, forms an integral part, it stands to reason that any deviation from the expected pattern of behavior will have a deleterious impact upon its operation. Originally there was no kingship, no king, no punishment, and no one requiring punishment, since people sustained each other through *dharma* but with the decline of *dharma* people became evil, so at last the gods fearing complete chaos, appealed to the creator god Brahma who produced an ideal monarch.

Invested with worldwide dominion, King Prithi arranged a social contract with the gods on behalf of humanity. So people were to live according to their inherited positions in society: the priestly brahmins, the warlike warriors, the hard-working farmers, and the lowly servants. That in 1917 the ruler of Karangasem, Gusti Bagus Djelantik, responded to a severe earthquake by calling for a revitalization of Hinduism was not unexpected. As a king, he believed it was his duty to restore the caste system in Bali, so that everyone would behave in an appropriate manner and please the gods through religious festivals and temple repairs. Even the Dutch colonial authorities were moved to contribute funds for the rebuilding of temples damaged by the earthquake.

Appropriate behavior is therefore seen as the key to private and public peace. A Balinese person should live in tune with *dharma*. If an individual does not, then he or she will pay the price in a future incarnation. Upon death, the *atman*, the "spirit," or perhaps better, the "self," is reborn in another corporeal form according to the degree in which an individual's karma is appropriate to his or her *dharma*. Because karma, the "actions" for which a person is responsible during a lifetime, determines future existences. In ancient India, the only escape from the endless round of rebirth was *moksa*, the "release" achieved by the spirit which had freed itself from all desire.

The householder was never expected to secure this level of enlightenment: the individuals most likely to do so were the meditative hermit and the wandering sage. Having cut themselves off from all the complications of social life, they alone had the chance of *moksa*. In Bali, though, this antisocial extreme was never fully embraced, possibly for the reason that the Balinese considered that a properly led life within a village community was the best route to a permanent dwelling place on Gunung

Agung, the abode of the gods and the deified ancestors.

Today the idea of *moksa* has been largely forgotten by the Balinese, who accept instead as their lot an endless round of rebirth. That is why children are taught to behave well, lest inappropriate actions lead to an unsatisfactory reincarnation. The lowest possible rebirth for an individual weighed down with bad karma is the form of a snake. When a snake unexpectedly enters a village, it is said to be seeking death in order to be reborn as a human being. Animals sacrificed during temple ceremonies are guaranteed a higher rebirth through the prayers said on their behalf at the time. Their blood propitiates the demons who might otherwise disrupt proceedings.

Reincarnation is restricted to kinship groups, blood relations. And the Balinese hold that it can only occur over three generations—grandparents, parents, and children—so that more remote ancestors are worshipped as family gods. Identifying a reincarnated ancestor is not unlike the Tibetan method of confirming the identity of the Dalai Lama: a child's behavior has to be just like his grown-up predecessor: "Granddad always did this or that." Definite confirmation can also be gained from a fortune-telling *balian*. One such expert recently explained the closeness of three cousins as their grandmother's reincarnation in all of them.

Only the rare spirit is freed from the cycle of birth, death, and rebirth, so that it can fuse with the unmoved mover of the Balinese cosmos, Ida Sanghyang Widi Wasa. Most Balinese hold that all the gods and goddesses are manifestations of Sanghyang Widi Wasa, who is sometimes depicted near the entrance of a family compound. The name means "divine order," being a mixture of Balinese and Sanskrit: *widi* is actually derived from the Sanskrit word *widhi*, meaning "order."

By no means extraordinary are the creative and destructive forces resolved in the figure of Sanghyang Widi Wasi. Cataclysmic though they appear as destructive periods alternate with those of renewal, this state of affairs is exactly how the devout Hindu expects the world to run. The long, slim body of Sanghyang Widi Wasa speaks of flawless spiritual beauty, beyond sensual charm, and yet still possessing the agility of the dancer. Quite possibly there is a definite reference to Shiva in Sanghyang Widi Wasa's pose, for in southern India, the source of most of the Hindu ideas which were exported to the Indonesian archipelago, Shiva is revered as Nataraja, the "king of the dance."

A south Indian bronze of Shiva Nataraja, "king of dance"

This less frightful aspect of Shiva appears in elegant southern Indian bronze statues, whose aim is to remind worshippers of his role as a cosmic saviour. The god appears encircled by a ring of flames, the vital processes of universal creation, and with one leg raised he stands upon a tiny figure crouching on a lotus. This dwarfish demon represents human ignorance, the delusions that must be overcome through wisdom to escape from the bondage of the world. In one of his four hands Shiva holds a drum, the sign of speech, the source of revelation and tradition; his second hand offers blessing and sustenance; in the palm of his third hand a tongue of flame is a reminder of destruction; and the fourth hand points downward to the uplifted foot, already saved from the power of delusion. Although the pose signifies the refuge available to Shiva's worshippers through asceticism, the Balinese eschewed this approach to *moksa* and sought enlightenment through religious festivals, performances of dance-drama and the creation of beautiful objects.

Such circumspection may not have been entirely misplaced, because Shiva has to be reminded of his immense strength. "By stamping your feet," a hymn proclaims, "you imperiled the safety of the Earth and scattered the stars of the heavens. But you dance in order to save the world. Power is perverse."

Ida Sanghyang Widi Wasa seems to be less important to the Balinese than Shiva, who lords it over Gunung Agung. Yet immediately after the establishment of the Republic of Indonesia, it was Sanghyang Widi Wasa who proved to be invaluable politically. In monotheistic Jakarta, Balinese beliefs were regarded as no more than crude superstitions and, as a consequence, their Austronesian-Hindu religion was considered unworthy of any financial support. Once it was appreciated how the Balinese believed in Sanghyang Widi Wasa as a supreme deity, however, no reason remained to prevent the receipt of government funding. As was pointed out then, Roman Catholics pray for assistance in their daily lives to saints and the Virgin Mary while believing in Almighty God. Not missed, too, were the less than straightforward Muslim practices in Java, where the faithful revere the island's heterodox saints, the *walis*, at whose tombs spiritual power is said to be heavily concentrated. Despite clerical disapproval, these saints' tombs are still places of popular pilgrimage. The stiff-necked officials in the Ministry of Religion finally conceded that prayers offered to the Balinese rice goddess Dewi Sri for a good harvest might be more than agricultural magic.

Alerting Jakarta to Sanghyang Widi Wasa's position in the Balinese pantheon was not a cynical ploy, because this deity's omnipresence is akin to the Hindu concept of *brahman*, or "holy power." Arguably it has been the most significant idea of Hinduism from earliest times to the present, since *brahman* represents the highest divine energy as well as the transcendent power within every part of the universe. This invisible cosmic force is the essence of all that we are and know. Every individual partakes of *brahman*, hidden though it is deep down in the spirit, so that all Indian spiritual exercises are devoted to its discovery. How to reach this fundamental resource and stay in touch with it; how to realize the divinity of *brahman*; this is the quest that has inspired the Hindu ascetic throughout the ages.

Although Indonesian law grants freedom of worship in the republic, it still claims to be a state based upon belief in one, all-powerful deity, Allah. Over ninety-three percent of the Balinese subscribe to Hinduism, but there are Buddhists, Muslims, and Christians living in Bali, in addition to the non-Hindu Bali Aga. The disdain of the Bali Aga for the caste system is also shared by an increasing number of Balinese, who have come to the view that strictly inherited status is incompatible with modern life. They note how absurd it is to treat a senior civil servant administering one of the eight districts of Bali as a *sudra*, a member of the lowest class. Having been promoted on merit, he ought to be regarded as a *satria*, or "warrior," traditionally the caste which provided the island's rulers. It remains to be seen whether everyone will eventually belong to the same social class, and then assume the status of the occupation they chose to adopt: priest, official, merchant, farmer, or worker.

Whatever the outcome of present-day reflection on the value of the caste system, the Balinese people still have to cope with the demonic forces active in their island. This is because their Austronesian-Hindu religion embraces the principle that for every good, positive, constructive side of existence, there is a counterbalancing evil, negative, destructive side. These two aspects of daily life are inseparable: they must coexist in dynamic equilibrium so that neither side becomes too dominant. Maintaining this critical balance between positive and negative forces is the ultimate aim of Balinese ritual observances.

Yet the notion of a necessary evil component in life on Earth is not restricted to Indian thought, nor indeed to Austronesian anxieties about the powers of darkness. In the Book of Job there is a classic statement of the necessity of suffering, which denies the traditional view that the righteous are favored by God and therefore prosper, whereas the wicked are overtaken by misfortune and calamity sent by God. All the time he suffers, his three closest friends doubt his righteousness but Job knows he is innocent. While his friends try to explain his suffering by examining his moral conduct, Job himself seeks an answer for his suffering by examining God's intervention in human affairs, unjust though divine action often seems to be. Job's explosions of grief show that even the most holy of men are driven by pain, loss, and the sense of divine abandonment. Even when covered "with sore boils from the sole of his foot unto his crown," Job still remains steadfast in his belief.

> Then said his wife unto him, Dost thou still retain thine integrity? curse God and die. But he said unto her. Thou speakest as one of the foolish women speaketh. What? shall we receive good at the hand of God, and shall we not receive evil?

Because Job has finally realized how prosperity can be more dangerous than adversity, he appreciates that God sent him a spiritual wake-up call of suffering. Even though the Book of Job concludes without giving any reason for Job's personal plight, it leaves the reader in no doubt that true piety requires no outward proof of success and that God's conduct is quite beyond human comprehension.

In justifying the wickedness of kings in the *Mahabharata*, Arjuna argues, "I do not see any creature in this world that lives without injuring others; animals live on animals, the stronger on the weaker… No act is entirely devoid of evil." This pessimistic Indian notion later evolved into a Job-like acceptance of earthly misfortune, so that evil came to be regarded not only as inevitable but also desirable. Possibly for the reason that the Hindu gods themselves are subject to passions, the universe could not avoid conflict at any level. One text goes so far as saying that Brahma "produced creatures in whom darkness and passion predominated, afflicted with misery; these were humanity." Another text tells us how he went on unintentionally to create demons. Shocked at this event, Brahma's "hair fell out and turned into serpents," making the creator god even more upset.

SPIRITS AND WITCHES

Less interested in the origin of demons, the Balinese are preoccupied with their continuous struggle against these malevolent beings who may appear in any guise. During a village exorcism, a priest will name scores of demons and their locations in the neighborhood. What he tries to do is persuade them to return to their abodes, at a safe distance from the village itself. Witches are a particular problem since they look like ordinary people. At night a *leyak*, or "witch," transforms herself into a ghostly light, even an animal, and roams the darkness in search of victims. A preference for attacking at midnight means that most Balinese stay indoors soon after sunset. Becoming a witch is dangerous, however, for the safe return of the spirit to the body can be problematic.

A belief in the ability of certain individuals to leave their bodies in a spiritual form is common in both East Asia and Southeast Asia. One *xian*, or Chinese "immortal," was condemned to limp through eternity when it took him longer than expected to complete a spiritual journey. Li Tieguai, the iron-crutch immortal, told his disciples that they would have to

A *leyak*, a Balinese witch

cremate his body if his spirit did not return within seven days. After the deadline, the disciples noticed their master's spirit was still absent and so they were obliged to do as he had instructed. A little later, Li's spirit came back but could not locate the body. Then, finding a dead man nearby, it decided to enter the corpse. As Li stood up, he felt something wrong with one leg and he realized that henceforth he had to inhabit the body of an ugly, lame beggar.

The accidental destruction of the body did not, of course, end Li Tieguai's immortality, but he paid a price for underestimating the length of his absence as a spirit. In Bali, trance draws upon the same shamanistic heritage, when it is said that someone in a trance has been taken over by another spirit. Shamans themselves, the *balians*, use out-of-body experience to find out the cause of an individual's problems. These Balinese "witch doctors" are able to penetrate *niskala*, the unseen occult realm, and consult a helpful spirit there. Usually a *balian* has a familiar with whom he regularly communicates. *Balian usada*, "healers," are high-caste men whose families specialize in such mystical medicine, deploying magic weapons as well as holy water.

Trance is associated with Rangda, the chief Balinese witch. Sometimes during dance-drama there may be dozens of men who go into a trance,

An old illustration of Rangda, queen of the witches

until Rangda herself leaves them rolling on the ground like stricken animals. The total number of trancers in Bali is unknown, as indeed is the exact cause of their sudden trances. But trance is believed to be the invitation for a spirit to come, *rauh*, into one's body. Whether it occurs at a dance performance or another ceremony, the person who goes into a trance is supposed to gain spiritual knowledge that could valuable to non-trancers. He may well, for instance, learn of the gods' attitude toward a village's religious observances. Keeping the gods happy is as critical in Bali as keeping the demons at bay.

Rangda is the name of an historical character, a villain in dance-drama and a goddess, so complex is her role in Balinese religion. Along with the good lion Barong, she is probably the best-known figure among the Balinese. The word *rangda* can be used to denote either a widow or a witch, while Rangda herself is worshipped by witches as the supreme witch. One reason for the closeness of widows and witches may derive from the Hindu rite of *sati*, the self-immolation once expected of a widow on her husband's pyre, a practice banned in India by the reforming governor-general Lord William Bentinck in 1829. The issue split Hindu opinion at the time because it forced a generation who had grown up with the rise of British authority in the subcontinent to face squarely the traditions that had shaped their society for millennia. To what extent *sati* ever spread to the Indonesian archipelago is uncertain, even though in 1904 two of a dead king's elderly wives chose to sacrifice themselves at his cremation. This example of *westaria*, or "self-sacrifice," would appear to have been exceptional, but the connection between the two meanings of *rangda*, widow and witch, remains suggestive. It would appear that a widow generates a degree of anxiety since she is still alive while her husband is dead: the implication being that she ought to have given up her own bodily form and followed his spirit wherever it went.

That Rangda is now regarded as Durga as well, "the inaccessible" aspect of the great Hindu goddess Devi is not really unexpected. The consort of unruly Shiva, Durga encompasses all the terrifying elements of female divinity. How in medieval India the terrifying Durga merged with Devi is outside the scope of this study of Balinese culture, but we should note that the springboard for Devi's final triumph as the supreme Hindu deity was the cosmic crisis caused by Mahisa. Without the dire threat posed by the buffalo demon Mahisa, neither Shiva nor Vishnu would have

Durga, the ferocious consort of Shiva

agreed to hand over their celestial weapons to Durga, the destructive aspect of Devi.

What lay behind this unusual myth is a matter of speculation, although an explanation might be the resurgence of goddess worship more ancient than the Indo-Aryan pantheon. Excavations of the so-called Indus Valley civilization, whose great cities of Mohenjo-daro and Harappa predate the arrival of the Indo-Aryans in India by well over a thousand years, has revealed hundreds of female figurines so that there must have been one in every household shrine.

Durga's defeat of Mahisa was greater than anything ever achieved by either Vishnu or Shiva. Because the buffalo demon was not easily overcome and in the titanic struggle "the Earth was shattered by his swift turns; the ocean, lashed by his great tail, overflowed on all sides; the clouds, rent by his swaying horns, broke into fragments; and mountains collapsed, cast down by the blast of his breath." As a result of Durga's triumph, Devi became the great goddess Mahadevi and absorbed virtually all the other Hindu goddesses. So it happened that Shiva and Devi came to be worshipped as the twofold personalization of *brahman*, the primordial substance that animates the universe. Supreme, Devi holds "the universe in her womb," while she "lights the lamp of wisdom" and "brings joy to Shiva's heart."

The inexorable rise of a female deity in late Hinduism could not but have an influence on the Balinese, although it is curious how this theological development led to the elevation of such an ambivalent figure as Rangda. Yet this witch goddess is never held to be totally evil through her connection with black magic, since magical power is present everywhere in Bali. "Rangda is only bad," a priest commented, "when someone disturbs her." Rather the *leyaks*, her female followers, are blamed for the trouble afflicting ordinary people. But Rangda's destructive inheritance is made clear in her appearance in dance-drama. Pendulous breasts mark her as an old woman, just as a lolling tongue, curling fangs, claw-like fingernails, and hairy knuckles denote her bestial nature.

The historical Rangda lived in the eleventh century. Her name was Mahendradatta, a Javanese princess who gave birth to Erlanga: in Bali she was known as Queen Gunapriya Dharmapatni, whose superior descent was reflected in the decrees issued by King Udayana. Udayana's choice of a Javanese bride was an indication of Bali's growing indebtedness to the culture of Java. The Majapahit conquest of the island in 1343 completed the process by sweeping away old Balinese customs, but the influence of Queen Gunaporiya Dharmapatni was so great at court that she is credited with the introduction of sorcery as well as secret rites among the nobility. After 1001, the queen is unmentioned in royal decrees, suggesting that she died before her husband. What appears to be her funeral monument, on a hilltop near Gianyar, places emphasis on her demonic character, since a woman is depicted as Durga dancing on a bull.

After her early death, the queen somehow became identified in Bali with Rangda. In the myth of Calon Arang, the widow-witch prefigures the witch goddess. Calon Arang, or Mahendradatta as she is also called, practiced black magic and, in disgust, her royal husband banished her to the forest and married again. The subsequent death of the king left Mahendradatta a widow. Although there already existed a rift with her son Erlanga for failing to take her side when she was banished, the thing which annoyed Mahendradatta most was that nobody was willing to marry her daughter. No matter the girl's exceptional beauty, no suitor dared to acquire a demonic mother-in-law.

In revenge for this slight, Mahendradatta went with her followers to a graveyard and there implored the goddess Durga to devastate Bali. The wish was granted, with the result that terrible epidemics broke out across the island. When a distraught Erlanga beseeched Durga's husband Shiva to help his stricken kingdom, the great god advised King Erlanga to apply to the sage Mpu Baradah, whose spiritual powers were sufficient to avert a calamity. It is even alleged that Mpu Baradah studied black magic in order to thwart Rangda, who then appeared in her most monstrous form. A sorcerer's duel rather than a straightforward struggle between good and evil, the Calon Arang story ends with the purification of Mahendradatta and her conversion to good works. The climax of the duel between Mpu Baradah and Rangda is the witch's attempt to burn the sage alive. It fails and Rangda resumes her human shape as Mahendradatta, so that she can be temporarily cleansed with holy water.

Rangda is often said to have been a high-caste woman from the eastern Javanese province of Girah. Even though her relationship with royalty is unclear in the tales which mention the black magic she performed there, the same problem provokes a nocturnal visit to a graveyard. Fear has condemned her daughter to perpetual spinsterhood. Without the corpse of a recently buried infant, Rangda cannot weave her dreadful spells. But the shunned daughter seems to have already accepted her fate and decided to follow her mother's profession as a witch. In Bali, the conflict with Rangda is settled by Barong, since Mpu Baradah assumes the shape of this good lion in dance-drama. Closely resembling a Chinese lion, Barong represents white magic and is the antithesis of Rangda.

RITES OF PASSAGE

The ongoing contest between Rangda and Barong brings us back to the Austronesian–Hindu belief in a productive balance between the forces of good and evil. The demonic element cannot be eradicated, nor indeed would a Balinese person consider it wise to try and do so. How this basic idea directly affects the individual is evident in tooth-filing, a rite of passage that aims at reducing human passions to a reasonable level. A specialist achieves this in adolescents through evenly filing off the six upper canine teeth and incisors. The ritual is supposed to moderate lust, anger, greed, arrogance, drunkenness, and envy. The lower teeth are left untouched, for desire and passion should never be entirely quenched. As protruding teeth are one of her distinguishing features, tooth-filing is something Rangda never underwent.

Six to eighteen years of age is reckoned to be the best period for tooth-filing, with boys undergoing the ritual earlier than the girls. Yet the filing of the upper front teeth has as much to do with beauty therapy as religion, because the Balinese find long canine teeth aesthetically displeasing. Even more, tooth-filing is believed to bring success in every endeavor, besides warding off sickness and evil influences. So serious are the Balinese about tooth-filing that no one would have it done without first consulting an expert on the calendar for an auspicious day. Tooth-filings are not held very often, with the result that families tend to arrange the ritual for a group of children, which often includes cousins. And of course the whole event makes liberal use of holy water.

Choosing an auspicious day for any event is by no means easy in Bali. Like most of the world, the Republic of Indonesia has standardized itself upon the Western calendar and shuts government offices on Sundays. But in Bali this calendar is overlaid by two very different ways of calculating time: the 210-day Pawukon calendar and the Saka lunar calendar. The Pawukon was brought to Bali by Hindu priests fleeing from Muslim Java, and its main purpose is the regulation of religious festivals. Its complexity comes essentially from its subdivisions: a week may be one day long or as long as ten days. A special calendar, called the Tika, keeps track of the most important weeks and days of the Pawukon cycle. The Indian Saka calendar, on the other hand, is more regular except that its year is only ten months in length. Named after a Scythian dynasty whose nomadic followers overran much of northern India during the first century BC, this calendar was introduced to the Indonesian archipelago by migrating Hindu priests.

Neither the Pawukon nor the Saka calendar really matches tropical Bali's year, since the island has no real seasons other than the vast difference in rainfall caused by its two monsoons. Torrential downpours during the Javanese monsoon are the sole defining event each year. But such is the respect in which the Pawukon and Saka calendars are held that only through consulting them together is it possible to identify the days on which it is safe to attend a tooth-filing ceremony, get married, hold a cremation, plant rice, make a fishing net or undertake a journey.

A section of an astrological calendar

In addition to the Pawukon, Tika, and Saka calendars, there are astrological methods of choosing appropriate days for action, or indeed inaction. Unlike some other astrological systems, the decisive event for a Balinese person is the day of the week on which he or she was born. Even though there are other factors that come into play, the popularity of astrological calendars, usually in the form of Kamasan-style drawings, reveals how seriously the Balinese take their predictions.

Besides the ritual of tooth-filing, a Balinese person is involved in a whole series of rites from birth to death. Even while still in the womb, the unborn infant is the subject of prayers and purification. At birth though, there is a burst of ritual activity whose aim is to protect the child from spiritual harm. The key rite of passage then is the treatment of the placenta, which is carefully wrapped in white cloth and buried by the front door of the parents' house. Wherever the grown-up child may later live, his or her happiness is unlikely to be perfect if they go far from this spot. The baby's bathwater is poured over it every day, and a little offering of food is placed there before the baby is fed. When giving her breast to her newborn baby, a mother will not neglect first to allow a few drops of her milk to fall on the ground, for the benefit of the buried placenta. She will continue doing so until rice replaces milk, when a few grains are deliberately spilled instead.

An equally important rite occurs when the umbilical cord drops, since this ends the impurity that is supposed to cling to the parents. Wrapped in a piece of white cloth, the umbilical cord is put in a small shrine above the baby's cot, so that demonic influences are kept away. Shiva's son Sanghyang Kumara is the deity charged with the protection of babies until they have lost their milk teeth.

During a child's infancy, the spilling of milk and rice is intended to satisfy the *kanda empat*, the four spiritual companions who stay with a Balinese person from birth to death: spiritual brothers for a male, and spiritual sisters in the case of a female. These *kanda empat* become particularly vital for a child's protection when the second set of teeth start to grow. At this stage a fifth companion appears to add extra strength to the spiritual cordon. Before going to sleep a Balinese is expected to have friendly thoughts about the *kanda empat*: if they feel slighted, they can turn nasty. When treated with respect, however, these spiritual companions act as a reliable defense against external forces as well as exercising a

A Balinese boy surrounded by the *kanda empat*, his personal guardians

calming influence over internal passions.

Among the Minangkabau, on the western coast of Sumatra, the rites connected with childbirth are even more pronounced, because these people form the largest matrilineal Muslim society now in existence. The secure social position traditionally enjoyed by women in Southeast Asia baffled the first European voyagers. Women were never the property of men, so that the Spaniards were shocked by how easy it was for wives in the Philippines to divorce. As in other parts of Southeast Asia, women played a major role in trade, and especially market places. As Stanford Raffles noted, "it is usual for the husband to entrust his pecuniary affairs entirely to his wife."

The matrilineal outlook of the Minangkabau people is perhaps best expressed in their description of men: they are "like ashes on a burned tree trunk," one gust of wind and they are gone. That is why the Minangkabau longhouse belongs to its women, and the mummified afterbirth of all its members, past and present, is either tacked to its interior columns or carefully placed beneath the floorboards. These physical remains are the unbreakable cord, the indissoluble bond, of each extended family.

Further Balinese rites of passage mark the progress of the child into adolescence and adulthood, including tooth-filing. The second set of teeth that follows the milk teeth are the gift of the sun god Surya, the creator god Brahma, and Dewi Sri, the rice goddess. At this point an individual is judged to be fully human and his childhood protector Sanghyang Kumara is dismissed. It is somewhat curious that this son of Shiva should be responsible for infants. The unpredictable nature of Shiva himself may be one reason for awarding Sanghyang Kumara this crucial role, since the Balinese will not have forgotten how the great god tore the head off Ganesa when the boy attempted to prevent Shiva from entering his consort Parvati's room. Either Shiva's own son or his nephew, the headless Ganesa was only restored to life when the still angry god gave him an elephant's head.

Sudden outbursts of fury, a trait of Shiva which must explains his residence on the summit of a still active volcano in Bali, indicate how far he is beyond human and divine conventions. Shiva has so many aspects—from stark asceticism through violent deeds and animal acts to sexual love—that his divinity is hard to grasp, not to menion portray. Late Hindu texts go so far as identifying Shiva with the totality of creation: his faces rule the five directions, while his forms represent the five elements, the sacrificer and the material world. "Out of fear of Shiva the wind blows, out of fear fire burns, and the king of heaven and death rush to their work."

For a devout Balinese, religion is less based on reflection and prayer than on intuitive experience in the community. The village priest, as with his counterpart in the great temples, endeavors to preserve the purity of his congregation by the production of holy water and the proper arrangement of religious festivals. The latter are always joyous, whatever they celebrate. Strange as it may seem, this is particularly true of cremation ceremonies, for the burning of a corpse is an occasion for gaiety and not mourning as it represents the completion of an individual's particular incarnation on Earth. The ceremonial burning liberates the spirit so that it can either merge with Ida Sanghyang Widi Wasa and become a deified ancestor resident on Gunung Agung, or undergo another incarnation in Balinese society.

Cremation rites are, in fact, very simple. A corpse can be cremated quickly, with just a few offerings and prayers, but cremations in Bali are rarely such modest affairs. Family pride, village status, and a desire to impress the spirits, all contribute to spectacular cremations. Over recent years a preference for elaborate ceremonial has led to a boom among craftsmen who specialize in constructing huge cremation towers and artistically designed coffins in the shape of winged lions, bulls, cows, and fish with elephant tusks.

The Balinese climate asks for cremation shortly after death, but families are not always in a hurry and a month or more may pass before the ceremony takes place. In most cases the corpse is buried and then dug up, although some poor Balinese are not cremated at all. An effigy can be burned instead of a corpse. Prior to the burning, the cremation ground is purified and, amid great hilarity, the corpse arrives along with its relatives and friends. After a final purification with copious quantities of holy water, the pyre is set alight and the corpse consumed by the flames. Ashes are then cast into a flowing stream, which carries them to the sea. Disposal in the sea itself is preferred and the family may decide to go there so as to ensure the ashes get to this destination. Often they are taken away from the shore in a small boat to prevent their being washed up on the beach.

Because of the vast expense of cremation ceremonies, which can cost 100 million rupiah or nearly $8,000 for a single corpse, there has arisen the practice of *ngaben masal*, or "mass cremation." Villagers involved pool their financial resources, using a collective offering that reduces the cost to no more than 20 million rupiah per family. At Blabatuh, a village in Gianyar, ninety-one bodies were cremated in late September 2014. *The Jakarta Post* called the event a "splendid send-off" and featured on its front page a mourner running past burning sarcophagi in the shape of lions, bulls, and winged elephants. The Blabatuh mass cremation is staged every third year because this is the longest period a corpse can be left in the village cemetery.

Where no body is available, through for instance drowning at sea or death happening in a remote location, a priest is able to make a sandalwood substitute for cremation purposes. This is considered a proper alternative. Babies who die before their teeth appear are not cremated; though they are buried in the ground, ritually striking the graves of those unfortunates is sufficient to release their spirits as effectively as cremation.

A second rite of final passage for the dead person occurs well after cremation, when nothing physical is actually involved. An effigy is burned, along with ritual objects, the remnants of which are again thrown into the

Ida Sanghyang Widi Wasa dancing above the world-turtle Bedawang and two *nagas*

sea. Afterwards the spirit of the deceased visits the family temple where a shrine has already been prepared for it. Accumulated karma then comes into play and the next life is determined accordingly. For those spirits burdened by very bad karma, however, a period of severe punishment has to be endured before reincarnation can occur. Their demonic tormentors take delight in inflicting the most painful torture, such as forcing them to stand beneath a *kris* tree. From its top branches a shower of daggers is thrown upon the spirits below.

In the Balinese cosmos the spirit has started yet another journey in the endless round of birth, death, and rebirth. For the island is regarded as the entire world. Knowledge of other places—Java, China, India, and Europe—does not influence this fundamental Balinese outlook in the least. According to tradition, the Balinese cosmos was created when the world-serpent Anantaboga made the turtle Bedawang the island's foundation. Other primordial powers contributed to the development of the cosmos, now represented visually as a turtle embraced by two *nagas*, the Hindu term for cosmic snakes, and surmounted by Ida Sanghyang Widi Wasa joyfully dancing above all creation. Many cremation towers feature this symbolic view of the cosmos, thereby confirming the continued satisfaction of the Balinese with their unique island home.

Chapter Eleven
BALINESE MUSIC AND DANCE-DRAMA

"The ceremony of blessing the instruments is performed, and the children are told to play a piece as a termination of the rite."

Colin McPhee

Like everything else in Bali, music is unique and ubiquitous. Out of all proportion to the size of the island, the incredible amount of music performed is a direct consequence of the Balinese belief that no event can satisfactorily take place without musical accompaniment. Whether it is a religious festival, a temple ceremony, a tooth-filing ritual, a birthday celebration, an engagement party, a wedding reception, a public funeral, or even an exorcism of demons, there is music. And of course, music always accompanies dance-drama, the apex of Balinese cultural activities. Music and dance are inseparable, as is the participation of a gamelan orchestra. Although gamelan to a Balinese person means "orchestra," the variety of gamelan instruments have one thing in common: except the drums which are used to direct a performance, the rest are percussion. Sometimes a bamboo flute is added but the striking of wood and metal gives the gamelan orchestra its totally distinctive sound.

The nearest equivalent to gamelan is without any doubt the melodious stone chimes so beloved by the Vietnamese. Chime-stone ensembles in Vietnam descend from ancient Chinese musical practice, since from earliest recorded times ancestor worship was connected with pleasant sounds. According to the *Book of Odes*, collected in China no later than the sixth century BC, ancestors were tempted to return to the world not only by the prayers of their descendants, but by the pleasing sounds of musical instruments and the delicious smells arising from magnificent bronze cooking vessels.

Sonorous are the bells and drums.
Brightly sound the chime-stones and flutes.

Together they bring down blessings
And ensure an abundance of grain.

A thousand years of being a part of the Chinese empire would have been sufficient to transfer such a custom to Vietnam, without the enormous influence of Confucianism which never slackened after the Vietnamese achieved their independence in the tenth century. For this moral philosophy the cornerstone of society is the family, whose members have a duty of showing gratitude to their forbears through offerings at the ancestral tombs and ensuring the continuation of the lineage. A mutual dependence of the living and the dead, of ancestors and descendants, has always been the fundamental element in Chinese culture.

For Confucius himself music had been very significant indeed. So affected was he once by ceremonial music that for three months "he did not know the taste of meat." Because Confucius sought an inner harmony of the mind and a balanced expression of emotion, the discipline involved in playing an instrument or singing greatly appealed to him. Although a lute was the instrument favored by his scholarly followers, Confucius expected them to be able to play upon the chime-stones which princes and aristocrats suspended from elaborate wooden stands in their residences.

It is more than an historical coincidence that in Bali the sound of gamelan music is believed to attract deities to temple ceremonies, in the same manner that bells, drums, chime-stones, and flutes encouraged the arrival of ancestors in Sino-Vietnamese worship. It shows a similarity of attitude across East Asia as well as Southeast Asia: nowhere was music ever viewed as mere entertainment.

Gamelan instruments are typically bronze. Some have keys, others are gongs. The keyed metallophones come in a number sizes and shapes with an assortment of mallets. In several cases they use bamboo resonators, above which the keys freely hang, but many have their keys simply laid over a wooden trough. The sound produced by the latter is protected by rubber pads that cushion bronze when it comes into contact with the wood. Padded mallets have a similar effect, causing long ringing tones. Gongs used in Bali range in size from tiny high-pitched ones to enormous ones of three feet in diameter. Often ten small gongs, arranged in ascending order of pitch and balanced with taut cords on a wooden frame

A gamelan orchestra at a dance-drama performance

rather like Vietnamese chime-stones, add melody to gamelan music. Most gamelan orchestras are directed by a pair of drummers, who set the rhythm and control the development of the composition. Their simple drums are made from a hollowed tree trunk with its ends covered by animal skins. Additional non-metal instruments are made from bamboo: a rattle, a xylophone, a flute, and a gong.

Gamelan sounds are still a surprise to many Western visitors. How far they influenced Claude Debussy's music is a matter of conjecture, but at the Paris International Exhibition of 1889 the French composer was taken aback by the gamelan orchestra that he heard playing there. Certainly the occasion marked the first trickle of maritime Southeast Asian music into Europe. Not until the 1930s, however, were the sounds of gamelan more widely available through recordings made in Bali itself. Then Colin McPhee, a Canadian-born composer living in New York, rushed to the island so as to enhance his own modern pieces with the gamelan sound. Even though he spent a great deal of time studying Balinese music, and indeed encouraging its continuation as a living art form, McPhee's enthusiasm for gamelan was not widely shared on his return to North America, since in 1938 the music of an exotic island seemed not a little irrelevant as the Second World War loomed. But he did much to raise the profile of Balinese culture through his advocacy of its musical heritage and, for many years after its publication in 1964, his *Music in Bali* remained the standard work.

Unlike the American anthropologist Margaret Mead, who had a fascination with the bizarre, Colin McPhee was attracted to the more refined parts of Balinese culture, and especially the musical performances he encountered in palaces and temples. He was uninterested in the supposedly Freudian aspects of daily life in Bali, which Mead typified as sexual repression, a cultural burden that weighed heavily upon the Balinese; its only relief comprised periodical performances of dance-drama. The witch Rangda, she was sure, represented the supreme example of such necessary emotional outbursts. Even though the good lion Barong would always put Rangda to flight, the Balinese still looked forward to another round in their age-old contest.

What had gripped McPhee's attention was the sound of the gamelan orchestra, which produced "tranquil, golden music." At one temple festival, he was utterly entranced by its playing. "Throughout the morning," he tells us in *A House in Bali*, first published in 1944, "the air was filled with sound that gladdened the hearts of all, causing the temple to ring with festive noise."

In his description of the festival, one of the first he attended, McPhee explains how such events are conducted. It is "a three-day honoring of the gods. On the evening of the first day the gods are invited to descend and enter the shrines prepared for them. For three days they are feasted and entertained. Before they leave, advice and favors are sought." Then he tells us, the gods are "ceremonially requested to depart."

Despite a slight delay, the arrival of the gods was announced through trance, and McPhee was able to ask where the gods stayed during their visit to the temple. He was told how they resided

in the tiniest of objects, apparently in stones, in bits of wood, in little golden figures. These precious objects were kept locked in the temple, to be taken out, purified and set in the shrines for the three days of the feast. At one moment this feast seemed scaled to the proportion of giants, at the next it was like a dolls' tea party. Images and stones were wrapped in the brightest of cloths, tied with golden sashes, set on silken cushions, while food was set out for them in the smallest dishes. Yet woe betide the community if the gods felt slighted and grew angry. Now, suddenly, they were titans; in their anger they could spread disaster in the form of drought and epidemics of plague.

On the afternoon of the second day McPhee watched a troupe perform *topeng*, a popular form of dance-drama which employs masks. Their plays center upon courtly events, with complicated plots often depending on mistaken identity.

As McPhee was delighted to discover, every Balinese village's ambition is to possess the best gamelan orchestra in the neighborhood. It is only very poor communities that do not have two or three orchestras to play for their festivals and ceremonies. Because instruments are not too difficult to construct, much can be done locally, although a first-class gong can only be obtained from an expert smith. Villagers are willing to pool their resources to purchase whatever parts of an instrument they lack, so that the wooden stands already carved get all the equipment they need. Buleleng gongs are the most expensive, possibly for the reason that from the late 1910s onward Singaraja witnessed a tremendous revival of music in a modern mode. Arguably the emergence there of *gamelan gong kebyar*, and its immense popularity throughout the island, has been detrimental to traditional gamelan. Meaning "bursting forth," *kebyar* refers to a style of music that features sudden changes in rhythm, embellishments and ornamentations akin to the improvisation usually associated with jazz. From the outset, emphasis was placed upon individual performance. Traditional gamelan is steady and sedate in comparison.

Yet as McPhee pointed out, Balinese instruments have always tended to be played with "nervous electric energy." They followed patterns "that broke the music into spangles, gave it light and fire, created tension so that the longest phrase could not die, but became instead an adventure. High and clear, they were forever changing, while below them the melody slowly uncoiled."

The Balinese do not write down their music. Rehearsal forms the method by which traditional compositions are learned and perfected. And the Balinese have developed their music to the point of having a special type of orchestra for every purpose, each differing from the others in both size and sound. For cremations the *gamelan gambang* is preferred for the austere sounds that come from its wooden xylophones. As *gambang* compositions are closely connected with classical verse, these orchestras tend to recruit Balinese players of a scholarly disposition.

Since music permeates Balinese life to a degree unimaginable in the West, the gamelan orchestra is an indispensable ingredient in dance-drama. As indeed Walter Spies and Beryl de Zoete note in their seminal study *Dance and Drama in Bali*, which was published in 1938, it is impossible to approach dance

> without allusion to the unfathomable world of tone and rhythm which is continually revealed in the rare and complicated texture of Balinese gamelan. It is the most direct yet mysterious expression of the Balinese temperament and genius, as impersonal as nature and as sensitively alive. One has the feeling as one listens that something of the brilliance and depth of the infinitely varied Balinese landscape vibrates in the resonance of metal, cowhide, and bamboo, by some intense sympathy which becomes articulate in rhythm.

They go on to point out how, even though Bali "is thought of a place where everyone dances, because dancing forms an integral element in the endless series of private and public festivals, nowhere in the world is dancing more specialized." It is quite singular "that though dancing accompanies every stage of a man's life from infancy to the grave, there is no spontaneous communal dancing, and among a people of peasants practically no seasonal dances."

Equally baffling to Spies and de Zoete was the informality of dance venues. They note how the stage "may be the village street, the graveyard, the temple-court, the ground outside the temple, the courtyard of a Balinese house, the outer court of a palace. Its floor is bare earth, covered in certain dances with palm matting."

For it is the context of a dance-drama performance that determines its degree of sacredness. The popular *barong* dance is actually a reenactment of an ancient ritual pared down for the benefit of tourists to one hour in length. That is why the masks are not the same ones as the ones used for temple rituals, for which only the most sacred masks are on display.

As there is no Balinese deity who presides over music and dance-drama, performers seek inspiration instead from their own ancestors, whose delight in musical events is taken for granted. What they hope to gain through their supplication is *taksu*, the spiritual force that guides the movements of a dancer's body as well as the fingers of a musician. And a Balinese audience is quick to recognize *taksu* when it manifests itself, because a performer can possess *taksu* one day and not the next. It is not dissimilar to the Welsh idea of *hwyl*, the sudden ecstatic inspiration which lifts a recitation or a song to an unexpected level of excellence. Much to do with an individual's mood or frame of mind, *hwyl* appears to take possession of the performer who is often quite unaware of the impact he or she happens to be having on an audience. At eisteddfods, the competitions regularly staged in Wales, the winners are invariably said to have triumphed through the gift of *hwyl*.

Except where they take a second part in a masked play, dancers sit and relax beside the gamelan orchestra when out of the action. Informality is the touchstone of Balinese dance-drama, with refreshments being served to resting dancers and musicians during a performance, but once involved again in the unfolding plot the same dancers spring to life. Their sudden movement somehow adds to the dramatic effect, since they seem to be propelled by a surge of supernatural energy back onto the stage.

"There is no smallest indication of a change of scene," Spies and de Zoete were amazed to discover. "The conversation of the characters alone indicates where they happen to be at the moment; in a marketplace, palace court, or graveyard, or journeying from one to the other." Whereas the leading dancers are comparatively free in their movements, "the comic attendants… must always balance each other, or balance their master." Subtle choreography makes sure that the chief dancers are not left on their own, so everything appears natural and unaffected.

Balinese dance-drama revels in its variety. It combines spectacle with sound, and is less interested in story than in presentation. The avant-garde French theorist Antonin Artaud identified the nonverbal, gestural nature of dance-drama when he witnessed a performance in Paris in 1931:

> In fact the strange thing about all these gestures, these angular, sudden, jerky postures, these syncopated inflexions formed at the back of the throat, these musical phrases cut short, the sharded flights, rustling

branches, hollow drum sounds, robot creaking, animated puppets dancing, is the feeling of a new bodily language no longer based on words but on signs which emerge through the maze of gestures, postures, airborne cries, through their gyrations and turns, leaving not even the smallest area of stage space unused.

Splendid display goes hand in hand with an exquisite style of dance that literally grips the spectators' attention. This is hardly surprising when, as in ancient Greek theater, the myths being explored in the action are so well known. Few Balinese in an audience would be unacquainted with the career of Ken Angrok, the eastern Javanese king who seized the throne with the aid of a magical *kris*. That he was eventually killed by the very same dagger does not figure in masked drama as any sort of judgment on his bloody usurpation. Rather his own violent death is treated as little more than the exhaustion of Ken Angrok's power: magic could no longer protect him.

Spies and de Zoete throw an interesting light on the role of dance-drama in maintaining Balinese culture. They write how

in Bali where wood and stone are always in dissolution, tradition is permanent and alive. It is not from any desire to perpetuate the past that the style of centuries ago is renewed again in stone or in dance, but because, despite their love of novelty, the Balinese have not really learnt any new attitudes, and cannot imagine a present which does not clothe itself in those which are immemorial. The gesture-language, the attitudes of the Balinese stage today, can be paralleled in the oldest stone figures in the temples, because the ritual knowledge which created the one still directs the other and is still the eye through which the Balinese views behavior in the dance world where artists and spectators are equally at home. The imagination of the audience as well as the skill of the dancer animates the forms and lives of the familiar ritual which is bound by indissoluble links to ritual in their own life.

That is why a dancer is untroubled by the burden of self-expression. During performances in Bali dancers seem possessed by the roles they perform: they never need to strive for celebrity like Western stars but, on the contrary, they are able to join the action without any awareness of themselves. They can readily do such a thing because every dance movement has been learned through a program of training and practice since childhood. Facial and body movements are so crucial that a lackluster dancer will soon be termed "threadbare" or "worn out."

Children are involved in dance from an early age. They hear gamelan music while still in the womb and, as babies, they are encouraged to dance with adult assistance as soon as they can stand. A village's communal hall is the place where most children really develop their dancing ability, while those born into artistic families accompany their elders and help them dress when they are they happen to be dancing in public. Simple observation and imitation is the way the majority of Balinese acquire a knowledge of dance, although there are teachers who take on promising youngsters and try to turn them into first-rate performers.

Similar arrangements now exist for young musicians, thanks to Colin McPhee's enlightened sponsorship in the 1930s of children's orchestras. Yet children as musicians were still not taken seriously for another three decades. Since then there has been a children's gamelan category in the annual Balinese arts festival. The impersonality of music and dance in Bali makes it easier to participate in public events, because there is not the self-consciousness that deters so many young people in the West.

It would be a mistake to suppose, however, that every Balinese community is dancing all the time, or that village societies are permanent institutions. Music and dance organizations come and go as their membership changes, but the need for dance at religious festivals ensures that a village is never short of trainee dancers for long. Nor is there ever any gap when it comes to a gamelan orchestra, since music is an indispensable accompaniment to dance. But no one learns to dance in a general way; a young person learns a particular dance, the training for which is necessarily specialized. For *baris*, one of most splendid of all Balinese dances, the elaborate movements imitate a line of warriors, the guardians of former kings. *Baris* means "a line," and its dancers are only seen brandishing their spears on important occasions such as temple ceremonies and cremations. There is also a solo *baris*, in which one dancer shows off his military skills. Quite different again is the *legong* dance, whose beautiful girls are supposed to be celestial maidens.

Apart from *baris*, there are several dances which are considered more sacred than others and are usually performed in the inner court of a temple. The most common is the *rejang*, a dream-like dance whose performers are unmarried females. In a slow procession, they advance with simple steps and arms outstretched, their tall headdresses of coconut palm fronds and marigold flowers setting off gorgeous costumes in red, white, and gold. Karangasem has always been famous for its various forms of *rejang*, partly through the generous patronage of its former kings. The dance is actually an exorcism, its purpose the driving away of demons that bring illness to Bali during the Javanese monsoon, which lasts from late November to March.

Another temple dance is the *mendet*, which dispenses with elaborate costume altogether. On the first and last nights of a village festival, women dressed in simple attire dance in welcoming or sending off the gods, depending on the occasion. They carry as offerings small flowers, holy water, and incense. Spies and de Zoete were very impressed by this offering dance, in which

> the offering was held in the right hand, the body swaying slightly to the right; the left hand, which is empty, was carried very slowly to the left, with raised fingers, then dropped and brought to join the right. Twice to the left and twice to the right the offering swayed, while the weight of the body moved imperceptibly from foot to foot. The forward step was always taken with the right foot, on every tenth beat, the whole phrase consisting of twenty-four. When the first step of the phrase was taken the offering was extended forwards, the weight falling on the left; and the left arm started again its long curve. It is impossible even to suggest the beauty of the floating, imperceptible progress of the mendet.

Just as slow is the *gabor*, another offering dance with two or three performers. The women who perform the *rejang*, *mandet*, and *gabor* are recognized as temple dancers. They need not be especially accomplished, because any woman can become a part-time priestess once purification with holy water allows her to handle holy things and take part in temple dances.

Since holy water features in every Balinese ritual, it comes as no surprise that there is a libation dance, the *mabang*. In a purification rite intended to rid a village of pollution or prepare its temple for a festival pleasing to the gods, *mabang* dancers are largely older men. But towards the end of the dance, all the men of a village join in the exorcism, often howling like dogs.

Utterly different are the trance dances that are also used to exorcise illness and other demonic afflictions. They are called *sanghyang*, meaning "holy," and imply that the dancer while in a trance has been taken over by a spiritual force. Now confined to remote villages in Bangli and Karangasem, *sanghyang* obviously represents the earliest, pre-Hindu dance form belonging to the Balinese. It is firmly rooted in the Austronesian tradition of spirit possession, the shamanism which is acknowledged throughout Southeast Asia. Faked trances recently staged for the benefit of tourists have not yet weakened the reputation of *sanghyang*, for these ritual dances are still regarded as sacred in Bali. One can only wish they remain that way. Better that the sudden trances which tend to occur during the *barong* dance should satisfy curious visitors, even though they are unlikely to witness them if their stay is only a brief one. This means that the witch Rangda remains the best bet for the supply of genuine trancers, since her undoubted ability to rouse these young men to fury often results in a frenzy of self-stabbing.

What Spies and de Zoete found really fascinating was trance-dancing, and its unexpected impact on dancers who "shudder and make strange sounds as they become possessed, and are evidently unconscious of their surroundings, though not in such a way as to prevent them from orientating themselves in space, which they do with perfect ease. Some appear exhausted afterwards, but quickly recover."

Such *sanghyang* dancers are specially chosen, often by observing which villagers are most susceptible to a trance state. As the Balinese frequently consult their ancestors via a medium, a *balian*, they are fully aware of the value of trance. Not every village has resident trancers, which explains why young men inclined to go into a trance will travel some distance to meet with others like themselves at the *barong* dance.

Apart from the practised trance of the *balians*, who are in the main women, trance seems to be a group phenomenon. Ordinary spectators at a religious ceremony or a dance performance will occasionally become trancers. But only very rarely do individuals go into a trance in the confines of their home compound. The strange visitations of trance intrigue the Balinese as much as they do visitors. Even though they are likely to joke afterward about the uncontrolled actions of someone in a trance, there is also recognition that a spiritual presence is manifest in the body of a fellow villager. Then villagers squat down, as they always do when a god is nearby, so as to be on a lower level and show respect. Only the attendants of the trancers remain on their feet in order to be ready to provide comfort when a trance is over.

Involuntary trance is quite distinct from the induced trance of the *sanghyang* dance, where the heads of the performers are held over incense smoke, prayers are recited and a choir sings at an ever-increasing tempo. Once a state of trance has been achieved, the dancers are brought to the stage with their eyes closed and then left to sway back and forth to the sounds of a gamelan orchestra. That they have already acquired second sight is illustrated by a *sanghyang* event recorded by Spies and de Zoete. They relate how a young girl in a trance indicated a desire to be carried to another village; half way there she met another trancer like herself and, holding hands, they returned to the dancing-place. To the bewilderment of the spectators, the two girls danced in perfect unison as if they had already practiced together. After a quarter of an hour, the guest trancer stopped dancing of her own accord, and was taken back home.

MYTH AND DRAMA

Although Balinese dancing must have originally been connected with ritual, if we are correct in supposing that *sanghyang* derives from a pre-Hindu religious ceremony, dance became more and more theatrical following the Majapahit conquest of the island. In dance-drama, even the most dreadful demons were gradually tamed for the amusement of an audience, yet the link with religion was never entirely severed because no temple festival could be considered successful without some kind of dance performance. And as trancers continue to demonstrate at the *barong* dance, powerful spiritual forces are always present when the good lion Barong confronts the wicked witch Rangda.

Yet the richest source for dance-drama since the Majapahit conquest of Bali in 1343 has been the stories contained in the two great Indian epics, the *Mahabharata* and the *Ramayana*. Javanese chronicles, romances, and legends have provided a useful supplement, but center stage is held by the Indian literary tradition that came to Bali with King Ketut Kresna Kapakisan. As an ex-brahmin himself, the new ruler could be expected to prefer the *Mahabharata* and the *Ramayana*, the joint repository of Hindu

The *wayang wong* masks of Rama and his abducted wife Sita

belief. The original version of the *Ramayana* is attributed to the sage Valmiki, who brought together bardic fragments and then, as Homer did in ancient Greece, reshaped them into poetry that set the standard for early Sanskrit literature. Study of both Indian epics reveals parallels with Homer, and especially between the *Iliad* and the *Ramayana,* which culminates with Rama's expedition to the island of Sri Lanka to recover his abducted wife Sita, or "furrow."

Both the Greek and Indian storytellers drew upon a shared mythological heritage that was recast to suit the different experiences involved in the occupation of Greece and the Ganges river valley, in the middle of which the *Ramayana* is mainly set around the city of Ayudhya. A real Mycenaean king might well have led the Greek armada to Troy, but Agamemnon's leadership has been absorbed into a tale of divine rivalry, of gods and goddesses settling their personal disputes by backing either the Trojans or the Greeks. Yet even with Helen, the human cause of the conflict, we are dealing with a goddess rather than a wayward queen. Hatched from an egg, this daughter of mighty Zeus was probably a tree goddess whose cult encompassed abduction as well as rescue.

The chief thing that the *Iliad* and the *Ramayana* have in common is the divinity of the abducted women, Helen and Sita. At the end of a protracted siege of the demon Ravana's stronghold in Sri Lanka, Sita is reunited with Rama; but he does not welcome her back as readily as Menelaus, Helen's forgiving husband, with the result that Sita is swallowed by the ground as a testimony of her innocence and purity. As someone who had fulfilled her *dharma*, she was able to call upon mother earth as a witness. Inconsolable, Rama followed her into eternity, walking into the waters of the Sarayu River. Vishnu is associated with the primordial waters, where between such incarnations as Rama and Krishna the great god slumbers on the coils of Ananta, the world serpent.

More than Krishna in the *Mahabharata*, Vishnu's incarnation as Rama in the *Ramayana* is always presented as a crucial divine intervention. He has descended to Earth in order to defeat of the demon host gathered by Ravana, whose name means "the screamer." It was a challenge that touched a nerve in Bali, since the island always had more than its fair share of demonic forces. The preserver god Vishnu was compelled to intervene in worldly affairs because Ravana, through penance and devotion to the creator god Brahma, had become immune to attack either from the gods or other demons. So unusual is the idea that severe austerities could ever be a means of acquiring immense power that we can only conclude that here is an instance of indigenous Indian influence on Aryan beliefs. The Indus Valley people who were overrun by these Indo-European invaders sometime between 1750 and 1500 BC appear to have been the first devotees of yoga.

Just how strong the *rishis*, or "sages," were considered to be in ancient India is evident in the humiliation of the sky god Indra. When this deity seduced the *rishi* Gautama's wife, in a similar manner to Zeus' sexual exploits in Greek mythology, the punishment meted out was nothing short of castration: the subsequent replacement of the divine testicles with those belonging to a ram merely served to underline the indignity Indra suffered. No other Indo-European god ever endured such a fate. The Balinese, however, have always been indifferent to yoga and the severities that preoccupied Indian holy men.

Undoubtedly Valmiki based the *Ramayana* on oral materials, but he had an eye on the religious dimension from the start for, unlike Shiva, there was never anything sinister in Vishnu's makeup that could stop him from becoming a savior deity. So in Balinese dance-drama Rama is the perfect hero: even his name places emphasis on goodness, since he is the one who "charms and shines." Capable on his own of dealing with demons like Viradha, described as "sunken-eyed, huge-mouthed, great-belled, a massive, loathsome, deformed, gigantic creature, terrible to behold," Rama does need assistance when tackling Ravana and this he obtained from Hanuman and his monkey army.

So versatile is Hanuman that he regularly delights Balinese audiences, despite being rejected by them as a deity. Monkeys are common enough in Bali for performers to know how to portray both their acrobatic skills and their mischievous side. These dancers' monkey masks are among the most expressive ones worn, with hair, widely carved eye holes to allow performers to convey a range of emotions, and a movable jaw, which can be manipulated to great effect. Hanuman's own mask, however, is more ornate and features protruding teeth as well as alert eyes. Above all, it is a reminder of the unselfishness of this stalwart character, who comes to Rama's aid without demanding anything in return.

In the *Mahabharata*, the other great Indian epic, the story begins with the birth of the blind Dhritarashtra and his younger brother Pandu.

Because of the blindness, Pandu ruled in Dhritarashtra's stead for some years, before retiring to a life of solitude in the forest. Pandu, "the pale one," had a skin ailment that could have been leprosy, so the entitlement of five sons was as uncertain as that of the hundred sons Dhritarasthra sired, when he came to the throne after Pandu's abdication.

As in ancient Greece, Indian kings were supposed to be without physical blemish. At Athens we know how magistrates, whose duties had previously been discharged by kings, in particular those who oversaw religious affairs, were once examined to make sure of their physical perfection. Ideally Greek and Indian rulers had to be paragons of health. Aware of the seriousness of his condition, Pandu never consorted with his two wives who presented the retired king with sons fathered by the gods. The third son Arjuna, "bright and shining," had Indra for his father. On the death of Pandu, Dhritarashtra welcomed back the five Pandavas to Hastinapura, his capital on the upper reaches of the Ganges, and nominated the eldest, Yudhishthira, as his heir.

This was deeply resented by Dhritarashta's eldest son Duryodhana, whose name means "hard to conquer." So the Pandavas prepared again for exile. Just before their departure, Yudhisthira lost everything in a gambling match with Duryodhana: his possessions, the freedom of himself and his brothers and their joint wife Draupadi. In this tremendous win Duryodhana was abetted by his uncle Sakuni, an expert gambler and cheat. He told Yuhisthira that a single throw of the dice would determine "a stake of exile in the forest when you or we lose." Only with great reluctance was Duryodhana persuaded to a compromise, whereby the Pandavas were permitted to retain half their possessions as well as Draupadi, provided they first went into exile for thirteen years.

At the end of this period the Kauravas, Duryodhana's kinsmen, were unwilling to let the Pandavas have their turn as rulers, and so the issue had to be settled through warfare. They battled for eighteen days, with breaks at night to refresh horses and men, on the Kurukshetra plain. It was during this protracted struggle that Krishna, who served as Arjuna's charioteer, revealed his true identity as the god Vishnu, and explained how the destruction of whole families signified nothing in the endless round of reincarnation. No matter the extent of the slaughter, nor the grimness of the hand-to-hand combat, there was nothing any of the warriors could do about the inevitable battle other than take part, a fatalism which recalls that of King Priam of Troy when he and Helen observed the enemy drawn up outside his city. Under no illusion about the might ranged against him, the old king tells Helen that "I bear you no ill will at all: I blame the gods. It is they who sent this terrible Greek host here." Priam simply has no choice but endure the relentless destruction of the Trojans on the battlefield.

The same acceptance of inevitable conflict is apparent in the *Mahabharata*. But in ancient India a permanent state of warfare was made less intolerable by two beliefs that the Balinese inherited via the Javanese: namely, reincarnation and immutable class distinctions. Except for leaving society altogether and becoming a hermit, Krishna tells Arjuna that, as a warrior, he has no choice but enter the fray, so that "good fortune, victory, happiness, and righteousness will follow."

Other sources for Balinese dance-drama include the *Panji*, a Javanese romance dating from the early eighteenth century. Also known as *Malat*, it comprises a long romantic poem in which a prince by the name of Panji, and his eventual princess, Candra, have a variety of adventures. They meet and are separated again and again. In spite of references to actual eastern Javanese kingdoms like Singhasari, the events related in the romance are legendary and turn upon mystifying impersonations. The principal characters communicate in Javanese with the result that most of the audience cannot understand them. But as in *wayang kulit*, the shadow theater, attendants and comedians provide a running commentary in Balinese.

As interested in courtly affairs is *topeng*, one of Bali's most popular forms of masked dance-drama. *Topeng* literally means "to press a mask against the face." Its stories revolve around the lives of Balinese kings, whose exploits are recounted during temple festivals. Usually five men dance all the roles by changing masks and headdresses. The three chief characters are Topeng Keras, a strong-willed minister; Topeng Keras Bues, another courtier with bulging eyes; and, last but not least, Topeng Tua, an old man with great dignity and inner strength. Topeng Tua has a childlike innocence that enhances the comic moments in the dance-drama, as when he discovers a flea in his clothing or a nit in his hair.

Wearing half-masks to enable them to explain events, clown-servants act as both storytellers and commentators. They bring up the problem facing a king and, after the dancer who takes his role, Topeng Dalem, has

Topeng Tua, the wise elder statesman

told the servant-clowns what action he intends to take, they gather other clowns to undertake the task. These *bondres*, or "clowns," sport masks with multiple rows of teeth, odd ears, and monkey features. In many respects, the *topeng* dance could be said to parallel the rituals of ancestor worship, since throughout a performance divine assistance is steadily sought, especially against misfortune and disease. Which makes it more than likely that the origins of masked dance-drama are to be located in exorcism rites.

Topeng dancers must possess a variety of skills. They have to move in time with gamelan music, while being fluent in several languages such as Sankrit and Javanese. Because *topeng* is looked upon as a vehicle for teaching history and philosophy, its performers are expected to have an understanding of early texts. Such knowledge starts in a dancer's own village, where the patronage of the local priest is essential, but once his reputation spreads abroad, he is invited to dance elsewhere. So respected are first-rate *topeng* companies that the Balinese government has employed them for information purposes: they outline such policies as family planning and health programs in villages and even on television.

More specific in its focus is *wayang wong*, the masked dance-drama that a Dewa Agung at Klungkung asked his dancers to devise at the end of the eighteenth century. Because *wayang wong* is based on the *Ramayana* and the triumph of Rama over the demons, Hanuman plays a key role in narrative, along with his monkey followers. Totally selfless, his bravery is unmatched and his devotion to Vishnu without compare.

Yet sacred *barong* masks are by far the most important Balinese masks, because as Spies and de Zoete point out,

> the barong play is another example of the impossibility of considering any dance form in Bali as dissociated from its social and religious significance. It is possible of course to watch the mythical beast, the Barong, dancing on roads or in the temple, in all its panoply of gilded leather and grinning mask, and admire its dexterous steps, without realizing that this amusing apparition is a philosophic symbol. For the Barong is at once the most familiar and most obscure figure in Balinese dance-drama, the most concrete and most abstruse, the most typically Balinese and the most universal.

Its long sagging body, built on a light frame of bamboo, is animated by two performers in a similar way to the European pantomime horse. But there the comparison stops, because the dancers inside the *barong* are as accomplished as anyone else who performs on the Balinese stage. The good lion has an endless variety of movements, ranging from rapid steps to crouching on the ground, from kicking the dust to swishing its tail around the head as if to keep off flies. So complex is the beast's character that only accomplished gamelan musicians can respond to its temperamental behavior. Sometimes Barong is discontented enough with a melody to clack its jaws as if trying to bite the sounds of the music.

When the good lion is pleased with a gamelan orchestra, it will lie down on one of the instruments while the musician continues imperturbably to play on as best he can. Often in appreciation a foot is placed on a drum. This enjoyable theater in no way diminishes the climax of the *barong* dance, the good lion's triumph over the dreadful Rangda. Another name for her is Matah Gede, or "the big unripe one," and refers to her human form prior to the transformation into a witch.

Rangda is *niskala*, the intangible world of Bali that can suddenly manifest itself in a frightening manner. She comes from darkness, the source of illness and death, whereas her lion opponent is the light, the antidote to evil. The half-naked men who go into a trance to assist Barong during the fight with Rangda are in effect a divinely inspired human shield

Barong, the good lion of dance-drama

for the protection of the audience. Their self-stabbing is seen as a necessary sacrifice to keep the powers of darkness at bay.

Whatever the ultimate origin of *barong* dance-drama, there can be no question that Rangda's defeat is a sign of Balinese confidence in their religious beliefs. Yet the Hindu–Austronesian outlook is far from simple: its apparently contradictory elements, such as the rites of ancestor worship and the expectation of endless reincarnation, often bewilders the visitor. For the Balinese think that all is well in their cosmos as long as there is an equilibrium of opposing forces. In dance-drama this is affirmed time and again when invisible enemies are contained, temporarily expelled, even exorcised. But, like Rangda herself, they will return to trouble Bali again, which helps to explain the underlying strength of the island's cultural heritage. Because Balinese dancers not only seek to amuse an audience, they battle against relentless demonic attack as well.

Chapter Twelve

BALINESE ART AND ARCHITECTURE

"Everybody in Bali seems to be an artist."

Miguel Covarrubias

So artistic did the Balinese people appear to this Mexican traveler in the 1930s that, in his book *Island of Bali*, Covarrubias launched worldwide the notion that their island home was nothing short of an aesthetic paradise. "Coolies and princes, men and women alike," he wrote, "can dance, play musical instruments, paint, or carve in wood and stone." Utterly remarkable was the presence in "an otherwise poor and dilapidated village" of "an elaborate temple, a great orchestra, or a group of actors of repute."

Determined to experience the real Bali for themselves, Miguel Covarrubias and his wife quickly moved out of the Dutch-owned Bali Hotel in Denpasar and took up residence nearby at a prince's lodging house constructed in traditional materials of mud, wood, and thatch. It was here that they met the artist and musician Walter Spies, who in 1927 came to live permanently in Bali. Previously he had been a musician in central Java, at the court of the sultan of Yogyakarta. The influence of Spies on the approach of Covarrubias to Balinese culture was immense, and in particular as regards the view that its creative roots were nourished by folklore and religious belief. So impressed was he with Spies that Covarrubias called him "Bali's most famous resident" and "an authentic friend of the Balinese and loved by them."

A footloose Russian-German émigré, Spies felt comfortable at last among the Balinese, for whom his preference for male partners raised no eyebrows. But he was arrested by the Dutch colonial authorities in 1939 for having sexual relations with underaged boys and sentenced to a term of imprisonment. The submission made on Spies' behalf by Margaret Mead, who was firmly convinced of the value of Sigmund Freud's view of culture, received scant notice from the Calvinist judges. They could not agree with her suggestion that Spies was merely seeking a "repudiation of the dominance and submission, authority and dependence, which he

195

associated with European culture."

Prior to his downfall, Spies was indeed a major influence in shaping modern Balinese art. At Ubud, he assisted the ruling family in turning this town into a centre for sculpture as well as painting. Along with Beryl de Zoete, an English expert on drama, Spies also wrote *Dance and Drama in Bali*, which was published the year before his dramatic arrest. Even though this study opened Western eyes to the richness of Balinese dance-drama, the lasting impact of Spies was on Covarrubias' work because *Island of Bali* has worn well, probably being the most read travel book on the island.

According to Covarrubias, "the effervescence of artistic activity and the highly developed aesthetic sense of the population can perhaps be explained by a natural urge to express themselves, combined with the important factor of leisure resulting from well-organized agricultural cooperation." His appreciation of the effectiveness of the *subaks*, the irrigation societies at village level, is correct, but Covarrubias might have added how these organizations, like all others in Bali, cannot be separated from religious observance, from colorful festivals arranged in honor of the gods and for which beautiful objects always have to be prepared. But he has a telling point about the popularity of Balinese arts and crafts, when he adds that there is no "centralization of artistic knowledge in a special intellectual class." As a consequence, "not only the aristocracy can create informal beauty, but a commoner may be as finished an artist as the educated nobleman, although he may be an agriculturalist, a tradesman, or even a coolie." Another worthwhile comment is the geographical context of Balinese arts and crafts. "Nothing in Bali," Covarrubias notes,

> is made for posterity; the only available stone is a soft sandstone that crumbles away after a few years, and the temples and reliefs have to be renewed constantly; white ants devour wooden sculptures, and humidity rots away all paper and cloth, so that their arts have never suffered from fossilization. The Balinese are extremely proud of their traditions, but they are progressive and unconservative, and when a foreign idea strikes their fancy, they adopt it with great enthusiasm as their own. All sorts of influences from the outside, Indian, Chinese, Javanese, have left their mark on Balinese art, but they are always translated into their own manner and they become strongly Balinese in the process.

The Moon Drum shrine at Pejeng

This openness to outside influence should not be regarded as anything unusual, considering how readily Bali accepted Javanese ways after the Majapahit conquest of 1343. Even present-day Balinese look upon this as the decisive historical event in the development of their culture.

In the company of Spies, Covarrubias traveled around Bali looking for examples of genuine "native" art, but their quest was largely fruitless. That they identified as "the most remarkable of antiquities" the Moon Drum, housed in the Pura Penataran Sasih temple at Pejeng, only reveals how little they appreciated this ritual object owed to mainland Southeast Asia. These massive drums, mainly originating in northern Vietnam, moved right down the length of the Indonesian archipelago and even reached distant New Guinea. Although the Moon Drum is actually of Balinese manufacture, this magnificent artifact imitates the Vietnamese method of bronze casting. The spread of the drums throughout maritime Southeast Asia indicates a network of early trading as well as a sphere of cultural influence that means Bali was never an isolated island.

What Spies and Covarrubias achieved, possibly without fully realizing the implications, was to demonstrate how Bali had always been an integral part of Southeast Asian culture. The Majapahit takeover of the island brought new Indian artistic styles along with Hinduism, but these had already been thoroughly Javanized, and especially in *wayang* painting. While Balinese art nowadays is mostly viewed in galleries and museums, traditional works were first placed in temples and palaces, having a definite spiritual charge.

The village of Kamasan in east Bali is the home of traditional Balinese painting. Once its resident painters served the kings of Gelgel, whose court was a few miles away. Their unique *wayang* style of painting is so-called because of its close resemblance to *wayang kulit*, or "shadow puppets," a form of theater still popular in Java as well as Bali. For centuries their performances have served as both a means of entertainment and religious instruction, since their plots are drawn from the *Mahabharata* and the *Ramayana*, the Indian epics which encapsulate the essence of the Hindu faith. Less adventurous than dance-drama in the use of Balinese folklore, *wayang kulit* is still improvised because there are neither scripts nor rehearsals. The puppeteer is at liberty to vary the narrative from performance to performance.

Wayang art at first appears as entirely two-dimensional to a Westerner, who is so used to perspective. A second look reveals, however, a subtle interplay of texture, line, shape, and color. Because Balinese texts talk about "giving life" in the creative process, the most traditional subjects are full of vigor and fascinating detail. Legend confirms this preoccupation with realism, fundamentally different though it is in concept from Western art. The ancestral artist-craftsman, Sangging Prabangkara, possessed such talents that nothing was beyond his genius. For the Dewa Agung at Klungkung he filled a palace with wonderful statues, painted a lifelike portrait of the queen, accurately depicted the creatures of the forest and the sea, and finally ascended upon a giant kite to record the heavenly realm. As he liked what he saw there, Sangging Prabangkara is said to have chosen to stay on. Many legends have collected around this charismatic figure, whose outstanding ability as the founder of Bali's artistic tradition recalls the awe in which the ancient Greeks held Daedalus, whose statues were said to be so real that they had to chained in order to prevent them running away. Among other things, Daedalus is credited with the construction of the first building fit for a king, something Sangging Prabangkara had also mastered because he designed the Klungkung palace at the time the Balinese court moved there in 1710 from Gelgel.

For Daedalus the critical breakthrough was the invention of the saw, an idea that his nephew Talus got from the jaw of a serpent. Out of jealousy, Daedalus is said to have killed Talus and fled from Athens to Crete, where he was warmly welcomed by King Minos, for whom he built the splendid palace at Knossos. Without a bronze saw he would have been unable to cut and dress stone used in its construction. But the king soon turned against Daedalus, whose name may be translated as "ingenious," and he was imprisoned along with his son Icarus. Rising to the occasion, Daedalus constructed wings for himself and his son; and as his son took flight, he warned Icarus not to fly too high, for fear that the wax holding the wings together would be melted by the sun, nor to fly too close to the sea, for fear that the wings would become too heavy because of moisture. Icarus disregarded his father's instructions and in his excitement soared higher and higher, till the wings fell apart and he plunged into the sea and drowned.

Less detail is available about Sangging Prabangkara's aerobatics, but it offers an intriguing parallel to the Daedalus legend. Whether or not the Balinese genius actually built the gigantic kite that he used to fly heavenward is not made clear, despite his unexpected disappearance like Icarus. Staying on in the heavenly realm is of course a convenient device for ending Sangging Prabangkara's amazing career: he could do everything, no royal request was too demanding, and so the gods may have decided to keep him with them. Possibly they were envious of his contribution to royal comfort in Bali, although his architectural achievements were meant to be as pleasing to gods and goddesses as they were to members of the royal family. Just as Daedalus built a dancing place at Knossos, so Sangging Prabangkara provided Klungkung with a venue for dance-drama, always a favorite of the Balinese deities.

In painting a portrait of Klungkung's queen, as well as those depicting the creatures he encountered during his expeditions through the forest and under the sea, Sangging Prabangkara would have used the same materials that still form the basis of *wayang* art at Kamasan today. These comprise a canvas of white cotton cloth which is sized with rice paste and polished with a cowrie shell. The rice paste sizing provides a smooth surface for painting: its consistency also permits the rolling up of the cloth without damaging the paint. Pigments are black, made from soot, and other colors derived from natural vegetable and mineral dyes. But Chinese ink has long been favored, and over the centuries the Balinese palette was extended through the addition of Chinese vermilion and bright yellow.

Different gods are painted in different colors, so that there is a clear link between color symbolism and the divine. The mighty Shiva is associated with white, a combination of all the colors, while Brahma appears in red, Vishnu in brown and not the blue invariably employed in Indian treatments of this savior deity.

It is not uncommon for several artists to work on a *wayang* painting. The master painter draws the outline first in pencil and his assistants fill in the colors. Finally, the master redraws the outlines, puts the finishing touches to the painting, and then leaves his assistants to polish it with a cowrie shell. At Kamasan, the production of art always seems to have been a family enterprise. Today the most senior of the *wayang* painters, I Nyoman Mandra, can be seen at work in the village along with his son and other close relatives. An obvious parallel is the master painter in medieval Europe, whose apprentices learned how to paint by contributing to commissioned works. The usual patrons then were churchmen who wanted frescoes for the walls of abbey churches and cathedrals as well as

I Nyoman Mandra at Kamasan, where relations help to complete his traditional paintings

painted wooden panels showing the saints and holy scenes.

Medieval artists were well aware of the merits of their paintings, since the twelfth-century Benedictine monk Theophilus in Germany could observe, with approval, how "the faithful soul sees the representation of the Lord's Passion expressed in art" and "it is stung with compassion." A similar emotion would have been evident in the Balinese viewer of *wayang* paintings, not least because the subject matter was inevitably religious with the exploits of Rama the most common of all depictions. His quest to save Sita from the clutches of the demonic Ravana was simply too good an adventure to pass over, since it enabled the painter to introduce the monstrous beings who lurk in *niskala*, Bali's own unseen world.

The far-reaching expertise of Sangging Prabangkara must account for Covarrubias' view the "the artist in Bali is essentially a craftsman and at the same time an amateur, casual and anonymous, who uses his talent knowing that no one will care to record his name for posterity." While this was the case before the establishment of Dutch rule over the entire island, the stylized nature of Balinese painting underwent a radical transformation during the colonial period and immediately after the attainment of Indonesian independence. Since then, individual artists have emerged who employ a mixture of Balinese and Western techniques. Traditional *wayang* painting continues to flourish at Kamasan but, in other artistic centers, painters have explored a more international approach to composition and color, stimulated as much by tourist demand as any desire to abandon a truly Balinese vision.

This upsurge of creativity was strengthened through the interest shown by foreign artists who have come to live in Bali, such as Arie Smit. This artist's studies of the Balinese landscape, with its temples, paddy fields, trees, mountains, and people, seem quintessential: even their two-dimensional quality suits the subjects that attracted his attention. A large number of Smit's works are on display today at the Neka Art Museum in Ubud. It was in 1960 that Arie Smit first got involved with local artists. Walking through the countryside, he saw two teenage boys amusing themselves by drawing pictures in sand while guarding ducks and cows. As they could not afford the school fees needed to secure a full-time education, he invited them to learn painting in his studio at Penestanan, a village to the west of Ubud. So keen were the boys to take up his offer that Arie Smit paid for someone else to do their farm work. Although these

Detail of a painting by Young Artist I Ketut Soki

youngsters, the first Young Artists, were given paints and shown how to use them, they were allowed complete self-expression. But like all Balinese paintings, their compositions are crowded with activity.

The inspiration behind the so-called Young Artists school of painting is Arie Smit's own approach to the Balinese landscape, which he described as the place "where sky meets the sea [and] there is play; reflections move, shapes dance, the horizon forms a strong line, breaks, is light, is dark. The horizon of a tropical sea is not a dividing line; it blends air and water, and sky and sea become one." Although the sixty-eight-year-old I Ketut Soki is the only Young Artist with a studio in Penestanan now, his works have lost nothing of the school's original verve.

Thirty years before Arie Smit's sponsorship of painting at Penestanan, the Swiss artist Theo Meier had collected paintings and encouraged local artists in Batuan, a village located well to the south of Ubud. The Batuan painters had already expanded on the traditional subjects which appear in the Kamasan school by adding folktale and dance-drama material. Many were indeed accomplished dancers themselves. A restricted palette of black, dark green, and brown gives Batuan paintings a distinctive appearance, when they depict village rituals and temple ceremonies. But Theo Meier was really interested in selling Balinese art to foreign visitors and, this commercial edge, combined with an unorthodox lifestyle, made him unpopular with other Europeans living in Bali. Moreover, he never gained the respect of the Balinese either; unlike Arie Smit who, after Indonesia gained its independence, received awards not only from the Balinese provincial government but also from the federal government in Jakarta.

A full discussion of modern Balinese artists, including the Young Artists, can be found in Adrian Vickers' *Balinese Art: Paintings and Drawings of Bali 1800–2010*. But Vickers cautions about jumping to quick conclusions about current developments.

> That the three domains of painting on Bali—art by the Balinese, art about Bali by Westerners, and art by other Indonesians—should be so linked tells us two things about the nature of Indonesian art: the sense of 'region' and 'center' in Indonesian art is complicated by the abundance of forms of art in Bali, and the shadow of colonial and tourist influences still hangs over the art of the Balinese and of other Indonesians.

Thus it is too early to identify this or that artist as being most typical of modern Balinese art. Yet absolutely transparent is the vast distance that separates their creativity from the hundreds of paintings on sale in "art shops," hand-painted though these bright pictures of birds and flowers usually are.

WOOD, STONE, METAL, AND FABRIC

Because stone that is really suitable for sculpture is unavailable in Bali, three-dimensional artists have had to rely on wood, not just for figures but also masks. The latter have been part of dance-drama from the beginning of the Majapahit era, but in the late eighteenth century *wayang wong*, or "masked drama," was boosted at Klungkung through the initiative of a Dewa Agung. This king asked his dancers to devise a new form of dance-drama based on the *Ramayana* story of Sita's abduction by the demon Ravana. Although the dancers still imitated the movements of the puppets in *wayang kulit* performances, they sang and danced wearing masks.

The mask carver is a specialized craftsman who has likely come to his calling via a family connection. Most of the mask makers live at Mas in central Bali, a village renowned for its woodwork. Top-quality masks command high prices and villagers have to save hard in order to secure a sacred Barong mask for their village temple. Only high-caste carvers are permitted to undertake this task, around which a whole series of religious ceremonies cluster. The selection of a sacred tree requires careful attention and the calendar has to be consulted for an auspicious day to cut out a piece of wood.

A priest is involved in almost every stage of the production process for Barong and Rangda masks and special ceremonies are arranged in the village acquiring these sacred artifacts. Inviting divine power to enter the masks, the priest conducts services in the village temple as well as the village cemetery. If they are judged to have been successful, and a newly made mask has received a spiritual charge, then the priest dons the mask and goes into a trance usually among the graves. Afterwards the mask is wrapped in white cloth and placed in the village temple.

Nearly all the sculptures lining the roads leading to Ubud have been carved from imported stone, or made from concrete using molds. Like some of the masks at Mas, they are intended for sale to tourists and usually end up in European, Australian, and American gardens. Traditional Balinese woodcarving served the needs of temples and palaces, and its subjects consisted of gods, heroes, and demons. Since the 1930s, though, sculptors have tended to use stone more than tropical hardwood. Their work never aims at artistic admiration: its chief function is religious, which is why the Balinese people put rice, fruit, and flowers before sculpted figures each day. The softness of the island's stone obliges constant renewal, and particularly in temples where sculptors have to replace moss-covered work on a regular basis. One consequence is that there is always employment for stone carvers, who never lack opportunities to perfect their skills.

Another traditional Balinese article sought by visitors is the *kris*, a dagger only worn now as fashion accessory. Once the *kris* indicated social status, with the result that some of them boasted gold and jewels in their decoration. The *pandes*, or "smiths," responsible for these daggers belong to a group largely outside the caste system. Quite a few families of smiths claim an ancestry preceding the introduction of the Hindu faith.

Balinese kings patronized the *pandes*, making them an adjunct of royal government and providing workshops within their palaces. Besides wishing to exercise a degree of control over the production of weapons, these rulers believed in the magical powers inherent in metal products. When the Dutch invaded Bali using rifles and machine guns, the *kris* had outlived its usefulness as a weapon of war and the only role left for it was a symbolic one. The most dramatic instance of this now are the blunt *krises* with which trancers stab themselves during performances of dance-drama. These young men seem to be consumed by anger at the arrogance of Rangda, but they never strike the actor who impersonates the wicked witch. And self-stabbing rarely, if ever, causes serious injury because the trancers are believed to be under the benign protection of the good lion Barong.

Only the blade of a *kris* is thought to be sacred, which is the reason for its safe keeping within a protective sheaf. Otherwise its potency might be strong enough to harm the owner. Quite unrelated to Hinduism, or any other imported religion, the *krises* of the Indonesian archipelago are locally manufactured cult objects which were feared as much as they were respected. The infamous maritime Southeast Asian habit of running amok, during which a demented individual can knife any number of people at random, is sometimes attributed to the blood lust of a certain *kris*. Many Balinese tales mention the immense power of *krises*, whose placation has always been taken very seriously indeed.

A prime instance of the power inherent in a *kris* is the weapon that once belonged to Ken Angrok, the usurper of authority in eastern Java. An ex-bandit, Ken Angrok was backed by discontented priests and introduced to Tunggul Ametung, a ruler he served as an enforcer of his far from popular decisions. The ruler's wife was the beautiful Ken Dhedhes, who fell in deeply in love with the hired strong man. Ken Angrok's priestly supporters encouraged the affair and advised the would-be usurper to obtain a magic *kris* from Mpu Gandring, the famous Javanese blacksmith. It would have the capacity to kill with a single thrust.

The blacksmith asked for six months in which to forge the *kris*. When Ken Angrok went to collect the weapon at the appointed time and learned it was unready, he seized the *kris* and stabbed the blacksmith. Before dying Mpu Gandring cursed Ken Angrok to be killed by the same dagger, and his children and his grandchildren to die by it as well.

With the unfinished *kris*, Ken Angrok still managed to assassinate Tunggul Ametung and marry Ken Dhedhes. Proclaimed king by a jubilant priesthood, Ken Angrok adopted the name Rada Rajasa and claimed descent from Shiva Girinda, or "Shiva of the Mountains." In 1221 he defeated another eastern Javanese ruler and doubled the size of his realm, henceforth known as Singhasari. But the blacksmith's curse caught up with the king six years later, when his son Anushapati obtained the *kris* from Ken Dhedhes and stabbed him in the back at a banquet. The queen had become tired of Ken Angrok and revealed to Anushapati that he was in fact the son of Tunggul Ametung, who had been assassinated.

Anushapati then became king of Singhasari and ruled until 1248, when during the excitement of a cockfight, his half-brother Tohdjaya grabbed hold of the *kris* and killed him with it. Tohdjaya was the son of Ken Angrok and a concubine. But the new assassin sat on the throne for just a few months and met his death in a palace coup fomented by his two nephews, Ranga Wuni, the son of Anushapati, and Mahisha Champaka, the grandson of Ken Angrok. Although these two princes ruled in turn, and appear to have met natural deaths, the magical *kris* had visited destruction upon the royal family over a couple of generations, as Mpu Gandring swore it would. When the second nephew died in 1268, having already abdicated in favor of his son, the ex-king was deified in the forms of both Shiva as well as a Buddhist saint. The event anticipated the extravagant claims to divinity made by Kertanagara, the last king of Singhasari, who in 1292 provoked the Mongol invasion of Java. This ambitious monarch had added Bali to his dominions a few years earlier.

A final artistic product of Bali that delights visitors are its textiles. In many ways they form the core of the island's culture for cloth is not only prepared for human garments, but also the coverings of statues, rocks, trees, small buildings, and even machines. On special occasions almost everything seems to be ritually clothed, including cars and buses.

Difficult though it is to trace the history of Balinese textiles in a climate that makes such short work of perishable goods, weaving was almost a monopoly of royal and priestly families in the pre-colonial period. As servants saw to the housework, the ladies living in these households had plenty of time on their hands, which allowed them to attend to looms. On a Balinese loom the warp is stretched between a heavy wooden frame and a kind of yoke held by the weaver's back. The weave is tightened by a long ruler of polished hardwood that slides over a bamboo drum.

Most famous of all cloths are the *ikat*, or "tied" textiles, whose threads are dyed before weaving begins. Of the range of naturally-obtained materials found in Bali, dyestuffs used to make blue-black and pink-red-brown colors predominate. These materials derive from mud, shells, insects, bark, and roots. Given the symbolic significance of white, red, and brown in religious art, it is transparent how woven textiles reflect this cultural outlook. Red, black-brown, and white threads are still believed by the Balinese to provide protection for the wearer. In their temples brightly colored offerings, cloths, and banners conform to the same cosmic pattern.

Perhaps the most internationally famous Indonesian textile is batik: its colors are applied to a white cotton material, using wax or rice paste to stop one dye from affecting another. When the dyes have been applied to the entire surface, the resist is removed by boiling, melting, or scraping. Overdying is now a popular method for making batik cloth, but traditional batik designs require the use of a brass pipe to control the wax. A perfect batik can take weeks of patient work. Settlers of Chinese origin in Java embraced batik as if it were their own, and added motifs such as the dragon and the phoenix which still distinguish these textiles from other local products. Today the typical Javanese batik, with its intricate pattern of designs, is a consequence of the rise of Islam and the overthrow of the Hindu kingdom of Majapahit towards the end of the fifteenth century. Balinese batik was spared this fate, so that its patterns remain true to pre-Muslim styles.

Ubiquitous in Bali, however, is *poleng*, a checkered cloth wrapped around ritually important objects. Its squares are black and white or black and red, and they represent the duality of the Balinese cosmos: *sekala*, the visible world, and *niskala*, its invisible dimension. During dance-drama performances, the witch Rangda's followers wear *poleng*, a clear reference to its association with the demonic world. Yet *poleng* has a positive side in that it thwarts evil spirits when covering the ground, since people who walk over the checkered cloth are guaranteed protection.

LIVING ARCHITECTURE

No less attention is paid to ritual in the Balinese approach to architecture, for their houses, like everything else in Bali, are animate structures. During

A traditional residential compound with its surrounding walls

the construction of the house the building comes "alive," an idea that is reinforced by naming its parts after a human body. As Covarrubias points out,

> a house, like a human being, has a head—the family shrine; arms—the sleeping quarters and the social parlor; a navel—the courtyard; sexual organs—the gate; legs and feet—the kitchen and the granary; and anus—the pit in the backyard where refuse is disposed of.

And similar to the Chinese concept of *feng shui*, or "wind and water," the house compound is carefully oriented in order to ensure the buildings and their occupants are most favorably positioned. Above all, its layout takes note of the Balinese compass, whose main points are linked to particular deities.

The two principal directions are *kaja* and *kelod*. Whereas *kaja* is defined as "upstream" of "facing the mountain," and in particular the volcanoes upon whose summits the deified ancestors are said to dwell, *kelod* means "downstream" or "facing the sea," an area full of malignant forces. In southern Bali, where most people live, *kaja* and *kelod* roughly correspond to north and south respectively. Correct alignment with the sacred volcano Gunung Agung is the orientation that really must be judged correctly. Once the go-ahead has been obtained from the spirit already inhabiting the site, and appropriate offerings presented to the gods, an auspicious day is identified for the commencement of work. Great care is taken over the placement of the wooden uprights supporting the roof: their bottoms should be nearest to where the roots were in the tree. For the "planting" of these timbers is at one with the organic nature of the Balinese house, an Austronesian belief that is evident throughout maritime Southeast Asia. Among the Acehnese of northern Sumatra, for instance, the house uprights are even referred to as being male and female and given auspicious-sounding names, such as king and queen.

Above all else, the satisfaction of the spirits of place is of critical importance. The *merajan* that so disconcerted Made Djelantik in Denpasra were placed on the tops of modern buildings in order to maintain the goodwill of these spiritual powers. *Merajan*, or "house temples," are as common in mainland Southeast Asia as they are in Indonesia. A friendly relationship with these spirits in Bali depends on their participation in village festivals, when residents ensure they receive offerings along with the gods and the ancestral spirits.

A Balinese residential compound is home to an extended family typically consisting of a married couple, their sons with their wives and children, their unmarried daughters, and the parents of the husband, if they are still alive. Like the Chinese again, the Balinese feel uneasy when they sleep without a wall surrounding their dwelling. Even the gateway of a compound has placed behind it an *aling-aling*, or a freestanding "blind wall," for the purpose of keeping demons outside. Chinese houses use screens instead, believing as do the Balinese that malignant spirits encounter tremendous difficulty in turning corners. But the Balinese have nothing resembling the deliberately curving lines of Chinese pathways, again a problem for spirits who move in straight lines.

The various pavilions of the house are distributed around a well-kept courtyard of hardened earth free of vegetation except for some flowers, decorative plants, and the odd tree. In larger compounds there are gardens, orchards, and pigsties. Because of its marked tendency to run wild and spread out in all directions, bamboo is not grown at all. Dealing with unwanted bamboo is an unwelcome task, and only old people undertake its removal because their closeness to death and reincarnation makes them much less fearful of the plant's potent power—a somewhat ironic attitude when it is recalled how dependent the Balinese have always been on bamboo, for buildings, water pipes, furniture, and even musical instruments.

The ancestral shrines are set off from the rest of the buildings in the compound by a low wall which provides a *sanggah*, or "family temple." The actual size of each temple is strictly laid down, and the advice of the village priest is sought during construction. Dedicated to the family's ancestors, most shrines comprise house-like buildings raised on pillars constructed with bricks or sandstone blocks. Other thatch-roofed structures are dotted about the compound too: these are for the worship of different deities whose primary task is guarding the occupants from malignant spirits. Balinese apprehension over the denizens of the unseen world has turned the dwelling compound into a spiritually fortified refuge.

The *umah meten*, or "sleeping pavilion," of the house owner is the first to be erected after the construction of the family temple. Next in importance to the family temple, the *umah meten* is usually a small pavilion standing on a solid platform, with a thick thatch roof surrounded by four windowless walls. High-caste families often add a veranda or porch in front of the entrance with another line of posts supporting the roof. In many ways the sleeping pavilion is the family's stronghold, where heirlooms and valuables are stored. Normally the head of the family sleeps in the *umah meten*, but being the only building in which privacy can be guaranteed, he moves out for the benefit of newlyweds or unmarried girls needing protection. They are shut into it at night, while the rest of the family sleeps outdoors on the veranda or in surrounding open pavilions.

Two other buildings of note are the *paon*, or "kitchen," and the *lumbung*, or "granary." The former is a simple structure, built on a low terrace with stoves placed along its rear wall. The latter, close to the kitchen, is more complicated than most pavilions because a principal feature is the wooden platform raised well above the level of the ground, for the purpose of keeping the family's rice supply away from hungry rats and mice. Since rice is not only the crop that sustains the Balinese people but even more a precious gift of the rice goddess Dewi Sri, the location of the granary receives special attention. Rice is usually threshed on the ground next to this building.

Although constructed on a grander scale, the *puri* or "palace" is not essentially different from a family compound. Walls offer protection from evil influences and members of the royal family live in separate pavilions. Where differences are most obvious are in the quality of the building materials used, the palace layout with a clear distinction between public and private sections, and the dynastic temple which proclaims the right of a king to rule. The dynastic temple is supposedly the center of the Balinese cosmos, though not of the entire island once there were several kingdoms in existence. As soon as the original royal house, founded by Ketet Kresna Kapakisan, lost its preeminent position, the Majapahit notion of a single cosmic center at the palace of the king could no longer be sustained. The Dewa Agung at Klungkung might still be looked upon as the supreme ruler, but other kings in their own palaces claimed to exercise a divinely conferred authority as well.

There are, in fact, nine *puri* of ex-kings left now and thousands of mini-palaces, which were built for minor royalty. Some are still inhabited by the descendants of these once-powerful families, others are simply places of tourist interest. Even though the temple in a full-blown palace is dedicated to a line of royal ancestors, the public can visit it on special occasions, unlike family temples in residential compounds. The royal shrines are indeed much the same as ordinary ancestral shrines, although they are more elaborately decorated. The *meru*, the pagoda-like towers with an odd number of thatched roofs that diminish in size toward the top, were raised by kings to show their respect for the gods. Eleven is the highest number of roofs ever put together, and these particular *meru* are dedicated to Shiva. Another feature of Balinese palaces that were thought to have attracted divine goodwill were water pavilions, maybe for the reason the water surrounding these buildings cuts them off from the mundane, from the distractions of everyday existence.

At Klungkung the bale kambang, or "floating palace," literally seems to float above a lily-filled pond, while the panels beneath its shingled roof are covered with *wayang* paintings of scenes from the *Sutasoma*, the fourteenth-century Javanese tale in which King Kertanagara plays such a prominent part. Quite likely Mpu Tantular, the author of this intriguing poem, deliberately set out to demonstrate the divinity of Kertanagara, Singhasari's charismatic ruler. By the time the *Sutasoma* appeared

Kertanagara was already long gone, but his Majapahit successors were keen to associate themselves with his memorable reign. After the regency of his mother, who was loyally assisted by Gajah Mada, Hayam Wuruk seems to have felt on his accession in 1350 that he needed to link himself somehow with Kertanagara. The greatest of all Majapahit rulers, Hayam Wuruk enlarged the influence of this maritime kingdom to its farthest extent, his prize conquest being that of Bali in 1343, since it re-established Javanese control over an island first overcome by Kertanagara nearly a century earlier. It was Singhasari's entanglement in Mongol politics that had caused its loss. So it looks as if Mpu Tantular was commissioned by Hayam Wuruk to boost his own royal prestige through the composition of the *Sutasoma*.

The Balinese are highly conscious of orientations, both in their daily lives and in their construction of buildings. Nowhere is this clearer than in their temples, the most cherished of all creations. Hardly anywhere is without a temple or shrine: in the 1950s it was calculated that there were 20,000 temples in Bali, a gross underestimation of the more than half a million places of worship now identified. There are family temples, clan temples, village temples, *subak* temples, field temples, market temples, as well as temples for particular gods and goddesses. And because a *pura*, or "temple," is a place to entertain the deities when they descend on a visit, they are open to the sky. They have no forbidding rooms, blackened with incense and occupied by awe-inspiring images: in fact, they tend to avoid divine representations altogether.

A typical temple with two or three courtyards surrounded by a low stone wall, each court leading to the next through a stone gateway, signals the basic simplicity of Balinese worship. So different from a Hindu temple in India, or indeed an Indian-inspired Javanese temple, is a Balinese place of worship that its design must have remained unchanged from the pre-Majapahit era. An early reverence for stone lingers in the megalithic thatched towers of the *meru*, as it does in the split monumental gateways between courtyards.

Of the courtyards forming a temple, the inner one is higher than the rest and underlines the notion of a mountain slope. It is situated at the *kaja* end and considered to be the temple's holiest section. Here relics are kept and shrines used for the presentation of offerings. Priests invite gods and goddesses to come down from Gunung Agung, stay in the thatched-covered shrines and attend ceremonies. They hear worshippers' prayers, receive offerings, watch the entertainment, and generally enjoy themselves. The gaiety of such religious occasions persuaded Jawaharlal Nehru on a visit in 1950 that Bali was "the morning of the world." Coming from the leaden atmosphere of the subcontinent, the Indian premier added it was "the last paradise," having noticed the lightness of Hinduism in the island, where a less rigid caste system has hardly been a burden for its inhabitants. Perhaps most significant of all, its lightness has also allowed most Balinese temples to remain communal property, since villagers take care of their fabric and only call upon specialists such a stone and wood carvers when they are required.

The middle courtyard, in a three-court temple, acts as a store. It also has a kitchen for the preparation of food offerings for the deities who stay in the inner courtyard during festivals. The outer courtyard is a public space, a gathering point for gossip, even a venue for cockfights. Animals are additionally sacrificed here in this courtyard to placate the demons. When an animal is killed in a sacrifice, however, it acquires merit enough to achieve reincarnation at a higher level, an aim that the prayers said at the time are intended to ensure. The copious quantities of blood which are shed during a cockfight is also believed to appease the demons. Vicious steel blades as sharp as a razor are attached to the right foot of each cock in place of a spur, which has been cut off. Severely wounded cocks fight until one falls dead, and the winner crows and pecks its fallen opponent. Hundreds of cocks are sacrificed in this manner every year.

Of the larger temples by far the most significant is Pura Besakih, first developed as a premier cult center under Ketut Kresna Kapakisan in the fourteenth century. Since volcanoes occupy such a special place in Balinese cosmology, and there is none more revered than Gunung Agung, the island's highest peak, it is to be expected that Pura Besakih stands on its southern flank. In the past the temple was the principal place of worship for the royal families of Klungkung, Karangasem, and Bangli, but today it is an extensive complex of twenty-two temples that are regarded as the focus of Balinese Hinduism. Here the last centennial purification of the island, the Eka Dasa Rudra, was successfully celebrated at a second attempt in 1979. A previous ceremony held in 1963 had ended with a rare eruption of Gunung Agung, many Balinese said because the island's communist governor Bagus Suteja insisted on the earlier and incorrect date.

The lotus throne at Pura Besakih dedicated to Brahma, Shiva, and Vishnu

Purification involves elaborate preparation of offerings, animals for sacrifice, prayer, and performance, all culminating in a grand ceremony after a month of intensive ritual activity. Tourists are kept away from Pura Besakih during this period, but thousands of Balinese pilgrims arrive to place offerings in one or more of its shrines. Worshippers from islands as far distant as Timor attend the Eka Dasa Rudra ceremony too.

The main temple, known as Pura Penataran Agung, is not surprisingly dedicated to Shiva, the chief deity ever since Ketut Kresna Kapakisan brought the Hindu faith to Bali from eastern Java. Yet the symbolic center of the whole temple complex is in fact the *padmasana*, or "lotus throne," located in this temple's first courtyard. The throne itself is dedicated to Ida Sanghyang Widi Wasa, the supreme spiritual being or holy power, who is manifest in the Hindu triumvirate of Brahma, Shiva, and Vishnu. Each of these great gods are honored with separate shrines raised above the throne and resting on the backs of turtles, doubtless a reference to the cosmic turtle Bedawang who acts as the island's foundation. In spite of dating from only the late seventeenth century, the lotus throne must indicate an older combined worship of the imported Hindu gods, just as the numerous *meru* dotted around Pura Besakih serve to emphasize the syncretic nature of Balinese religion, since no god or goddess is ever completely overlooked.

Part Five

ALMOST PARADISE

Dancers at Singapadu

Chapter Thirteen

ROMANTIC ENTHUSIASTS

"There must be something special about an island which can so fascinate a foreigner."

Dr. Made Djelantik

Of these fascinated foreigners the most enthusiastic was certainly Miguel Covarrubias, whose *Island of Bali* is familiar to nearly all visitors to the island. Published in 1937, this book encapsulates the pre-Second World War view of Balinese culture. From the moment he saw the island's outline from his ship as it approached Buleleng, Covarrubias was enchanted by Bali. Wonder, amazement, and delight awaited him and his wife; their reactions overflow the pages of *Island of Bali* and not just from the words, because the author's own drawings enhance the book's charm. This is the reason for it outlasting all other travel books about Bali.

Once across the mountain range which separates the northern district of Buleleng from southern Bali, the most populous and culturally developed part of the island, the first impressions of Covarrubias were happily confirmed. He notes the traveler's relief as

the fog vanishes, and the air becomes warmer and clearer. Tropical vegetation reappears, and riding among tall palms and enormous banana trees, he enters Bangli, which is at last like the Bali of the photographs. With lessened suspicions, he rides through many beautiful villages and fantastic ricefields covered with every shade of green.

Although disdainful of the numerous gift shops in Denpasar, and their piles of mass-produced "Balinese art," Covarrubias soon began to discover the real Bali in the town's "dirt-paved lanes… where the peace is not broken by mad automobiles running over pigs and chickens" and there were "the typical mud walls of the compounds, the thatched gates protected by mysterious signs—a dead chicken nailed flat on the wall, or a little white flag inscribed with cabalistic symbols."

Here was "the proper setting for the lithe brown-skinned women returning from market with baskets full of fruit on their heads and for the men in loincloths sitting in groups around the baskets in which they keep their favorite fighting cocks. Energetic women thresh rice or bathe quite unconcerned in the ditch by the roadside, and serious naked children play with a cricket they have just captured. From behind the walls come the occasional tinkling of practicing on a gamelan."

Powerfully drawn to this world, Covarrubias and his wife quit the Bali Hotel and moved into a pavilion owned by a local prince, whose father had fallen in the 1906 *puputan* at Denpasar. There they encountered Walter Spies, an expatriate who reveled in Bali's artistic heritage: he had already done much to stimulate creative activity at Ubud, where he was welcomed by the ruling family. At his house near the town he introduced Western ideas about art to hundreds of painters and sculptors. What Spies tried to do was move Balinese art on from the traditional Kamasan approach to composition, which was based on the stylized figures in *wayang kulit*, or "puppet theater."

Spies took Covarrubias under his artistic wing and guided him round the island's treasures. Covarrubias relates how he and his wife "roamed all over the island with Spies, watching strange ceremonies, enjoying their music, camping in the wilds of West Bali or on the coral reefs of Sanur." On a second visit in 1933, however, a more systematic approach was adopted in order to gather material for *Island of Bali*, since Covarrubias knew that an account of Balinese culture would require more than just a collection of photographs with explanatory captions. But the return visit was at first a disappointment because

> the tourist rush was in full swing and we heard that missionaries, unknown in Bali up to the time we left, were making converts, and everyone talked of trouble on their account. In Denpasar a great many women had taken to wearing clumsy blouses, the young were developing a contempt for Balinese ways, and the people complained of poverty, another novelty in Bali.

Yet beyond the discontent of Denpasar, which along with Singaraja was always the place most susceptible to change, Covarrubias soon found how Balinese life went on as before.

Because "no two festivals are carried out in exactly the same manner and no two temples exactly alike," Covarrubias decided to identify "the general principles [which] are the same everywhere." Without a formal training as either an anthropologist or an orientalist, however, he felt *Island of Bali* was necessarily "limited to present a bird's-eye view of Balinese life and culture, both of which are inextricably bound to their deeply rooted beliefs and their logical and harmonious living."

In view of the monumental misjudgment reached during the 1930s by the American anthropologist Margaret Mead, who thought Bali "teemed with excessive ritual" and its inhabitants were confined in some kind of socio-religious straightjacket, the amateur approach of Covarrubias is much to be preferred. The Mexican enthusiast uncovered a cultural dimension that continues to engage discerning visitors today. Yet he was wrong about the island's fate, since its "living culture" has not entirely disappeared "under the merciless onslaught of modern commercialism and standardization."

A reason for Balinese resilience is undoubtedly the communal solidarity of the villages, where most people still live, even if they belong to a conurbation such as Denpasar. Having already thwarted the communist-inspired reform program of Bagus Suteja in the late 1950s and early 1960s, there is no indication that modernization will weaken village support for the island's culture in the near future. Covarrubias glimpsed this aspect of a "well-coordinated form of agrarian socialism" when he pointed out how "the inherent unity and cooperation of Balinese communities had kept feudalism at bay." As he concludes:

> The nobility met with an insurmountable passive resistance to any encroachments upon the autonomy of the villages and had finally to content themselves with the collection of tribute from their "vassals." The common people tolerated the princes, but even today they consider them as total outsiders and in most social and administrative matters the villages remain entrenched against all interference from their noble landlords, now appointed as go-betweens between the people and the Dutch Government, mainly to the same office to which the threat of boycott reduced them in the past—the collection of taxes.

What Covarrubias appreciated, of course, was the way "their social organization not only is best suited, but is essential to their manner of living." Without its strong village communities, Balinese culture simply would not survive.

EXPLORING THE IDYLL

Spies also helped Beryl de Zoete to write an equally enthusiastic book on Balinese dance-drama. A fringe member of the Bloomsbury group, de Zoete traveled extensively in Asia, documenting its theatrical traditions. Her lucid prose was a foil for Spies, who provided the background for *Dance and Drama in Bali*, which was published in 1938. But she admitted that it was Spies' musical knowledge and his genius for vivid imagery that inspired several of the most notable passages in the book.

According to de Zoete, Bali was shaped by "a metaphysical view of life." There is a "harmonious disposition of man's life between the womb

Dance-drama performance staged for tourists at Singapadu, near Denpasar

of the mother and the womb of the toy cow in which he is finally burned," something that is clearly reflected "in the relation between man and nature." Sustaining this social harmony, she firmly believed, was the islanders' view that Bali formed a complete cosmos. She writes that

> everything has a part in the pattern, every humor in a man's body, every sensation, every faculty of his mind as well as every being of earth and sky, every tree, plant, and animal. It is impossible to define the correspondence which one certainly feels between the Balinese people and their surroundings. It is of course the most natural thing in the world. Yet it seems to us strange and exceptional, because we have lost the art of inhabiting a landscape without disturbing it, of being part of it with all the elegance of natural things, plants and birds and animals. The gods enjoy intelligible delights, architecture, music, dancing, offerings of flowers and fruit; those incredibly beautiful offerings made out of the simplest elements into the utmost elaboration.

She adds, "everywhere in Bali there is the same mingling and interchange of simplicity and elaboration." And it is this essential gracefulness of Balinese living that finds its fullest expression in dance and music.

Although *Dance and Drama in Bali* only claims to be "an introduction to Balinese dancing," its coverage of the island's tradition of dance-drama has never been surpassed. Subsequent studies of the performing arts lack the immediacy of de Zoete's prose, although they often contain extra information that helps to illuminate the Balinese stage. Conscious of this lack of detail, de Zoete offers an apology "for the untechnical treatment of dancing in the book," but she really need not do so. Like Covarrubias' tremendous excitement in *Island of Bali*, doubtless stimulated by the guidance of Spies as well, *Dance and Drama in Bali* outshines everything else when it comes to relating how the different dances are performed.

Whether describing the "little girls who appear like small golden idols in the *legong* dance, and render with astonishing refinement and skill its complicated evolutions," or the various movements of the warriors in *baris*, a dance which ranges from the wielding of weapons to the quieter gestures of courtship, de Zoete never loses the interest of the reader caught up by her own amazement at the sheer virtuosity of all the performers.

As enthusiastic was Colin McPhee, whose absorbing interest in

A *baris* dancer at Singapadu

Balinese music took him all over the island, visiting villages where accomplished musicians lived. He informs us in *A House in Bali* how he had hoped to

> discover some book, some ancient writing that had to do with laws, the theory of music. But none existed, it seemed, which struck me as curious, since there were books on everything else imaginable. As I talked with older men, hoping to gain a clearer insight into the form and construction of the music they had been playing, their answers were vague and hesitating. Laws existed in their minds, and I could learn more in a half-hour of observing than I could in an afternoon of conversation.

So McPhee came to realize that Balinese music was only learned and perfected through practice, through taking part in preparation for public performances.

The gamelan captivated McPhee, who encountered this distinctive Balinese sound on gramophone records in New York and Paris. In the French capital, however, he also heard gamelan live when a group of musicians and dancers from the village of Peliatan in Gianyar performed at the Colonial Exhibition. But McPhee was also encouraged to go to Bali by Covarrubias, since the Mexican explorer happened to be in Paris then. From 1931 until just before the Second World War, McPhee proceeded to make a detailed study of the gamelan and documented its music in Western notation for the first time. When he left for the United States, he had collected all the material he needed to write his most famous book, *Music in Bali*. It took McPhee twenty-five years to complete this task in California, where he died in 1964. Some of his friends believed his final illness resulted from nostalgia, a yearning for the island's culture that he described so well in *A House in Bali*.

Enthusiast though she might well have been in Bali, Margaret Mead's response was decidedly muted and a sign of her personal disappointment with the Balinese idyll. Even before the island received the Hollywood treatment in the 1950s, with films such as *The Road to Bali*, there was a marked tendency to regard it as a second Eden. In this film Bob Hope and Bing Crosby flee from "a pair of matrimony-minded girls" in Australia to Bali, where they encounter Dorothy Lamour playing a beautiful princess.

Her attire was more suited to Thailand or India than maritime Southeast Asia, but this did not trouble Paramount Pictures in the least. Such cultural niceties were as unimportant as the film's location, since *The Road to Bali* could have been shot anywhere: it was in fact nowhere, the entire production taking place inside a Hollywood studio.

Margaret Mead arrived from London, with her third husband Gregory Bateson, in 1936 after stopping at Singapore to join a tour of Makassar, before heading south to Bali. Mead's fieldwork in the South Pacific appeared a perfect preparation for her investigation of Balinese culture, but surprisingly this turned out to be far from the case. Once again Spies was instrumental in guiding Mead around Bali, but for her the exuberance of Balinese ritual and art was disturbing enough to categorize the culture as schizoid. Deeply indebted to Sigmund Freud's view of human nature, Mead was bound to see the *barong* dance as a prime example of sexual repression. She was sure that Balinese men lusted after nubile *legong* dancers until they were suddenly transformed into hags like Rangda, the terrifying witch.

Even before Gregory Bateson and Margaret Mead publicly announced their findings about the Balinese people, Spies was baffled by their overriding concern with schizophrenia, but he was either too amused or too polite to criticize it. He might well have quoted Bronislaw Malinowski, the doyen of anthropology, whose experience of life among the Trobriand islanders of Melanesia led him to write:

> In the study of primitive folklore and native decorative art, we shall find elements which may prove almost refactory to scientific analysis and yet will have to be recorded. Here the anthropologist may have to cease to be a mere analytic man of science. He may have to become almost an artist.

In spite of the term "primitive" being inappropriate as a description for Bali, Malinowski was correct in identifying the importance of an intuitive dimension in its culture. Because the seen, *selaka*, and the unseen, *niskala*, cannot really be separated for any length of time: Rangda is always ready to challenge the good lion Barong.

In his rejection of the absolute argument of psychoanalysts, who contended that Freud's theory of the Oedipus complex was the "primordial source… the fons and origo of everything," Malinowski wrote that it could never be "the unique source of culture, of organization and belief." Carl Jung, the other colossus of psychoanalysis, broke with Freud over this theory too. He became convinced that the individual possessed a personal unconscious and a collective unconscious; the former is filled with material peculiar to the individual, whereas the latter houses the common mental inheritance of mankind—the archetypes, or primordial images, which "bring into our ephemeral consciousness an unknown psychic life belonging to our remote ancestors. This psychic life," Jung suggested, "is the mind of our ancient ancestors, the way in which they conceived of life and the world, of gods and human beings."

In Bali it could be said that this archetypal inheritance is evident most of all in dance-drama, where the earliest Austronesian anxieties are explored, contained, and to an extent, resolved. The island has moved at one level into the modern world, but the Balinese people still have to deal with the unseen. They cannot help but feel the continued power of *niskala* within themselves.

An Ubud-style painting of white starlings

Chapter Fourteen

DETACHED OBSERVERS

"According to Balinese belief, the Goddess of the Lake and the God of Mount Agung share dominion over the island, a concept that is taken literally by the inhabitants of the mountains, who point to the side of the lake where the power of the goddess stops and the dominion of the gods begins."

Stephen Lansing

Margaret Mead's notion of a repressive Balinese culture, of the regulation of daily life that lay behind the violence of the trancers during the *barong* dance, had been attacked by a leading Dutch psychiatrist as soon as she made her point of view public, but such was her eminence as an anthropologist that it still became widely known anyway. Neither she nor her husband Gregory Bateson were qualified to undertake psychoanalytical research, but this fact hardly seemed to matter. And nobody bothered to point out how little Balinese they actually spoke, let alone use the language to explore the innermost thoughts of the islanders.

Schizoid is how Mead termed the Balinese. There was "not an ounce of free intelligence," she claimed, "or free libido in the whole culture." Such a negative conclusion appears so odd now that it is easily forgotten how anthropologists once studied non-Western societies in the quest for specific things. Mead set out to research the cultural aspects of schizophrenia, which she thought Bali must have in abundance. Up to her death in 1978, she remained steadfast in supporting the correctness of her opinion, disdaining any value in what Miguel Covarrubias had called the "measured rhythm" of Balinese life.

When Denny Thong, an Indonesian doctor in charge of a mental hospital in Bangli, finally met Mead in a New York restaurant, he was surprised at her lack of interest in his comments. Thong said, "Mead was an excellent conversationalist but a poor listener. Whenever I disagreed with her, she raised her walking stick!" As he relates in *A Psychiatrist in Paradise*, published in 1993, the Indonesian doctor was eager to ask Mead if she realized that in small Balinese villages in the 1930s the sight of a large Western woman with light hair and blue-grey eyes would be fearful to small children. Not only would Mead's visage be out of the daily experience of the children, but her features happened to resemble those of the demons and witches that were a part of Balinese folklore.

Oblivious to any suggestion that she never got close enough to these Balinese villagers to really understand their child-rearing practices, Mead was dead within a few months of the meal with Thong.

Totally different in his approach to mental illness among the Balinese was Denny Thong himself, who hailed from Banka, a small island off the coast of western Java. He had been appointed to direct the only mental hospital in Bali and, not long after taking up his duties in 1968, he realized the best way to make progress was to combine modern methods with certain features of traditional Balinese medicine. Such a detached outlook won over many Balinese who still looked upon the *balian* as the best person to treat mental illness. As Thong went as far as appointing one of these traditional healers to the hospital staff, everyone was reassured of his good intentions.

Crowning the hospital's work in Bangli was an annual temple festival when over a thousand people came to make offerings and pay their respects to the gods. The participants were current patients seeking help with their treatment, former patients giving thanks for their cure, and the families of both groups, pleased at last that they could express their gratitude in a traditional fashion. Skeptical though some Western visitors were about such events, there was no question that Thong had tapped a deep root of Balinese belief which brought positive results for all involved.

Quite remarkable was the relationship of trust and mutual support that developed between the hospital doctors and the *balian* I Nyoman Jiwa, who had joined the staff. This traditional healer provided invaluable assistance in diagnosing and treating patients, although Thong's daring experiment was a subject of criticism in other Indonesian islands. Western-trained psychiatrists deeply resented the credibility that it conferred upon the *balians*. Indeed, by the 1980s the Indonesian medical establishment was so tired of the international reputation enjoyed by Thong's unusual method of dealing with mental disorders that he was summoned to Jakarta for a face-to-face meeting with the Directorate of Medical Health. Despite still working in Bali on several projects under the auspices of international agencies, Thong was transferred elsewhere. He tells us, "the news was a blow to me and my family... My wife was born in Bali and has always lived there; for her, the idea of leaving her extended family seemed horrendous." One valuable outcome, however, was his book *A Psychiatrist in Paradise*, which an American working then with traditional healers told Thong he really must write. Its account of his time in Bangli is a fascinating read for the layman as well as the open-minded specialist.

STUDYING THE *SUBAKS*

Even more detached than those of Denny Thong were the observations of Stephen Lansing, an American anthropologist who was the first person to appreciate the importance of the *subaks*, the village irrigation societies upon which successful rice cultivation depends. He understood the crucial role played by Bali's temples in helping the *subaks* manage the ecology of the rice fields. His seminal work *Priests and Programmers* demonstrated in 1991 the contrast between Balinese farming systems and the new methods recommended by Western consultants.

When new strains of rice were introduced in the 1970s, on the advice of the Asian Development Bank, the Indonesian government insisted that constant cropping should replace traditional cropping patterns. Soon there was chaos in water scheduling and the uncontrolled spread of pests. Harvests failed and the Balinese faced famine. The Bank now acknowledges that the change had been catastrophic and only when farmers returned to traditional methods did their harvests recover. Fortunately for Bali the reason for this urgent reinstatement of traditional ways was explained in detail by Lansing, who divined the key contribution made by water temples.

The subtitle of *Priests and Programmers—Technologies of Power in the Engineered Landscape of Bali*—reveals the nature of Lansing's insight. What Lansing grasped was the extent to which the island's agriculture was the product of a thousand years of communal effort. The ruggedness of Bali meant that irrigation methods used in Java and other parts of Southeast Asia were unsuitable here. Well before the Majapahit takeover in the fourteenth century, Balinese rulers had encouraged the clearance of land and the construction of irrigation systems by the *subaks*. Because a *subak* area comprises land watered from a common source it drew farmers together and ensured that channels and tunnels were always properly maintained. At the Museum Subak in Tabanan the sheer scale of their work is illustrated by displays of the traditional tools and methods that were used down the ages.

Membership of a *subak* introduces almost every Balinese man to the workings of a well-organized group devoted to the maintenance of the village economy. Regular meetings allow any member to express his views, irrespective of the number of terraces he may own. And the local *subak* temple acts as a focus for communal effort and a reminder of the generosity of the gods. Worship is given to the supreme deity Ida Sanghyang Widi Wasa and Shiva as well as Dewi Danu and Dewi Sri. At the entrance of a *subak* temple, which is usually built next to a main irrigation channel, there is also shrine dedicated to holy water itself. From these temples each year *subak* members accompany village priests to Pura Ulan Danu, the chief temple belonging to Dewi Danu on the northern shore of Lake Batur, where they make offerings to the lake goddess, agree with her priest about the quantity of water they should receive for their paddies, and return home with some holy water.

Neither the Dutch colonial administration, nor officials appointed by the Republic of Indonesia, ever understood the *subak* system. Hence the temporarily disastrous disruption of its operation during the late 1970s and 1980s. Without close cooperation between priests responsible for the distribution of water and the farmers working the rice fields, there is no chance of keeping crops safe from pests and diseases. Only the burning or flooding of a paddy after harvesting prevents pests from moving to a neighboring field.

Lansing outlines the simple but effective way in which water temples and *subaks* work together. He notes how

> each shrine or temple is associated with some particular component of the irrigated landscape. A local irrigation system begins with a spring, or, more often, a weir in a river, which diverts part or all of its flow of water to an irrigation canal. Beside each weir or spring is a shrine. The congregation of the weir shrine consists of all the farmers who use the water originating from this source. The principal deity to receive offerings at the weir is called the "Deity of the Weir" (*bhatara empelan*). Offerings are also made at the weir shrine to the Goddess of the Temple of the Crater Lake, who is said to make the rivers flow.

A ceremony at a *subak* water temple; a *subak* channel (*below*)

The crater lake goddess is of course Dewi Danu, whose willingness to share her bounty makes her almost as popular as Dewi Sri, the sacrificed rice goddess. "The irrigation canal that takes off from the weir," Lansing continues, "eventually reaches a block of terraces. This spot is usually a kilometer or more downstream from the weir and is marked by a major water temple." It is "a walled courtyard containing a shrine where farmers can make offerings."

Water temples control the distribution of water through sluices and floodgates, so as to ensure that the flow irrigates the paddies without uprooting plants, and in particular newly planted seedlings. They also determine periods of fallow. Their role in bringing together *subak* members through an agreed cycle of planting, growing, and harvesting rice, along with tackling the problem of pests, is the key to Bali's successful ecosystem.

Since the publication of *Priests and Programmers*, Lansing has continued investigating the *subaks*. Perhaps his most revealing finding is the reason why upland farmers are willing to share water with farmers downstream. It is in their interest to do so. By synchronizing the flooding of rice fields, pests are kept down for the benefit of all. Underlying this productive cooperation is the Austronesian basis of Balinese religion and the belief that nothing is actually inanimate. The temple of the lake goddess Dewi Danu, the Pura Ulun Danu, possesses no coercive powers like a Dutch colonial officer or an Indonesian official, but its authority over the supply of water for agricultural purposes is unquestioned by the Balinese. And it is difficult to see how any other attitude could exist, for the water flowing down the irrigation channels is none other than Dewi Danu herself. For her divine essence is as essential as Dewi Sri's productivity to a good harvest, which is why their temples are so often next to each other. Together these two indigenous goddesses of water and rice have sustained Bali's culture throughout recorded history.

A PRINCE'S VIEW

Last but not least, Made Djelantik is an equally detached observer. We are indeed fortunate that his Dutch wife persuaded this prince to write an autobiography, published in 1997 as *The Birthmark*. The second of the king of Karangasem's sons, Made broke the princely mold by training as a medical practitioner in Holland. His older brother Gede succeeded to the throne in 1950, the year that Balinese kingship was abolished by the newly independent government in Jakarta.

A dual perspective as a Balinese prince and a Western-trained doctor gives Made's observations an acute edge. Importantly, he witnessed the effect of the tremendous changes that overtook Bali during a large part of the twentieth century, from Dutch colonialism through the Japanese occupation to the establishment of the Republic of Indonesia. Made Djelantik's family home, the Puri Agung Karangasem at Amlapura in eastern Bali, no longer has any function in Balinese society and is no more than a tourist attraction. It is presently inhabited by one of Made's nephews, who acts as a glorified caretaker.

In a sense, Made Djelantik had become an outsider as soon as he went to the Netherlands in order to study medicine. Right down to the 1930s ordinary Balinese people called Java by the name of Jawi, which also meant "abroad." Even though the Djelantiks could claim descent from Erlanga, who ruled eastern Java centuries before the Majapahit conquest of Bali, the larger island remained terra incognita. But the position of Made's father as a *stedehouder* ensured that his two oldest sons were admitted to reputable Dutch schools in Java.

Returning home during a school holiday in 1937, the two brothers found great excitement in the royal palace because

> the whole population of Karangasem was frantically busy with preparations for the seven-day-long *maligya* festival to be held... in honor of our ancestors, who had been cremated years earlier. After consultation with all the priests in the region, Father had concluded that the proper time had come to perform the *maligya* ceremony, particularly on behalf of his late uncle and predecessor Gusti Gede Djelantik. As is customary, there were numerous deceased close relatives whose souls would join the principal spirit in his ascent to the highest of the heavens.

The purpose of the *maligya* ceremony, Made points out, is assisting cremated ancestors to find a secure place at the summit of Gunung Agung, the abode of the gods. "In this highly symbolic ritual the souls are represented by *puspas*, flower effigies consisting of sandalwood, certain ingredients, decorated with silver or gold and each provided with a

The Dutch artist Nieuwenkamp on his bicycle: a bas-relief at the Pura Meduwe Karang

scribbled palm leaf for identification."

On the seventh day, at the climax of the rite, "four beautiful ceremonial towers were carried together with about twenty similarly elegant but smaller towers in a mile-long colorful procession to the sea at Ujung." The young schoolboy enjoyed the magnificent event and even recorded it with a film camera, but he could not help asking a high Hindu priest about the presence of a Buddhist colleague. Made was told that it made the "service to God more complete." When he dared to ask which god this was, the answer was not unexpected. It was

> Ida Sanghyang Widi, the One and Almighty, who can have three appearances to us, Brahma the Creator, Wisnu the Preserver, and Siwa the Destroyer, who brings us back to the Almighty.

Not entirely satisfied with the explanation and unwilling to cause offense by asking further questions, Made later admitted that he "was too busy filming and running about the entire time," as he needed to keep ahead of the column winding its way between green and yellow paddy

236

fields to the coast, that "the spiritual essence of the day—the returning of the purified souls (symbolized by the effigies) to the infinity of the sea— wholly escaped him."

But the film was a great success and delighted all who saw it on a screen in the palace afterwards. Since his older brother Gede was going to be the next ruler of Karangasem, there was scope for Made to fulfill his ambition and become a doctor. After finishing his secondary education in Batavia, he sailed to Europe and, in spite of the German occupation of the Netherlands, he qualified as a doctor, married a nurse, and came to appreciate the kindness of the Dutch people, whose lack of racial prejudice stood in stark contrast to his earlier experience in Bali and Java.

He also discovered Dutch interest in Bali. So taken was he with W. O. J. Nieuwenkamp's *Wanderings over the Island of Bali* that he gave up hot meals in restaurants for a month in order to buy the out-of-print book. Nieuwenkamp was one of the earliest artists to produce prints of Balinese scenes for a Western audience. Between 1904 and 1937 he walked and cycled around Bali during his frequent visits, buying the works of local artists and recording his own impressions of the island. Now he is commemorated in a bas-relief at the Pura Meduwe Karang, a large temple not far from Singaraja on the northern coast. It shows the artist peddling away on his bicycle. What impressed Made most was the accuracy of Nieuwenkamp's observations, plus "the love that shone throughout the text." Reading the book in his lodgings, it made the medical student "feel that there must be something special about an island which could so fascinate a foreigner."

Dr. Djelantik's return to Bali after the surrender of Japan was not quite as Made expected. His father received his Dutch wife without any reservations, as indeed did the rest of the royal family, but the colonial authorities were unsure of his loyalty and so he was posted away from the island. After independence, however, Made was able to practice medicine in Bali and he provides in *The Birthmark* a gripping account of the 1963 eruption of Gunung Agung as well as the bloody aftermath of the Jakarta coup two years later. But in the late 1960s he was recruited by the World Health Organization and worked in Iraq, Somalia, and Afghanistan. His contract ended in late 1979, just before Afghanistan was invaded by the Russians.

Postscript

BALI TODAY

Bali stands at a crossroads. According to the direction it chooses to take, the future of this fascinating island will be determined for the rest of the century. So far the resilience of the Balinese people has allowed its unique culture to survive both colonialism and nationalism, but a new threat is now emerging in the guise of mass tourism. How this is handled over the next few decades remains the crucial challenge.

Snake-like lines of foreign tourists, waiting for clearance through immigration at Ngurah Rai airport, are a sign of increasing pressure on the island's resources. Without a comprehensive plan for tourism, there is bound to be a steady decline in the quality of the Balinese experience, which makes a visit so memorable today. Already paddy fields have been sacrificed for building purposes and around some temples cheap tourist shops have sprung up. As yet, these straws in the wind are negligible: talk of easing the regulations governing the height of buildings is not. A coconut tree presently marks the upper limit for every building, meaning that the skyline of Bali remains a natural one.

Once again there are Javanese entrepreneurs seeking to take advantage of Bali's attractiveness to foreign tourists, although this is nothing like the blatant exploitation of the Suharto years. Then intimidation was used by this Indonesian president to get his way in the island, for the benefit of his own family and his closest supporters. Yet the Balinese provincial government still needs to resist Jakarta's dictates.

The fact that politics in the capital are so confused hardly assists Bali. The struggle for power among the political elite there does not augur well for the smaller islands in the Republic of Indonesia. Perhaps the headline in *the Jakarta Post* best summed up the 2014 election to the House of Representatives: "New fresh-faced, star-studded House feared inept."

For most Balinese people national politics seem irrelevant. They are more interested in family affairs and age-old ceremonies that keep demons at bay. In this respect, though, there is a growing concern about the number of Javanese who have come to settle down as farmers, especially in Jembrana. The terrorist bombs at Kuta in 2002 and 2005 are a constant reminder of a deep religious divide that hard-line Muslim groups in Jakarta are only too willing to exacerbate. Their recent opposition to the appointment of a Christian of Chinese descent as the city's governor was duly noted in Bali.

Yet there is no immediate cause for alarm. So deeply rooted are Bali's Austronesian–Hindu beliefs that the islanders are unlikely to see their society disturbed in the near future. That is why visitors should embrace its singularity with affection and not expect any accommodation of foreign ways. What makes Bali worth visiting, after all, is this difference: the island is unlike anywhere else.

Glossary

arak	a strong drink made from rice
Arjuna	an Indian hero in the *Mahabharata*
atman	the imperishable spirit in Hindu belief
Austronesians	the maritime peoples who settled the Indonesian archipelago
avatara	or "descents," especially the Hindu god Vishnu's incarnations
bale	a house or pavilion
Bali Aga	"original Balinese"
balian	a shaman or traditional healer
bandesa	a village priest
baris	a dance based upon military movements
Barong	the good lion of dance-drama
Bedawang	the world-turtle that supports the island of Bali
bhuta-kala	"earth demons"
Brahma	the Hindu creator god
brahman	"holy power" in Hinduism
Calon Arang	the legend of Rangda the witch
caste	Indian-inspired hereditary social divisions
Danghyang Nirartha	the influential Javanese priest who came to Bali in the sixteenth century

Dewi Danu	the indigenous lake goddess
Dewi Sri	the indigenous rice goddess
dharma	the Hindu concept of duty
Durga	the fearful consort of the Hindu god Shiva
Eka Dasa Rudra	a month-long festival held at Pura Besakih once every century to appease Shiva and purify the Bali
gamelan	Balinese percussion orchestras
Gunung Agung	"great mountain," Bali's highest volcano
Hanuman	the monkey ally of Rama in the *Ramayana*
Ida Sanghyang Widi Wasa	the supreme Balinese deity
jina	a Javanese term for an enlightened person
Kala	Shiva's demonic son
kanda empat	the spiritual companions of every Balinese person
karma	the Indian notion that an individual's deeds automatically determine the next incarnation
Kebo Iwo	the giant champion of King Bedaulu, the last Balinese ruler before the Majapahit conquest
Kertanagara	the charismatic king of Singhasari
kris	a short dagger of ritual significance
Krishna	Arjuna's charioteer, an incarnation of Vishnu
legong	a dance performed by young girls
leyak	a Balinese witch

Majapahit	the eastern Javanese kingdom that conquered Bali in 1343
merajan	or "temple house" belonging to the spirit of a place
Meru	the Hindu cosmic mountain and the name of the towering pagodas in a Balinese temple
moksa	"release," the enlightenment that ends the endless round of rebirth
naga	a Hindu cosmic serpent
niskala	the intangible aspect of existence: literally "the unseen"
odalan	a temple festival
padmasana	"lotus throne" dedicated to Ida Sanhyang Widi Wasa in the forms of Brahma, Shiva and Vishnu
pandes	the clan of smiths
pawukon	the Balinese 210-day calendar
perbekel	the secular head of a village
pura	a temple
puri	a palace
Rama	an incarnation of Vishnu in the *Ramayana* epic
Rangda	"widow," the chief Balinese witch
ruah	"trance"
Rudra	"howler," the destructive side of Shiva
saka	the Hindu lunar calendar

Saraswati	the Hindu goddess of learning
sekala	the tangible aspect of existence: literally "the seen"
Shiva	in Balinese Siwa, the great Hindu god who occupies Gunung Agung
soma	the ritual Hindu beverage associated with immortality
stedehouder	a high Dutch colonial rank
subak	"irrigation society," the basis of Bali's success in growing rice
Surya	the Hindu sun god
taksu	the spiritual inspiration of a great performer
tika	a special calendar tracking important events in the pawukon cycle
topeng	masked dance-drama
toya	"holy water," sometimes *tirtha* from the Sanskrit for "river crossing"
Vishnu	in Balinese Wisnu, the Hindu savior god
xian	a Chinese immortal

Further Reading

In spite of its fame as an international tourist destination, there are surprisingly few general books about Bali. The present volume is an attempt at filling this publishing gap between academic studies on one hand and tourist guides on the other. As some of the books recommended here are inevitably specialist treatments of Balinese history and culture, an explanation of their contents is offered in each case. Others are fortunately more accessible, so that readers will have little difficulty in following their discussion. It should be pointed out, however, that these books do not constitute a complete list of available titles, but rather they reflect the author's personal preferences as introductory accounts of a truly unusual island.

Perhaps the best place to start any attempt to come to grips with Bali and the Balinese is *The Birthmark: Memoirs of a Balinese Prince* by Dr. A. A. M. Djelantik, which was published in 1997. From the number of references made in *Bali: A Cultural History* to Made Djelantik it ought to be evident how much the author values his insights and opinions. A member of the Karangasem royal family, this prince-turned-medical practitioner cast an astute eye over the profound changes which overtook Bali during the course of the twentieth century. Almost as interesting is *Against the Odds: The Strange Destiny of a Balinese Prince* by I. Pucci and illustrated by A. A. M. Djelantik. Published in 2004, this collection of watercolors and anecdotes covers the main events of the doctor-prince's fascinating life.

A longer historical perspective can be found in *Bali in the Nineteenth Century* by Ide Anak Agung Gde Agung, who was born at Gianyar in 1921. A distinguished political and diplomatic career was interrupted by a refusal to endorse President Sukarno's concept of "Guided Democracy." After his release from prison on the overthrow of Sukarno in 1965, Ide Anak Agung Gde Agung became Indonesia's ambassador in Vienna and, following his retirement, he devoted himself to historical research. His *Bali in the Nineteenth Century*, published in 1991, remains the best treatment of the immediate precolonial period. It actually carries the story down to the *puputans* at Denpasar in 1906 and Klungkung in 1908, which together ended Balinese independence. This book may be read in conjunction with W. A. Hanna's *Bali Chronicles: Fascinating People and Events in Balinese History*, published in 2004, because the narrative begins with the arrival of the first Europeans, the Portuguese.

For an overall view of Bali in the context of the Indonesian archipelago from early times until the present, the reader might care to consult my own *A History of Southeast Asia*, published in 2014. What this study endeavors to do is pay proper attention to cultural issues, a dimension of modern Southeast Asia which simply cannot be ignored. Without an awareness of its cultural heritage, there is no possibility of appreciating the political and social choices that are currently available in each nation state.

Although much more academic in approach, Clifford Geertz's *Negara: The Theatre State in Nineteenth-Century Bali*, published in 1980, still provides an essential background to the Balinese monarchy. It examines the idea of the royal court as a cosmic center as well as the roles played by the irrigation system and the temple in the island's politics. As Geertz notes, "the master image of political life" has always been "kingship." This notion is explored, along with the rest of Balinese culture, in *The People of Bali* by A. Hobart, U. Ramseyerand, and A. Leeman. Part of a series entitled "The Peoples of South-East Asia and the Pacific," it was published in 1996.

Possibly the most important Balinese study ever written is J. Stephen Lansing's *Priests and Programmers: Technologies and Power in the Engineered Landscape of Bali* (1991). The spotlight that Lansing focused on the island's amazing irrigation system saved its inhabitants from suffering a prolonged period of poor harvests. Not only did this study of water distribution confirm the value of traditional methods of rice cultivation, but even more it demonstrated to the world how ecologically sound was the Balinese approach to natural resources. "Whereas Marx regarded nature in terms of linear evolutionary progress," Lansing concludes, "a Balinese farmer may be reminded instead of the intricate patterns of the tika calendar, or the interlocking cyclical melodies of the gamelan orchestras."

As yet, no satisfactory account of Balinese religion has been written. Several works may be read but they are partial. By far the best is F. B. Eiseman's *Sekala and Niskala: Essays on Religion, Ritual and Art*, published in 1990. Its strength derives from the author's long residence in Bali and his sympathy for the island's culture. The freshness of Eiseman's observations is delightful, including his personal experience of tooth-filing.

Rangda, Bali's Queen of Witches by Claire Fossey is, as the title suggests, concerned with the demonic side of Balinese beliefs. Published in 2008, this short study helps to clarify the ongoing battle between Rangda and the good lion Barong, the most popular of all Balinese dance-dramas, and the one that tourists are most likely to see performed. For an explanation of Balinese religious iconography there is C. Hooykaas' *Religion in Bali*, published in 1973. This slim volume consists of a collection of photographs with a commentary. *Time, Rites, and Festivals in Bali* by I Gusti Nyoman Darta, Jean Couteau, and George Dreguet explains the meaning of various daily rituals. Published in 2013, its illuminating text is supported by contemporary drawings.

Although *Island of Bali* by M. Covarrubias, published in 1937, deals with the island's culture in general, it has interesting things to say about Balinese beliefs. Miguel and Rose Covarrubias had arrived in 1930 and the book they compiled together is more than a tourist guide: it suffers from a typical pre-Second World War outlook, tending to concentrate on the "artistic" character of the Balinese people, but there are valuable descriptions of ritual events like cremation. An excellent commentary is included in *Sutasoma: The Ancient Tale of a Buddha-Prince from 14th Century Java*, translated by K. O'Brien in 2008. This story features the charismatic Javanese ruler, King Kertanagara of Singhasari, whose reign did so much to shape kingship in eastern Java and Bali.

Much better are books dealing with Balinese art and architecture, music and dance-drama, as well as textiles. Most welcome of all is *Balinese Art: Paintings and Drawings of Bali 1800-2010* by Adrian Vickers, which was published in 2012. Splendid illustrations and an informative text make this book a model for future specialist studies about Bali. Vickers is also the author of *Bali: A Paradise Created*, an accessible account of Balinese history and culture in spite of its declared aim "to bring to a wider audience important scholarship on Bali." It was published in 1989. More recently Vickers published *A History of Modern Indonesia* (2005), a short account of what today is the fourth largest country in the world with a population of over 220 million. Among studies of individual artists, *Arie Smit* by S. Neka and D. Sudarmaji, stands out. Published at Denpasar in 1995, it can be obtained in Ubud's Nekar Art Museum, where many of the remarkable works of this Dutch-born Indonesian painter are on display. Other useful books on Balinese art are *Ida Bagus Made: The Art of Devotion* by K. McGowan, A. Vickers, Soemantri Widagdo, and Benedict Anderson, published in 2008, and the catalogue of the Museum Puri Lukisan, a treasure house of traditional art situated in Ubud. Whereas the former work celebrates the paintings of a prominent local artist, the latter reveals the range of Balinese talent right across the island during the twentieth century. The museum also features exhibitions of other artists; in 2014 it was the turn of I Gusti Nyoman Lempard, whose beautiful house and garden still stand opposite Ubud market.

For the performing arts there is one exceptional work, *Dance and Drama in Bali* by W. Spies and B. de Zoete. A seminal study by two enthusiastic observers, it was acclaimed on publication in 1938 for shedding new light on human culture in general, and not just Bali's own amazing contribution. What undoubtedly surprised everyone at the time was the astonishing variety of forms that exist in Balinese dance-drama. A more up-to-date survey is *A Guide to the Performing Arts of Bali: Balinese Dance, Drama and Music* (2004) by I. Wayan Dibia and R. Ballinger. Just as instructive is M. Tenzer's *Balinese Gamelan Music* published in 2011.

Quite incredible in its scope is R. Watson's *The Living House: An Anthropology of Architecture in Southeast Asia* (1990). This wide-ranging survey of maritime Southeast Asia covers dwellings for both the living and the dead, because ancestors share with deities a prime importance in its indigenous beliefs. In Bali, of course, the acceptance of the Hindu idea of reincarnation has removed the necessity of permanent abodes for the dead, but roofed shrines are constructed in gardens for the periodic visits of deified ancestors. More specific is J. Davison's *Introduction to Balinese Architecture*, published in 2003.

Not to be forgotten are Balinese handicrafts such as textiles. These are discussed in R. Maxwell's *Textiles of Southeast Asia*, where attention is drawn to the offerings of clothing that the Balinese make to their gods and goddesses. In some instances the material is decorated in gold thread with figures from the Hindu epics. China's influence is equally clear in both textile design and the respect shown for its coins, which are believed to possess abundant supernatural power. *Textiles in Southeast Asia* was published in 1990. And, last but not least, readers will enjoy J. Slattum's *Balinese Masks: Spirits of an Ancient Drama*, published in 2003. This study of the art of mask making and the function of masks in dance-drama is truly revealing.

Index